It's How
You Play the Game

Table of Contents

Foreword

IT IS TO FRANK KING, chairman of the organizing committee of the Winter Games in Calgary, that we owe our gratitude for having undertaken, with verve and meticulous detail, to relate, under the title *It's How You Play the Game*, the story of these Games, from the birth of a dream to its culmination, which allowed me to call these Games "the best Olympic Winter Games ever organized."

It is to Frank King's credit that throughout his account, which reads like a novel, he has concealed none of the bright or dark parts of the adventure, and has skillfully revealed the complexity of it. Of course, as in any work with an autobiographical element, the author gives his own slant to the events he describes.

I wish every success to *It's How You Play the Game*, the credo of a man totally committed to his task. This testimony will enrich the one-hundred-year history of the Olympic movement. It will also provide valuable help to all those who in the future will have the perilous yet uplifting honor of organizing Olympic Games destined in their turn, I dearly hope, to become the best Winter Games in Olympic history.

JUAN ANTONIO SAMARANCH
PRESIDENT
THE INTERNATIONAL OLYMPIC COMMITTEE

Preface

THIS BOOK IS BASED on my recollections, on notes, and on published sources. Conversations are reproduced from memory, so naturally the words appearing here in quotation marks are not the exact ones that were used. Passages that are set in from the text and in smaller type, however, are reproduced word-for-word from speeches, letters, articles, and (in one case) a novel.

Putting on the Games was from start to finish a team effort. Although some people on the team are mentioned in the main text, I could only mention a fraction of them. In fact, many incidental references to individuals were chopped out by my editors, who complained that the cast of the story grew too large. I protested in vain. Other omissions or errors in the text are my own.

I would like to dedicate this book to everyone who helped make the Games happen, including everyone who helped out over the years in one way or another. In particular, though, I'd like to thank the 12,310 members of Team'88: the board of directors, staff, and games-time volunteers during the Games. Without the help of every last one of you, the Calgary Winter Olympics would not have been the success they were. It was a pleasure working with you all.

THANK YOU TO (IN NO PARTICULAR ORDER) THE OCO'88 BOARD OF DIRECTORS • TERRY ROBERTS • GERRY BERGER • WALTER SIEBER • LYLE MAKOSKY • BOB KASTING • JIM WORRALL • RALPH KLEIN • NORMAN WAGNER • GEORGE DE RAPPARD • PAULA ANDREWS • DIANE HUNTER • DON SPRAGUE • DICK POUND • BOB NIVEN • ROGER JACKSON • JOHN LECKY • WENDY BRYDEN • GEORGE CORNISH • BOB HOLMES • BARRY MITCHELSON • IAN DOUGLAS • MAURICE ALLAN • LEE RICHARDSON • JANE EDWARDS • BOB BRAWN • BOB LAIDLAW • BILL WARREN • PETER LOUGHEED • THANK YOU ALSO TO THE OTHER MEMBERS OF TEAM'88 • LORRAINE ANDERSEN • IRIS ING • ERIKA VAN

OYEN · JEANETTE ZIEHR · BARRY HARRISON · SHARON LEMIRE · HEINZ PENNER · TRACEY FAULKNER · DON AUSTIN · NORBERTO RODRIQUEZ · ANITA SPENCE · MIKE O'DELL · NAN HUGHES · MARION HARKNESS · JOHN DUNFIELD · CATHRYN MULLIGAN · VICTOR BLANCHETTE · GREG RESNIK · DANIEL TAIT · STEPHEN PONIECKI · HARVEY SPITTAL· STEVE MACDONALD · KENNETH CALBERRY · CY JOHNSON · CAROL MALONEY · MONIKA SEYMOUR · DOREEN YOUNG · BRENDA MAYDER · WILFRED OAKES · LANE KRANENBURG · JANE SALZL · SUSAN GOODWIN · ANNA CHRISTIANSEN · JACK MACKI · CHRISTOPHER WILLIAMS · RALPH GUREVITCH · JUDITH STABLEFORD · DAVID MACKIE · GAIL WEEKES · CAROL DOBBERTHIEN · JACKIE PODBORSKI · GORDON MCALLISTER · JEFF KELSO · JEFF MILLIARD · SHARON NEALE · GREG MATHIESEN · JOHN BROWER · LUCILLE NEYRON · REED HENTZE · DAVID DORE · BJORG UNGARIAN · MARY JANE HUSSEY · ANDREA MARTINIUK · HELEN TYTULA · DAVID SMITH · PEGGY SIMPSON · KATHY BRUCE · KELLI HANLEY · LORRAINE SHARPLIN · DAVID MCARTHUR · PETER GREEN · ALISON WALKER · CAROL JOHNSTON · DANA BEAUPRE · PAUL FIELD · TRENA GUEST · CATHE LIMACHER · MAX SLIGHT · BRIAN PAGE · PAT BJORNSON · JOHN CLAYTON · ALAN THOMPSON · KATHY LYMER · COLLEEN PETERS · JOHN NESBITT · STEPHEN IRVING · SUE NELSON · KARL KRATS · CAROL KLIMPEL · MICHEL GADBOIS · PHILOMENA HO · IAN EADIE · MARJORIE ROULEAU · DONALD ELLIOTT · ALISON ESSERY · BRUCE SHULTZ · PAMELA HORNFORD · MALCOLM CARMICHAEL · IRMA PHILLIPS · PAULA COWAN · TOM FRANK · JAY MACGILLIVRAY · RICK LANG · MARTHA GRIGGS · ELEANOR ROBERTSON · ALAN SCOTT · BEV MACKENZIE · SHERRI SEARS · STEVEN ULLATHORNE · ANNE CHAZAUX · SHELLEY GALLAGHER · GERRY CARVELL · CHRIS OLIN · MAUREEN BEDARD · JAKE BORN · ANN GARGULA · BARBARA FRIEND · HUGH HAM · JANE WRIGHT · JOANNE MCLEOD · EILEEN JOHNSTON · IRIS TURAGLIO · SHELLY MCNIE · DEBBIE CARTER · LAURIE BROWN · MARC BEAUCHEMIN · THOMAS ERIKSEN · TOM WOOD · ALAN STANHOPE · SANNA HULT · BOB CADMAN · BILL RICHARDSON · CLAUDE ROMNEY · IRENE BANDURA · CHARLES BOWLES · BRIAN HOWES · BOB JEARY · ROBERT HENDERSON · JEAN BENNIE · HARRY RIPLEY · SAHBRA SALEM · GORDON TALBOT · BEVERLY BERKHOLD · LINDA KING MASLECHKO · KATHY PHILLIPS · BARBARA ROWE · MAISIE MCCHASNEY · DAVID ARMSTRONG · KEN LYSTER · MARG QUAN · PABLO FERREIRA · LYN JURISSON · PAUL PELLICANO · ANNE WALKER · MARK WOITAS · CINDY RODERIQUE · NED BURNYEAT · STU RICHARDSON · FLORENCE LAU · DORIS TIPPETT · PHYLLIS HEMMING · DAVE DERWENT · JANE CARLSON · MONNIE SAUVE · DIANE WEBER · BILL WASHBURN · SANDRA GREENSLADE · SUSHILA KRISHNAN · DONNA LARSEN · JIM WEED · JANE HUTCHESON · JOYCE KRUSKY · MARK REVELL · DARREL WARREN · GORDON HANN · BARB KENNEDY · BARBARA HILL · TROY SEDGWICK · BRUCE WHITAKER · VALERIE SILBERNAGEL · ED FRASER · JARROD MILNE · GRAHAM BENNETT · LAL DE SILVA · JAMES WATSON · CHRISTINE HENZEL · CINDY SAVAGE · MERV ESHELBY · GERRY BADER · GORDON MCMANUS · PATRICIA SIMS · LINDA WILLIAMS · BOB KALEF · BOB MARSHALL · JENNIFER BURROWS · GORD SIMONIN · KENNETH DASKEWECH · DEE LAISNEZ · ANN TOOMBS · GERRY LUNN · BEVERLEY CAMERON · PETER PERREN · RHYLL MAIKLEM · SANDI JARRETT · ROBERT FOXFORD · MICHAEL HOLY · SUSAN WANAMAKER · WAYNE PATTON · HELGA SCHLENKER · CANDY STRUTHERS · TRISH WALLS · JIRI SOJKA · DIANE POOLE · BRENT RONALD · SUE-ANN MITCHELL · BRUCE HICKS · A. ADDISON · GENE BROPHY · DALE SPURRELL · WAYNE SCHULTZ · LAWRIE BONNEY · HELEN FISCHER · DONELDA EDMONDS · JOANNE MARTIN · MARK BOONSTRA · GEORGE BELL · CHARLOTTE MACNAUGHTON · STEPHEN PHELPS · JANE SANDERCOCK · ERNEST MATTERN · COLIN CLEGG · MIREILLE DELESALLE · BRUCE LIBIN · JANET CONWAY · MAUREEN BRASS · DARRYL DESPAS · JAMES MURPHY · LINDA WELLS · KEN UNDERHILL · MARGARET SWAN · LARRY ALGEO · ROBERTA BUNN · BEV HUTCHINSON · GORDON KUKEC · SHEILA POWELL · SHEILA SMITH · CAL STENE · LES GOROG · DAVID CLARK · TONI IRONSIDE · SHIRLEY VIERTELHAUSEN · FREDA NEWMAN · DEIDRE YOUNG · LAWRENCE HIGHCOCK · RAJU PAUL · DEBBIE YUEN · LYLE HANNA · RITA MIX · KARIN BRYAN · KC JESSUP · JENNIFER ZEBALLOS · JEFFERY ROBINSON · MAE O'DELL · SHARON CORNFIELD · JASON HICKS · REYN CHESHIRE · MARJORIE CHRISTIE · HANK BLAKEMAN · MARK BEDLINGTON · CAROLE YUNKER · DOUG MENZIES · MURRAY GILCHRIST · JIM MUNRO · GERRY DOUTRE · JEFF SANGSTER · AL MUNRO · TERRY BODY · IVAN RADOSTITS · MARIA ROBERTSON · MARILYN WILSON · LEE BROOKES · TREVOR MUELLER · ARNE MATIISEN · DOROTHY DALIK · PATRICK DUNNIGAN · ELEANOR WILLIAMS · BRIAN SOUTIERE· DON KREUGER · HERSCHEL SEGAL · DIANE POMEROY · MICHELE RILEY · HEATHER GARDINER · LISA COX · LEONARD MCKETIAK · RONALD BRYANT · ANDREA ROBERTSON · PETER BOLAND · WILLIAM SATTLEGGER · HAL STANLEY · JAY RYAN · BEATRICE PELUSO · ROBERT BAIN · LYNNE RAPPELL · GARRY GILLIS · NORMAND BOUCHARD · MATTHEW MURRAY · GAYLYNN SCHECHTEL · HUGH MAYO · ZOE NIKOLS · JOEY SILVERMAN · GORDON GRAHAM · ROBERT RIVARD · ROBERT PITTS · DAVE DE BIASIO · DOUG MAHER · WILLIAM MORTON · JOHN RISEBOROUGH · BRENDA DAVISON · B. THORNTON · DEIRDRE RICHARDSON · BILL BENEDICT · STAN JAYCOCK · MARIAN TVEIT · PATRICIA PETRYK · MARIANNE KASTELEN · THERESA FARRELL · RAYMOND JONES · GEORGE BAILEY · CATHY SAWCHENKO · GRANT SMILLIE · MONTY FORD · SUSAN HUTCHISON · RICHARD GLENN · MARSHALL WILLIAMS · TOMISLAU ZIVIC · EDMUND HARRIS · BARBARA FORREST · WALLY DEXTER · GREG WIEBE · PERCY MCDONALD · JOAN SCOTT-BROWN · ROBERT DAVIES · MAURICE GUIBORD · NICK KAZIMIR · NORMAN DEVITT · RANDALL GREGG · DAVID HEWITT · CAROL JOLLIFFE · SHARON REIMER · PAUL KJAER · SUSAN DEEGAN · SANDY BABUSH · PATRICIA FAWCETT · DARRIN DEMALE · DAVE CARLE · TERRI BROWN · AGNES COTE · STEPHANIE STENGLER · CAROL TANNER · MEL MERRELLS · ELAINE MACDONALD · DARREN DEAN · DAN VERNER · SONIA SABA · LYNNE DUNCAN-FRENCH · FRAN HART · PATRICK MELANSON · DOMINIQUE LACEY · JANICE SHARLOW · KELLY WARDLE · JOHN DUFFY · BILL DICK · EARL PERKINS · MARK LYLE · LEN THOMPSON · JUDITH BARLEY · BONITA KINAKIN · PAT BACEDA · DENISE CONNORS · DORIS URCH · JOY HEMMINGS · URSZULA SZULCZEWSKI · FRAN RISHWORTH · RICHARD MASTEL · ANNE ALLIBONE · LYNETTE PAARUP · MADELEINE VIEN · VAL WOHLGEMUTH · SUSAN BARNOFF · HILKKA WALLIS · RUTH SIDEBOTTOM · JEANNINE SIMPSON · BILL AVERY · LYNDA HEARNS · FRANCES METHERELL · JULIETTE JOHN · SCOTT OWENS · J.F. SENECAL · LINDY ARNDT · TODD REICHARDT · DAVE KAWALAUSKAS · ARMIS RUSSELL ·JEANNE KARCZ · ELSIE BENS · ELIZABETH MCRAE · CHRISTINE KING · CATHERINE ARNHOLTZ · HORST KIRMAIER · CHRIS SHANDLEY · LORRAINE NICOL · ROBERT ADAMS · JENNIFER STEWART-SMITH · ROBERT HASLAM · DOROTHY GAREN · JINYEO KIM · MARILYN WATT · HELEN CARTER-EDWARDS · AZIZEH SALEH · JOYCE CROWELL · DONNA STECYK · JULIA SMAAK · DEBORAH ARMSTEAD · BOB GENTLES · MARJORIE FRASER · PATTI YOUNGBERG · PAMELA HEYWOOD · CAROL JAMES-DAVIES · JOHN JABLONSKI · SHONA LOWE · EDWARD DEMCHUK · KEVIN ROSE · DOROTHY LEONG · DOLORIS VOGEL · SHELLEY WEARMOUTH · BRETT BERG · KATHY YOUNG · LARRY SPILAK · DIANE MCGREGOR · LYLE TRAWICK · ROBIN MORGAN · ANNA DEPALO · DON RAE · JOYCE BRUNEAU · BLAIR LOUDEN · DIANE COX · DINA DELORENZO · REASA WRIGHT · KIM MCKINNEY · GEORGE STUETZ · DIANNE HOWE · FLO GAINER · JACQUELINE DENIS · MICHAL PATTERSON · ROBIN SMITH · KEVIN ANDERSON · AUDREY HOOGE · LORNA GARDNER · MARY ANDERSON · GUY DOLL · TOM HEGI · LOUISE PANNENBECKER · KEVIN FLAMING · PAM RHUDE · SUE WILLIAMS · JAMES HANLEY · NETTIE STOWKO · ED GREEN · PAUL NANNELLI · LARRY LEGROS · SUE WOIT · MICHEL LAVIGNE · RICHARD SLATER · DONNA DUKART · MARIAN BEXTON · KATHY HILDEBRAND ·JUNE MCINTYRE · BOB THOMAS · DAVID HEBENTON · MEREDITH SIMON · RAYMOND ELIAS · JILL MAJOR · BRUCE YAMAMOTO · BARBARA MORRISON · ANNE BRADBURY · ANDREW LEITCH · FRANK HENDERSON · NANCY HOGG · JUDY SOUTIERE · HELEN LEE · JANET GATES · BARBARA KUPFERSCHMIDT · BORIS GANCHEV · ALEX FERGUSSON · JENNIFER WARD · ANNE WILSON · MYRON SEMKULEY · CLAIRE POTVIN · PAT STROME · LILY HENIGMAN · ROBIN FOWLER · LLOYD GAUTHIER · FRITZ BECKMANN · ALLAN BRAUSSE · INEKE SMIT · CHRIS JOHNSON · BARRY ADAMS · THORNEY BAILEY · HATCH RAWNSLEY · BOB HOLLINSHEAD · VICKY GASSER · TINA SNOW · LOREE WADDELL · JOAN FREEMAN · ANDREW LOCKHART · DEAN WEBSTER · JOHN THOMAS · TERRY CAMPBELL · LORRAINE CARLSTROM · DONALD

CHAPTER ONE

The Flame

"God keep your land glorious and free!" The words of Juan Antonio Samaranch, president of the International Olympic Committee, rang out across the darkened stadium. Sixty-two thousand people were there, and around the world more than a quarter of the human race was listening and watching on television. It was the evening of Sunday, February 28th, 1988, and the XVth Olympic Winter Games were coming to an end. The mood in Calgary's McMahon Stadium this evening had been jubilant, and, as the last few minutes of our Games ticked away, deeply sad as well.

"These have been the best-organized Olympic Winter Games in history," Samaranch had proclaimed a few minutes before, to a roar of appreciation from the crowd, who sat waving candles. The candles were ordinary white ones, and each was equipped with a red plastic wind guard that made it look like a tiny Olympic torch. From where I stood behind Samaranch, on the silver-painted stage at one end of the stadium, they looked like a sea of flickering stars. I was flying high with excitement. I felt how good it was to be there, to be a Calgarian and to be a Canadian.

WILCOX • CARY ALEXANDER • JEAN LUTHY • ELAINE PROCH-SCHIERMAN • WAYNE ROSBERG • CHRISTINE WILDERMAN • JAMES MCGOVERN • NANCY CLARK • DONNA HOBBS • THOMAS CUMMING • LAURA FOLTINEK • JOAN NEWTON • ISABELLE YVON • HELEN THOMSON • DEAN NELSON • DEBORAH BALAN • WENDY WALKER • HEATHER WIENS • JODI ANTONIUK • BETTE-JUNE HOLLINGTON • TRICIA WILKINSON • DAVID MELVILLE • CAROL HUMMEL • AUDRA HOLLINGSHEAD • BARBARA ROBINSON • FRITH POWELL • MARY FRANK • ROSS PHELPS • KENNETH PAULS • RAYMOND COLLIVER • RAYANNE DELAINI • MAUREEN HALL • AL TARLETON • DAWN PARKER • BEV FULLERTON •

"On behalf of the International Olympic Committee I now declare the XVth Olympic Winter Games closed," Samaranch said, but the crowd answered him with a chorus of dismay. "No! No!" they shouted. No one wanted the Games to end and the Olympic flame to go out. No other Olympic host city had ever resisted the departure of the flame so openly, but Calgarians had played the game differently from the beginning. I was happy with their reaction and relieved that our efforts had been so well received. I was proud to have been a part of it all.

With Samaranch's words a 10-year project and a 10-year dream came to completion for me and for those I had worked with. I thought back over the years—the first talk of organizing an Olympic bid, the struggle to understand the workings of international sport, our winning the bid at Baden-Baden, the efforts to forge a partnership to fund the Games, the infighting and the teamwork, and learning to play the games behind the Games.

For me the beginning had been unexpected. It had come at a meeting nearly 10 years before of the Calgary Booster Club, a group of local businessmen with an interest in developing amateur sport in the Calgary area. At that meeting, my friend Bob Niven and I had volunteered to look into organizing an Olympic bid. In the years that followed, there had been moments when the Olympic dream had seemed about to shatter, and we had held it together by the skin of our teeth and the seats of our pants. At first, many people within the Olympic movement had not taken us seriously, because we were outsiders. We'd had business experience, but none of us had ever organized a large-scale sporting event, let alone the Olympics. Gradually and methodically, however, we had gathered more and more good people around us, and, as the team had grown, so had the momentum. Eventually, we had become unstoppable—partly because we had refused to believe in letting ourselves be stopped.

By the time the XVth Olympic Winter Games ended on that February night, there had been over 20,000 of us on the organizing team. For every athlete in the limelight, there had been 10 people behind the scenes, working to make the show possible. Throughout the Games, the public had seen over and over how the Olympic spirit pushed athletes to the pinnacle of accomplishment; at the same time, I, as an organizer, had seen how the Olympic spirit inspired our volunteers.

The Olympic spirit is an inspiration to pursue excellence—to strive, as the Olympic motto says, to be swifter, higher, and stronger. It is also an inspiration to embrace brotherhood—to work, in the name of sport, for peace and harmony among human beings everywhere. The Olympic spirit chooses sport as its model, but it really applies to all of life. When you catch the spirit, you know you've got it. And once you've got it, others catch it from you. It's contagious.

The Olympic flame is the Olympic spirit's symbol. In Greek mythology, the secret of fire was stolen from the gods, who lived atop Mount Olympus. In the modern Olympic ritual, a flame ignited by the sun is carried by torches from Olympia, in Greece, to wherever the Games are being held.

For the Calgary Games, we had held a cross-Canada torch relay, and the response of Canadians to the ritual had been overwhelming. Thousands of people had stood in bitter cold for hours just to get a chance to see the flame, to hold it, to take a little bit of it away with them. They had broken into spontaneous choruses of *O Canada*, something you don't see very often. Some people, in a curious combination of the magical and the mundane, had lit candles from the torch and carried the flame home with them to light the pilot lights of their furnaces—a down-to-earth and very Canadian way to keep it burning eternally!

When IOC President Samaranch declared the Games over, when the five-ringed flag had been lowered and the Olympic flame in its great copper cauldron extinguished, the dream seemed to end for the moment. But to many, the dream lives on.

I was lucky enough to have a part in Calgary's Olympic adventure from the first Booster Club meeting until the final flicker of the flame. Because I was there in the back rooms from start to finish, I wanted to tell the story, providing many

CLIFFORD MCPHERSON · DEBORAH BARNABE · KEN VOGEL · ROD MAIER · BRENT HARRIS · SHEILA GUREVITCH · LINDA LUSTINS · BILL CARSON · JIM SULLIVAN · SONYA BULYCZ · MARILYN CAMPBELL · JURGEN DAUTER · ARLENE BETKER · DALE COLE · ANTHONY HAMPSHIRE · PAT WATSON · FRANK BREISCH · TOM SEARS · NICK LUNDHILD · BERTHA DAVIS · JEFF GLASS · KYLE KEITH · PATRICIA FISHER · WILLIAM PEPLER · CRAIG BILLINGSLEY · DWIGHT CARROLL · CAMERON PORTER · DORIS MIRKOVICH · JEAN BOUCHARD · GERALD POLACK · JAN SOBEL · WARREN WILLIAMSON · DONNA ZAROWNY · SEAN CASSAR · RONALD BIGSBY · DUANE ALLEN · AUDREY

details never made public before. It is the story of the pride and pain of people working together. It recalls innovative business tactics, together with emotional peaks felt world-wide. It is the story of the indomitable spirit of the people who made it all happen.

Chapter Two

Modest Beginnings

I like to believe in the sturdiness of an enterprise
that begins modestly.

Pierre de Coubertin
FOUNDER OF THE MODERN OLYMPIC MOVEMENT

I had no idea that something special was about to happen as I arrived at the Booster Club meeting and pulled up a chair beside my friend Bob Niven. We chatted about life in the Calgary oilpatch while we waited for President Bill Nield to call the meeting to order. There was nothing out of the ordinary on the agenda for the meeting, and I expected it to be routine. Instead it was a turning point in my life, the beginning of events that would eventually touch millions of others.

As the minutes of the meeting later showed, "It was moved by Jack Wilson and seconded by Lorne Scott that the president appoint a committee to study the possible involvement of the club in obtaining the 1988 Winter Olympics for the Kananaskis area and that the club pay incidental costs related thereto."

When Bill Nield asked for volunteers to serve on the new committee I looked at Bob, who said, "Why don't we go for it?" and we did.

LYNNE HANDY • DONNA RAMSDEN • JOHN BRISTOWE • GARY BIANCHINI • NOREEN SCHEIRMAN • RALPH VIGNA • JOHN (JACK) CADMAN • BOB MACKENZIE • TRACY JOHNSON • JENNIFER HATFIELD • CHRISTINE PEZARRO • RICHARD HAGON • JULIE YOON • DAWN BEATON • JUDY BECK • SEAN FITZGERALD • STUART MACDONELL • JOHN SHIPLEY • GWEN HNATIUK • JACQUELINE GHITTER • PAT RODRIGUEZ • CALVIN HOWELL • LORRAINE CRAIGIE • JIM SIE • WAYNE PETRYSHEN • GEOFFREY GRAVES • KAREN LOOMAN • LYANN ROSS • WILLIAM KAZIMER • ROBERT BAKER • MARLENE LOEWEN • ROGER BOUVIER • FLO BROWN • ERNIE SOLLID • DARRYL WHILLANS • SHARON KEELAGHAN •

The idea to try to bring the Olympics to Calgary didn't come out of the blue. It was inspired by an older project of the Booster Club. The club exists to raise money for amateur athletics. In the mid-1970s we had started trying to raise enough to build a "field house" in the city—a large indoor training facility that could be used for a variety of sports, including track and field. There was no such thing in Calgary back then.

We had tried to get money from the provincial government to build a field house, arguing that Edmonton had received more than its fair share of provincial funding for sports facilities. We had gotten nowhere. Then someone had suggested to us that if we really wanted provincial funding, we should get Calgary to sponsor a major international sporting event. You don't get any more major than the Olympics.

I remember arriving home that night after the Booster Club meeting. When I told my wife Jeanette that Bob Niven and I were going to investigate the feasibility of organizing an Olympic bid, she said, "You've got to be kidding!" Nevertheless, she was intrigued by the idea, and as her enthusiasm awoke it reinforced my own. The possibility still seemed remote, but I felt that it could happen.

I'm not sure why Bob Niven decided to get involved in the Calgary Olympic bid, but I know why I did. My visits to the Montreal Olympics in 1976 and the Edmonton Commonwealth Games that summer in 1978 had impressed and moved me, making me aware of the full potential of such sporting events.

The Montreal Olympic Games were something of a good news–bad news story. The Games were a sporting success, but the people of Montreal were left burdened with heavy taxes to pay for the financial mismanagement of the construction of Olympic facilities. Yet people who saw the 1976 Olympics remember the special feelings generated by the first visit of the Olympic Games to Canada. Jeanette and I had gone to Montreal without high expectations. We expected to see only a pretty good track meet. Instead we came away with a feeling of joy, achievement, and national pride. We were hooked on the Olympic Games.

The summer of 1978 added to our good feelings about the Games because it was a golden summer for Canadian sports. The Edmonton Commonwealth Games provided all that is good about international sporting events. They were financially well-managed, produced great athletic competitions, and, most of all, sparked a revived faith in Canada as a country. The 1978 Games provided Edmonton with a complete set of Olympic-standard sports facilities without making taxpayers suffer the way they had in Montreal.

The Montreal Games had the high emotional impact always associated with Olympics. The Edmonton Games demonstrated that good Games could entertain and inspire as well as be well-managed financially. With those two events as background, I soon became obsessed with the idea that Calgary should assume a place in the top echelon of international sporting cities. It wasn't until years later that I realized how deeply the Olympic movement touches many people, just as it had us. Bob Niven and I had frequent lunch-hour meetings together to talk about the enormous investigative job ahead. We had one big advantage: we knew virtually nothing about the Olympics. At the beginning we couldn't see the real problems; if we had, we might have quit early on. Instead, we forged ahead. We agreed to divide the work. I took on responsibility for organizational and political aspects, as well as figuring out the bidding procedure and how the Games would be financed. He agreed to take on the technical aspects, finding out about the sports involved, the facilities needed, and how much the Games would cost.

Losing is an Important Part of Winning

We soon learned that the idea of hosting the world's most inspiring athletic event was a dream that had been dashed for Canadians on six previous occasions. Of the six formal Canadian bids for the Olympic Winter Games that had been rejected by the International Olympic Committee, three had come from Calgary. For almost a quarter century Calgarians had aspired to host the Olympic Winter Games, but after three unsuccessful bids it seemed an impossible goal, and the architects of the bids had moved on to other endeavors.

LYNN PACE · SONNY O'SULLIVAN · DARLENE LINDSAY · PETER BALOGH · GWENDA PARDOE · NANCY JACQUES · TERENCE MCKIMM · CAROL RICHARDSON · SEAN MCLEAN · BILL HASEGAWA · CHERI GLEASON · MAUREEN WOODSKE · KEN HOLDEN · KATHY SCALES · MAUREEN DONAIS · RON FRIDAY · LINDA KOT · JEAN HUGILL · ILSE HADDAD · DAVID BROOKS · ROBERT SEVICK · MICHELLE MAGDA · ROBERT CHURCHILL · CORINNA GORSKI · MARK WATERS · PATRICIA MAHONEY · DONNA MCGINNIS · TED PETERSEN · ELIZABETH BURKE-GAFFNEY · RON BEIRNES · GLENDA JONES · LESLIE NORMAN · CATHY LEHEW · JEAN SILZER · ROB BAILEY · PEARL SNYDER · SANDY

Six times Canada had failed. Why? For starters, it was evident that Canada was far behind Europe in its influence over winter sports. Of the first 14 Olympic Winter Games, 10 were held in Europe—and all the winter sports federations have European presidents. At first glance it appeared to us that Canada was a third-world country as far as the international winter sports community was concerned. Our first job therefore became to understand the workings of international sport.

We learned that the Olympic movement has three main parts: the International Olympic Committee (IOC), the National Olympic Committees, and the International Sports Federations. The IOC is in charge of the whole Olympic movement and is responsible for putting on the Games every four years. The National Olympic Committee in each country trains and selects the athletes to represent the country, and the International Sports Federations make and administer the rules in each sport.

The IOC was established in Europe late in the nineteenth century. It selects for its members people it believes will help spread the aims of the Olympic movement throughout the world. Not all countries have an IOC member; others have two. The Olympic Charter, adopted by the IOC and modified from time to time at annual sessions, provides the rules that guide the movement. The strength of the IOC stems from the simplicity of its rules. There is no attempt to implement tight controls, and the development of sports programs within each country is completely autonomous.

In order to present a bid to the IOC to host the Olympic Games, a city must first obtain approval from the National Olympic Committee in its own country. The city must then convince a majority of the IOC members that it deserves the honor of hosting the Games. So we faced a complex and competitive two-tier lobbying process: first the Canadian Olympic Association (COA), then the IOC.

Those who had been involved in Canada's past Olympic bids were almost uniformly pessimistic about our chances of success. Most felt bidding again was a fruitless exercise—that it was arduous and highly political, and that it was doubly

HORNE • JANE WALLACE • BOB COUCH • GRANT HENNEBERG • TOM LEITHEAD • MICHELE MCKENZIE • DOUG SMITH • MARIE WILLIAMS • MARGE DAVIDSON • DENNIS KERBER • SANDRA WEBB • ALLEN SMYTHE • JEFFREY MARSTON • RANDY JAGGARD • BRUCE MAY • KEITH EVELEIGH • ROSVITA VASKA • ERV SCHIEMAN • RONALD WARD • ROSS SALMON • LAURIE KOLBA • RON SANDRIN-LITT • VIRGINIA CARR • FRANK ZAJICEK • CAROL PEDERSON • DENIS ETHIER • WENDY SINGENDONK • RONALD FRANCE • RON FOSTER • SHERRY SMITH • ALLISON WESTLAND • DAVID SHEPPARD • CHRISTINE PAGENKOPF • GORDON MCPHEETERS • ROBBI JAMES • WAYNE PAKENHAM • MICHAEL GINDL •

difficult for Canadians because we were so far removed from the decision-making process of the IOC, whose headquarters are in Lausanne, Switzerland.

From the beginning we refused to accept gloomy prognoses. Instead we decided to examine in detail each of the three previous Calgary bids for structural flaws. Many of the former key Olympic bid organizers had scattered to the four winds, but two organizers in particular, Ernie McCullough, a former Olympian, and Art Smith, a former MP, provincial MLA, and city alderman, had played crucial roles in other bids and were still around to talk with us.

Calgary's previous bids had been orchestrated by the Calgary Olympic Development Association (CODA), founded by Ernie McCullough. CODA's first bid, in 1959, to host the 1964 Winter Games, had not been a serious effort, but simply an attempt to raise the IOC's awareness of Calgary's interest and pave the way for a future bid. Immediately after the decision to award the 1964 Winter Games to Innsbruck, Austria, CODA set about fine-tuning a more serious bid for 1968. The second presentation was a strong one, but Calgary lost out narrowly to Grenoble, France. While the IOC is close-mouthed about its reasons for selecting some sites and rejecting others, a factor in the decision seems to have been the politics of geography: since the 1960 Olympic Winter Games had been awarded to the U.S. (Squaw Valley), and Mexico City was favored to win the bid for the 1968 Summer Games, the committee apparently wanted a European rather than a North American venue for the 1968 Winter Games.

Art Smith told us about Calgary's strong bid for the 1972 Winter Games and how organizers had been confident of a victory. The 1972 Winter Games bid team, however, led by Edgar Davis and including Peter Lougheed, Art Smith, and Hans Maciej, didn't take into account the awakening of environmental groups to the implications of holding a major sporting event inside Banff National Park. Prior to the 1972 bid, those groups had not been well organized, but after Calgary's narrow loss to Grenoble for the 1968 Winter Games, they gained a new sense of urgency and organized a massive letter-writing campaign to the IOC that greatly damaged the third Calgary bid. Just before the voting, the president of the IOC, Avery Brundage, openly communicated his concerns about the Calgary bid and read out excerpts from environmentalists' letters threatening disruption of the Games with protests and demonstrations. In the end it was not surprising that Calgary lost to Sapporo, Japan, again by a narrow margin.

International forces seemed perpetually determined to keep Canada from winning, and the CODA bid team became disillusioned and bitter. Art Smith remarked during interviews at the Sapporo victory, "While we were singing the Olympic anthem, we were being goosed by the Olympic torch!" This odd metaphor was a reference to the fact that the Calgary bid team had not expected to face the open hostility of IOC President Brundage.

The things that had made Calgary lose its previous bids were all things we felt we could change. We agreed that the Olympic Winter Games should not be held in a national park, and decided to exclude that option from our plan. Despite the pessimism among people who had been involved in past bidding our excitement about the possibilities of winning the next bid grew by leaps and bounds. Our investigations uncovered another more serious problem, however. From the beginning we knew that Calgary did not have all the facilities needed to host the Olympic Winter Games. But as we studied the requirements more closely we were shocked to find that Calgary had no world-class winter sports facilities at all. For example, the city's best hockey rink, the Stampede Corral, had served us well for 30 years, but 14 other Canadian cities now had larger and more modern arenas than Calgary.

Canada was ranked third in the world in speed skating, but was without even one usable refrigerated track. It had been more than 13 years since a major ski area had been developed in Alberta, and nowhere in Canada was there a bobsleigh or luge track. Calgary was like a growing boy who had always got by in jeans, had now outgrown them, and had nothing better to wear for a big occasion.

The lack of established facilities in Calgary presented a reason to fear failure in competitions against better-equipped

European bid cities. But Calgary's lack of sports facilities had originally motivated our bid, and perhaps it would help motivate the IOC as well. By allowing Calgary to build all-new facilities, the IOC could take a dramatic step forward for winter sports. Together we could build a complete set of sports facilities better than those existing anywhere. We began to see a chance to do enormous good through becoming a host city for the Olympic Winter Games. We decided to raise our goals beyond those of our predecessors and not only win the bid, but make the Calgary Winter Games the best ever.

The concept of pursuing excellence—of being the best in the world at what we were doing—began to dominate our thinking.

We showed the Booster Club some of the books from previous bids, each containing inspiring pictures of sporting events and new facilities. The books were impressive and they awoke the members' competitive spirits. Realizing how far behind Calgary was in developing sports facilities, the Booster Club supported the idea of a bid with equal parts of doubt and enthusiasm.

The First Team

Every successful venture is built around good people, so getting the right players on our team became a priority. Soon Bob Niven and I had recruited other Booster Club members—Jack Wilson, a former Olympic hockey player; Bill Nield, a financial administrator; and Fred Wuotila, a clothing merchant. From that small group we began to build a stronger and stronger team of supporters in the community. It would take a super team to achieve the new standards of performance we now had in mind. The concept of quality is contagious. We quickly began to reject anything that was only mediocre and chased after perfection.

I had heard that Roger Jackson, a former gold-medal Olympian, had recently been appointed dean of physical education at the University of Calgary. Roger had won a gold medal in pairs rowing at the 1964 Olympics in Tokyo. He knew a lot about the Olympics, since he was a member of the

TATTERSALL • TROY TARNOWSKI • GEORGE DIAMANT • PATRICIA GILLESPIE • SHARON LAWSON • LYNDON WESTERBERG • PETER SIGG • KELLI ROTH • ALLAN KENNEDY • BEVERLEY BRODIE • KIKA GRANDI • PATRICIA COMPTON • CHUCK FOWLER • DOUGLAS LOEWEN • STEVE HOLLO • LESLIE JOHN • SCOTT HERRINGTON • CAROL COOK • TRISH SHEPARD • JOHN JOHNSTON • ANGELA BELL • MAURICE BUCK • JOANNE CUCHIRAN • TERRY FLOOD • LEONARD HOWLAND • VERONICA ZELNICEK • ANNE MATKALUK • MAUREEN MEDDINS • SUSAN MONTGOMERY • MARNIE FISHER • LARS SILFVERSWARD • KENNETH PICKARD • KELLY STAN • STEVEN HARRINGTON • LOIS LONG •

COA and had just retired as director of Sport Canada, the federal agency responsible for amateur sport. It was obvious to me that Roger would be a tremendous asset to our bid and I had to make sure we recruited him.

On the drive up to the university I pondered the best way to explain our plan and our dream to Roger Jackson. As I spoke to him the expression on his face was quizzical, as if to say, "It's a wonderful idea. I couldn't possibly say anything against it, but do you think you can actually bring these Games here?"

What he actually said was that his new job and family responsibilities didn't allow him enough free time to help us.

There are turning points in any major undertaking and for us this was one. After listening to Roger Jackson's polite refusal, I said, "That's the wrong answer. It's too important for Calgary. We need your help. You must be involved." Roger appeared amused and taken aback by my directness and agreed to think it over. Later he accused me of twisting his arm, but when I called him back after a few days his answer was, "I'm in." Our first team was beginning to take shape.

An IOU from Iona

Meanwhile, Bob Niven was churning out cost estimates. It was frightening because the figures were enormous. It became clear, based on the costs of the Innsbruck, Sapporo, and Grenoble Winter Games, as well as the ones about to take place in Lake Placid, that holding the Games would cost at least $200 million. But unlike most of the previous host cities, we needed much more in terms of new facilities. The Calgary Winter Games would not be cheap.

Our tiny team of Olympic bidders created a business plan that outlined the essential ingredients for success. To pay for building new facilities we would need the support of all three levels of government. The Olympic lottery, created to help pay Montreal's Olympic debt, was already making huge amounts of money. Canadians took to their first form of legalized gambling, later called Lotto Canada, with a passion. Perhaps people everywhere love to buy lottery tickets because they believe it is one way to make their dreams come true. Lotteries are deceptive. They tell you that in order to win, you don't have to work, you only have to be lucky. In real life, the reverse is true.

The total gross revenues of the national lottery were approaching $1 billion and we felt the federal government was in a good position to use that new-found money for new projects. Nearly $400 million had been used to pay for Montreal Olympic facilities from 1976. Why not for Olympic facilities in Calgary for 1988?

Roger Jackson arranged a breakfast meeting with his former boss, Iona Campagnolo, the federal minister of Fitness and Amateur Sport, to discuss financing the Calgary facilities. We also invited Calgary Mayor Ross Alger, who had been generally supportive of our bid. The mayor was away, so Alderman Stan Nelson came in his place. The breakfast meeting with the minister was set for 7 a.m. at the Four Seasons Hotel in Calgary.

Roger and I had not planned a formal agenda for the meeting. Our intention was simply to test the minister's attitude toward funding support for Calgary's Winter Games. We had barely introduced the subject to Mrs. Campagnolo, however, when she caught me off guard by asking, "How much money do you need?" We hadn't even prepared a definitive answer to that basic question.

My mind flashed to the sheets of cost estimates prepared by Bob Niven. Bob had done all the legwork necessary to understand the various costs experienced at Sapporo, Innsbruck, and Lake Placid; we had sat together and, in only one night at my family's kitchen table, converted Bob's research into a full-blown budget. We had mulled over the numbers and begun an educated guessing game—throwing in a million or two here and there until we had done our best to balance what we needed against what we wanted. Later, the kitchen-table budget numbers gained undeserved credibility when the local media published them. After that the numbers were cast in stone. Later Bob and I often joked that we defended them as if even we had been taken in by their apparent authenticity.

MCMILLAN · RICHARD QUAST · JEFFREY BADYK · JACK MCMANUS · TERENCE THOMPSON · PEGGY MARSURA · HUGH MCLEOD · JENNIFER NIVEN · KIM JOHNSON · DAVID HOLMES · SHARLENE CRISS · BEVERLEY IVERSON · ANN SMITH · TAMMY HIROSE · PETER MARTIN · PAUL LANGE · LANE PETERS · CAROL ANNE FAULKNER · DIANA ALBERY · BONNIE NIEMI · SUSAN HARGRAVE · WALTER WONG · CYNTHIA PIDBORCHYNSKI · TOM WARD · HARRY KUHARCHUK · PAT CHAPMAN · LESTER PARDOE · GLENN MCBURNEY · ARMIN KUHME · FIROZ SHAH · JOAN MATTHEWS · JIM ANDERSON · VICTOR EMERY · JOSEPH LANGLAIS · LESLEY BARLASS · JEFF FITZGERALD · ARNIE MILLER · CRAIG

When Iona asked how much money we needed, I recalled that our numbers showed total costs for previous Games starting in the range of $200 million, and we needed more. So I blurted out, "We need $200 million from the lottery program." As I spoke, Roger Jackson's eyebrows vanished over his forehead in an expression of alarm. Two hundred million dollars seemed a huge number, probably far more than we could ever expect from one level of government. Perhaps I'd made a mistake in asking for so much, but the minister was already nodding thoughtfully. There was a long pause. Finally she answered, "I don't think that's inappropriate at all. In fact, I think that should be quite do-able."

Roger's eyes flashed relief. Off the cuff, going by instinct, we had landed in a comfort zone. The magic figure of $200 million became the focal point for all future financial negotiations with the federal government. Iona, Roger, and I all felt strongly that the money should come from the national lottery. We wanted to avoid asking the government to divert tax revenues from more important uses, since any such diversion would have given citizens a reason to be against our plans.

Iona Campagnolo probably understood more about what we were doing than we did. So Roger and I let the minister teach us about the lottery system. The outcome of that meeting was better than we had hoped. Everywhere else we were being told we were crazy. Iona Campagnolo was the first to share our vision—to say, "You can do it, you must do it, and I will support you all the way." Roger and I practically floated out of that meeting, and the encounter made a strong impression on Alderman Stan Nelson for his report back to the mayor.

Getting Things Rolling

With the support of one potential partner in place, we moved quickly to gain support from the Province of Alberta and from the City of Calgary. With important meetings in Calgary, Edmonton, and Ottawa, I felt like a juggler with three balls in the air.

Since many of the facilities we required could not be built within the city itself, we needed big provincial dollars. Our strategy was to use Calgary's need for a new hockey rink as the focal point of our discussions.

There had been talk around Calgary about a National Hockey League franchise coming to town, but without a major new arena, that was unlikely to happen. Two groups, one headed by Vancouver entrepreneur Nelson Skalbania, and another by a popular local oilman, Doc Seaman, were negotiating to bring the Atlanta Flames hockey team to Calgary. It was something everybody wanted, but the tiny 6,700-seat Stampede Corral was simply not NHL calibre. A new arena for the Olympics could be our ticket to gaining the city's support.

Mayor Alger was quick to see the advantage in building a hockey arena that could attract both the Olympic Winter Games and an NHL franchise. We had the attention of our second government partner; now all we needed was support from the Province of Alberta.

I arranged to see Peter Trynchy, minister of Recreation and Parks for the Alberta Government. Trynchy was receptive to our plans but not as eagerly supportive as I had thought he would be, considering that Alberta had recently hosted the successful Commonwealth Games in Edmonton. Perhaps it was because he, more than anyone else, knew the serious risks involved in staging international games.

In December 1978 I went to Ottawa to see Jack Horner, the minister of Industry, Trade and Commerce, to pin down federal support. As Alberta's only representative in the Trudeau cabinet, his endorsement of our bid was essential. In a brief three-minute meeting in a hallway of Canada's parliament buildings, Horner promised his support for our effort. I'm not sure he grasped the full impact of the project, but I accepted his commitment gladly.

At the meeting of the Booster Club in January 1979, Bob Niven and I were able to report that we now knew what was required to prepare our bid, and that all three levels of government had committed themselves to some degree of support. Iona Campagnolo's $200 million in lottery funds were critical; we were sure she had given us a serious commitment. Although Jack

Horner had added his support, we felt he could not necessarily be relied upon to come through in concrete terms. Peter Trynchy had offered a cordial but less-than-firm handshake deal on behalf of the Alberta government, and Ross Alger had urged us to proceed on the basis that the crucial support of City Council could be obtained when the time was right.

We told the Booster Club that we had decided to revive the original Calgary Olympic Development Association (CODA) as a vehicle to make the bid. We appointed 13 CODA directors, including Mayor Alger and charter member Art Smith. I would be chairman of CODA and Bob Niven its president. The Booster Club provided $35,000 in seed money, but we were to raise all other funding from private sources.

It was a humble beginning—but we had begun.

Going Public

It was time to take the bid to the public. In deciding when we should make the announcement, we knew we had a serious competitor hot on our heels: Vancouver, a city that had itself made two unsuccessful Olympic bids to the IOC, both recently. The Vancouver bid was not yet public, but somehow we got wind of it, probably through a contact within the COA. Many people assumed Vancouver would be a shoo-in next time around, especially with the participation of the fabulous new Whistler-Blackcomb ski resort.

We needed the Canadian Olympic Association's endorsement to take our bid to the IOC. To win that endorsement we would have to eliminate Vancouver from the competition. That would not be easy, because Vancouver had recent bidding experience and we knew virtually nothing about the game. We took the challenge seriously and stepped up our effort.

We wanted to get the jump on Vancouver by going public with our announcement first. Late in January 1979 we heard the Vancouver bid committee was about to announce its bid, so ready or not we were caught. We picked February 2nd for our inaugural press conference at the Westward Inn—not Calgary's finest hotel, but all we could afford.

Despite the scramble, I was confident when I took the podium and announced:

> The Calgary Booster Club has reorganized the Calgary Olympic Development Association (CODA) to prepare a bid on behalf of the City of Calgary for the 1988 Olympic Winter Games. We are about to embark on a campaign to fulfill the dream that one day Calgary will have the distinction of hosting this great international event.
>
> In assessing the criteria for an Olympic bid we naturally had to consider the potential hazards and pitfalls. We are sensitive to the excessive cost overruns of the Montreal Olympics and the environmental concerns of previous Calgary Olympic bids. These problems will not be overlooked when the final plans for the 1988 Winter Games are prepared.
>
> We accept the fact that there may be many such concerns that could pose very real problems for our future bid hopes. However, we will not allow ourselves to become intimidated from the outset by the fear of failure, or Calgarians may never experience the pride of hosting the Winter Olympics, and Calgarians may lose the more tangible and lasting benefits of Olympic facilities and Olympic recognition.
>
> We are reminded that Edmonton also faced many real and potential problems before it set out to present the Commonwealth Games in 1978. All Albertans and Canadians stood tall with pride beside our Edmonton neighbors as they successfully delivered one of the finest world-class Games ever held. The Winter Olympics are an even greater undertaking, and Calgarians are equal to the challenge.

I talked about our plans to build major new sporting facilities and the benefits that would result. The long-term legacy was of paramount importance, we believed. I continued:

> We already know that many millions of dollars will be required to finance this construction. We expect to finance the Games from public subscriptions as well as funding from all three levels of government and private sources. This money will be spent in the Calgary area, creating income and job opportunities for many inside the Calgary economy. The legacy of Olympic facilities left in place after the Games for public use must be self-evident.
>
> Not least among the benefits of staging Olympic Games is the positive impact on the growth of amateur athletics. Calgary will be the focal point of world interest during the Winter Games of 1988.
>
> The inspiration of the Calgary Olympics will endure long after the Olympic flame has been extinguished. Canadians of all ages will use and enjoy superb Olympic facilities for years into the future. The Olympics will be more than an immediate benefit. The Games will provide a heritage for our children.

RICHARD DVORAK • SHERRON PATTERSON • GLYNARTH HOWELLS • NEIL MCKENDRICK • KEIKO HATCH • MARTY KERNAGHAN • ROBERT TOKARYK • DON HEASMAN • BILL WOODS • SCOT BULLICK • ANDRE CHOW • JOHN SHARPE • JAMES STOREY • CAROL HERN • SYLVIA SPARKE • GWEN MULDREW • GABRIELE GULLISON • BOB GEHLEN • BRUCE MOHR • JENNIFER DUNCAN • CAROL ATKEY • HARRY HACKL • JULIA HAMILTON • THOM ULEVOG • HARRY TINGLEY • ROY WILLIAMS • RAYMOND MCKAY • JAMES HAIGHT • TRACY MACLEAN • RONALD HUYBERS • LISA FREEMAN • KERRY BLACK • DEAN TREMAINE • MARGARET HART • KENNETH MOORE • EVELYNE TODD • HERB GOODWIN •

I finished with a plea to the media to help us tell our story in order that the public might be able to understand the Olympic bid and participate in it. Back then I figured that, since the Olympics were an obviously good thing, the media would simply be our ally. Later they would be our adversary on more than one occasion. I have learned from those experiences never to underestimate the media's ability to find the downbeat angle on a happy story.

We had an excellent turnout of reporters but most of them were puzzled and skeptical. Who were we, after all, to announce our bid with such fanfare? We were unknown to the Calgary sporting establishment, untried and naïve. We had no facilities, no experience in bidding, and no money to support our bid. How could we hope to succeed where those before us had failed?

Ken Newans, a local radio and television sportscaster, looked puzzled. When it came time for questions, he raised his hand first. "I'm sorry Mr. King," he said, "but I've never heard of you before. What have you done?"

"I'm not surprised you haven't heard of me," I replied, explaining that my background was simply that of a businessman who cared about his community and had been involved with the Booster Club.

"Sports and business have to be combined if the Games are going to be successful," I said. "I believe the people of Calgary want the Games but there will be tremendous resistance to any additional tax burdens. For that reason the Games will be organized by people with a business background combined with a love for sports. We expect to be supported but not controlled by all levels of government. We will use the strength of the people in our community to avoid the problems of Montreal. We will ask people to give much, not to take from the project."

Newans ran out of the room and phoned his station to report that Calgary's fourth bid for the Olympic Winter Games had officially begun.

JEFF SIMUS · GWYNETH JORGENSEN · RICHARD MAKI · HELMUT SCHODERBOCK · TOSHIKO TAMAOKI · SUSANNAH HAMER · GERRY DE IURE · KIM LAKER · DANIEL MATO · THOMAS SMITH · VLADIMIR SHUSHKOVSKY · BRENT KIRKPATRICK · HARVEY CHUSID · ROY KELLY · CURTIS SAGER · KEN LEONG · SHAWNA STEWART · SUSAN MAGEE · BRIAN SUDEYKO · MARY BOZARTH · HAROLD GOLDSTEIN · YOKO GALVIN · PAMELA DEADMARSH · GABRIELE CHRISTEN · KEN STUART · WALLY CRAIG · JOSEPHINE BENEDEK · KATHLEEN GALLINARI · MEGU WHYTE · JEFFREY THOMAS · ANN GARNEAU · ROBERT GINGERA · MICHAEL KONOPCZYNSKI · MAUREEN TYNAN · JOHN WATSON ·

Reaction to our announcement was overwhelmingly positive. An editorial in the *Calgary Herald* the next day summarized the reasons we were so enthusiastic about making the bid:

> Calgary and Alberta as a whole would be left with an even richer and more productive legacy if the 1988 bid (or subsequent tries) were successful. . . .
>
> There are risks associated with a bid of this kind. They're worth taking unless Calgarians are content to continually play the backwater might-have-been game while cities such as Edmonton move further and further ahead on the cultural and recreational front.
>
> Alberta's oil won't last forever. Now is the time to lay the foundations for a more viable tourism industry—winter as well as summer.
>
> Bid for the 1988 Winter Olympics? By all means, and with every ounce of enthusiasm Calgarians and Albertans can muster.

Exactly three days after our press conference, Vancouver announced its own candidacy. We suspected that Vancouver, too, had rushed its announcement, so as not to be too far behind us. But we had beaten them to the first punch.

We played down Vancouver's announcement and gave press interviews saying that Vancouver's bid was simply a reaction to our own proposal. Our opening salvo worked; the *Calgary Herald* headline read VANCOUVER WANTS OLYMPICS TOO. It was the first step toward turning the tables—making us the innovative frontrunner and them the copycats. The first game had started, and it was a game we did not intend to lose.

MAURICE SHUGARMAN · CHRISTINA ARVIDSSON · PHILIP GOODHALL · LAURIE LANGENHOFF · GAIL EDGELOW · DIANNE BROSSEAU · JOHN DUNBAR · PETER HEEMSKERK · DON DAVIS · YVON LAVERDIERE · HARRY WARREN · LAWRENCE WILLMER · GARY WAGNER · DODIE ANDERSON · GAIL COSTELLA · TONY SHARPLES · RON CAMPBELL · CHERI JONES · GEORGE RAE · TOM DUNN · BUCK LAVOIE · DENISE KADATZ · NADINE ADOLPH · JENNIFER FOWLER · FAY SETO · LYDDA LUTSENKO · RON RHODES · B.J. ERSSON · SHERRY BEITEL · DEANNA ALMDAL · MELANIE HAYDEN · JOE HOSPODAREC · PATRICK MACKASEY · JOYCE TSANG · MAC MCCAFFREY · LOIS ADAM · DAVID

CHAPTER THREE

The First Round

The future belongs to those who believe in the
beauty of their dreams.

ELEANOR ROOSEVELT

W E HAD ONLY eight months left to plan our bid to the
Canadian Olympic Association (COA). In that short
time we had to find suitable sites for downhill skiing,
cross-country skiing, biathlon, ski jumping, bobsleigh, luge,
speed skating, hockey, and figure skating, as well as the media
and athletes' villages, main press centre, and international
broadcast facilities. We didn't get much sleep during those
months, what with working hard at our regular businesses by
day and CODA by night.

A Little Site-Seeing

Bob Niven discovered an existing proposal for a major
commercial skiing development in the Spray Lakes Valley east
of Banff National Park. We consulted Ken Read, Canada's top
alpine skier, who provided us with preliminary advice on
downhill skiing site selection. We developed a novel idea to
build an outdoor speed skating oval inside the thoroughbred

HENDRICKSON · STEVEN DAVIS · COLIN LUMBY · KEN BLIMKIE · JOON CHOE · REX BARKER · MARJORIE NELSON · MARY BOONSTRA ·
DAWN STEWART · QUINN MARTIN · HILDA WOZNI · WADE NORTH · PATRICIA LENGAUER · CAROL WOJTOWICZ · DONALD STONE · ISABELLA
OSTMAN · TERRY GERMAIN · LORRAINE NELSON · CAROL PHILLIPS · DAVID SPEERS · CLAUDIA COLLINS · GERALD EDWARDS · SHELLY
LOGAN GORDANIER · RODNEY LODON · SIDNEY CRAIG · CHERYL BEATTIE · MIKE MOORE · PETER CROMER · DEANNA CROFT · JOANN
JENSEN · SABINE FINKENSIEP · E.Y. PERREAULT · GLEN HOLMAN · HENRY DE PAIVA · PETER SCHACK · CRAIG SMITH · LUANNE MORROW ·

racetrack at Stampede Park, making use of the existing grandstand with its partly enclosed viewing area and 17,000 seats.

The student residences at the University of Calgary were an ideal spot for the Olympic athletes' village. We were pleased to learn that plans were already under way to expand the number of rooms to meet the demands of a growing student population. We also asked the City of Calgary to provide housing for the media that could later be used to meet the need for senior citizens' homes and low-cost housing.

Early agreement had been reached on the need for a new Olympic coliseum for hockey and figure skating as part of the city's support for our bid. An old 60-metre ski jump at Mount Norquay in Banff National Park was available, but we needed 70- and 90-metre jumps for the Olympics, and we had determined to stay outside the national park to preserve the support of the environmentalists. So we decided that Bragg Creek, a beautiful wooded area about half an hour's drive west of Calgary, would be a good place for the Nordic winter sports. We retained Underwood McLelland Associates to do the preliminary engineering designs to help us put together a professional presentation.

The Canadian Olympic Association evaluation team arrived in September 1979 to inspect our proposed sites. We were becoming reasonably conversant with most of the winter sports but were concerned about our lack of real knowledge about bobsleigh and luge. We asked Vic Emery, Canadian Olympic gold medallist in bobsleigh for 1964, to come help us. He accompanied us with the COA evaluation team to the bobsleigh hill we had chosen in the Spray Lakes Valley. He had never seen the area before. Looking around he said, "Well, where is the bobsleigh run going to be?" The COA team were out of earshot.

"Right here," we answered brightly. "Here on this hill right in front of you."

"That's impossible," he whispered, glancing around to make sure the COA people didn't hear. "That slope is at least twice as steep as you want for bobsledding."

We had a few seconds to let that sink in while the COA evaluators walked over. "Which hill are you going to be using for bobsleigh?" they asked.

"That one over there," we replied nonchalantly, pointing to another, much gentler slope down the valley a discreet distance from our original choice. We were instant experts designing an Olympic bid on the fly.

If it seems, in retrospect, that we didn't know what we were doing, it's because often we didn't. Time pressures were enormous and we were not just planning a bobsleigh run, we were planning everything needed for Olympic Winter Games. Starting from scratch, we had literally a few weeks, working as volunteers in our spare time, to make all the final decisions. Our competitors in Vancouver had only to dust off a competent bid already made once before to the IOC.

A Run for the Money

The years 1978 and 1979 were busy ones for me. On top of my day job and my work with CODA, I was busy in January, February, March, and the first half of April training for the biggest challenge of my life.

It was a time of heady growth for my company, Turbo Resources. In early 1978, Turbo had been negotiating to buy a packaging plant from Joe Womersly, the president of an eastern-Canadian company. Joe and I had haggled for weeks over the terms of the acquisition but remained $1 million apart in price. Finally Womersly suggested, only half jokingly, that we should settle the dispute with an eight-mile foot race around the city. I had been a competitive long-distance runner in university, but hadn't done much running for nearly 20 years. I returned his challenge, saying that considering the big money at stake, the race should be something a little more difficult . . . like the Boston Marathon. The idea of running in the prestigious Boston Marathon held a certain appeal to me, and since I was a few years younger than Womersly, I assumed I'd have a good chance of beating him. Womersly obviously had different thoughts because he quickly accepted my million-dollar challenge. We were too late to register for the Boston

Marathon that year, so we had to postpone settling the bet until April 1979.

My friend Bob Brawn, president of Turbo, was incredulous when he learned that I had arranged to run the Boston Marathon to settle our money difference. I was shocked too, when I learned that Joe Womersly ran marathons regularly! I'd never run anything longer than a 10-kilometre race, and in the last three years I hadn't run any distance greater than the last three blocks to the Calgary Petroleum Club.

The Boston Marathon was almost a year away, but I put off training because I was so busy. Joe, meanwhile, ran two marathons. Then we hit a snag: in order to register for the Boston run, you had to have run a previous marathon in three-and-a-half hours or less. Joe's times were both slightly over that figure, and I had never run a marathon at all. Neither of us was qualified to sign up.

Joe sought the intervention of a friend of his on the Metro Police marathon committee in Toronto. He got his friend to falsify Joe's time in the Toronto Police Marathon and fabricate a record for me. It was cheating, but in a sportsmanlike spirit. The times we gave ourselves were both three hours and 30 minutes—the minimum we needed to qualify for the Boston race. It was the only way we would be able to tackle the challenge.

I trained all that winter, going from my normal 185 pounds to a rakelike 158 pounds. Jeanette often called me "turkey neck." During many late evenings training on the 12-mile footpath around nearby Glenmore Reservoir, I had time alone to develop ideas for our Olympic bid. On cold Calgary evenings in January and February I would often return home at midnight from a 90-minute run covered in hoarfrost created by my breath. Local residents must have thought they had seen the Abominable Snowman.

Our whole family accompanied me to Boston in April to support me in this wild wager. The starting area for the Boston Marathon was a mass of humanity. Each runner has a starting number that tells him or her where to go in the lineup to start the race. The worse your times on previous marathons, the

SHYMKA • JOYCE WILLS • ANDRE LIPTAK • TRACY NAULT • ROD SMITH • DOT SMYTH • NANCY VAN VEEN • GORDON LANGLOIS • JAMES WOOD • TOM STOREY • DIANE RASCHIG • MARNEY FLEMING • AGNES REWUCKI • MICHAEL STERN • MICHELLE VANCE • JILL BURNS • RUSS TYNAN • JOHN TESSMAN • RENEE SMITH • MARLENE BELLAMY • GERRY ALCAZAR • ALBERT SNIDER • BARB POFFENROTH • ALLEN MASSINE • KERRI SPRUNG • CATHY PRIESTNER-ALLINGER • BRUCE MCCARTNEY • BARBARA MCKAY • KEN YOUNG • CATHERINE COOPER • CATHERINA VAN DEN AKKER • RONALD DUFORT • JANE PATERSON • NEIL ROBERTSON • EVELYN BARTON • PHYLLIS BANKS • LOGAN

farther back in the pack you are supposed to start. I went to the appointed place but Joe was nowhere to be found. I searched everywhere. Finally it was noon, the gun sounded, and we were off. Like every first-time marathoner, I wanted to start running immediately but there was no way to get going with 10,000 people in front of me. It took me seven minutes to walk to the starting line. Bill Rogers, the eventual winner, was already one-and-a-half miles down the road—and I hadn't even started yet.

Gradually the crowd of runners spread out and I was under way, pushing past people and searching for any place I could find to open up. I felt very strong as the adrenaline pumped. I felt great. After the first eight kilometres, I passed a huge time clock that indicated I had run the first leg in 33 minutes. I had 34 kilometres left to go, and was moving far too fast if I hoped to make it all the way. I slowed down, but kept a steady pace. After nearly an hour of running I noticed the familiar figure of Joe Womersly ahead. It dawned on me why I hadn't seen him at the proper starting point—Joe had started near the front of the mob and saved himself a seven-minute walk to the start line. I had been duped. I ran up behind him and grabbed his rear end and shouted, "God will get you for this, Joe!" He laughed and yelled an appropriate obscenity as I pressed on.

That day I pushed champion Bill Rogers to a new Boston Marathon record. I also pushed 5,220 other people to the finish line ahead of me. I finished in three hours 22 minutes, just ahead of Joe Womersly, who had chosen the wrong day to break in new running shoes. Our company saved $1 million, but more importantly, I found myself able to do something I thought I could never do. I extended myself to achieve a goal because I wanted it badly. There was a substantial incentive to succeed. It was a valuable lesson for me.

Turning Weaknesses into Strengths

We had to sell our plans to the Canadian Olympic Association. Unlike our competitors in Vancouver, our bid team knew little about the bidding process and even less about the people who made the final selection. That meant we had our work cut out for us. We tried to turn our lack of knowledge to our advantage by using it as an incentive to leave nothing to chance. There were 35 voting members in the COA, so we committed their names and personal background information to memory. We had to know our "customers" before we could convince them to trust us with Canada's seventh bid for Olympic Winter Games glory.

We watched Vancouver's lavish promotional activities carefully. We were happy to let Vancouver invite COA officials out to see what their city had to offer. Once the COA directors had accepted the Vancouver invitation and arranged to fly to that city at the Vancouver bidders' expense, we invited the COA people to stop over in Calgary on the way home. We saved some big airfare costs—money we didn't have. Our low-budget strategy also gave us a chance to leave the last impression on our guests as they made their way back from B.C.

We heard stories from COA officials coming away from Vancouver about having been entertained in Vancouver's top restaurants, on boats, and at mountain lodges. We didn't have a budget for lavish entertaining, so we simply invited COA visitors to our homes to dine with our families. The dinners were low-key and friendly, and because they were personal they worked. Our new friends in the COA told us that Vancouver's main selling argument was, "We've got the Pacific Coliseum, we've got Whistler Mountain, we've got almost everything. All we have to do is put in a bobsleigh run and a speed skating rink and we're ready to go. We don't have the handicaps Calgary has."

Handicaps, however, can be handy. Murray Costello and Gord Renwick, head honchos of the Canadian Amateur Hockey Association, came to Calgary en route from Vancouver. Like others before them, they had been convinced that Vancouver had a big advantage over Calgary because all its hockey facilities were already in place. But by now we were used to turning lemons into lemonade; I reframed the hockey comments to suit our situation. "It seems to me," I said, "if you choose Vancouver there will be no new facilities developed for hockey whatsoever. As you said, they already have a fine arena. But if Calgary gets the Games, we will be able to build the finest new hockey facilities in the world, and hockey in Canada will benefit for years to come." We won their support.

Calgary would not just hold an event in isolation; we would focus on building sport for the future of all of Canada. The legacy idea became a main goal of the Calgary Games.

The legacy we envisaged took three forms. First, we wanted to leave new sports facilities—places for people. Every great city has great places for recreation and cultural activities. Second, we wanted to leave a legacy of money. We began developing plans for funding the operating costs of the facilities after the Games, and for funding the training of future young athletes. Finally, we wanted to create a legacy of people: not only athletes, but coaches, officials, and spectators who enjoyed participating in sport.

Having developed a selling strategy, we needed tactics and style. We used a technique that served us well. We based our appeal to visiting experts on three magic words: "Please help us." The COA experts were happy to give us the benefit of their expertise, and they spent hours telling us what we should do to win the bid against Vancouver. The more they helped us, the more our bid became theirs. We spent a lot of time listening and not much time talking.

Unfortunately, Iona Campagnolo was no longer sports minister, having lost her seat in the 1979 election that brought a minority Conservative government to power in Ottawa. As soon as Steve Paproski was named the new federal sports minister, I arranged a meeting with him to begin the process of re-establishing federal support.

Steve Paproski was a former Edmonton Eskimo football player, a resident of Edmonton, and an old friend of Jeanette's father. We had met before. I hoped that I might have an inside track with him. In any event, I had to build back the $200-million pledge we had received from Campagnolo.

I went to see Paproski shortly after he was sworn into office. We talked a little about Edmonton and I congratulated him on his election. Then I detailed the $200-million commitment that had been made and stressed the importance of support from the government. Since we also wanted Calgary to be selected over Vancouver I said, "And we would appreciate anything you could do to help Calgary."

"Of course, I am an Albertan," he said with a wink and a large Chiclet-tooth smile. "I expect you will have my support."

"Anything you can do, any word you can say to colleagues or others of influence that will help Calgary, would be very much appreciated," I repeated.

"You can count on that."

I was stunned, however, when Paproski then informed me that the Conservatives were thinking about allowing the provinces to take over the lottery business in the interests of improved federal-provincial relations. In an incredible fit of generosity the federal government was preparing to abandon nearly $400 million in annual revenues in exchange for a $25-million annual royalty indexed to cover inflation. I cautioned Paproski that the Olympics and other events of national significance could not be held without big money being made available. I stressed that a condition of our existing funding commitment from the federal government was that it be from non-tax sources. We were adamant that taxpayers not be burdened with the same kind of bills as they had been in Montreal.

In spite of our protestations, soon afterward the Clark government quietly abolished Lotto Canada. It was a serious blunder. The Tories walked away from an established source of funding for national sports programs in exchange for a meagre share of the proceeds from the provinces and a soon-forgotten thank you. Later governments would regret this careless largesse.

I rose and moved to leave by the same door through which I had entered, but Paproski blocked my path and gently escorted me through a back hallway exit. As we went by his outer office, I understood why—the Vancouver Olympic bid delegation was waiting to see the minister, all smiling in anticipation. They weren't far behind us no matter where we went, but at least they were still behind us.

Back home, City Council had demanded we secure a positive recommendation from the Calgary Parks and Recreation Commission. The commission consisted of a group of volunteer citizens who worked closely with Commissioner Bob Welin to screen proposals affecting the recreational life of Calgarians. I packed up my now-familiar slide show of skiers, skaters, and tobogganers, and gave the appropriate "Dream of a Better Future" speech to the Parks and Recreation Commission. The chairman asked several penetrating questions before calling upon his colleagues on the commission to support the CODA bid. He was Bill Warren, a prominent local lawyer and past president of the Booster Club. The commission supported CODA unanimously, and Warren became a major force on Calgary's bid team.

At the end of July we succeeded in firmly establishing the City of Calgary's support when council passed a resolution endorsing the bid and empowering CODA to pursue it on behalf of the city. That left the problem of pinning down provincial government support. By August 1979 we had still not received final confirmation of the Province of Alberta's participation in the Games. They wouldn't say yes and they hadn't said no, and the deadline for printing our written presentation to the COA was fast approaching. The provincial commitment was of crucial importance.

The province finally sent CODA a letter of support but it was a milquetoast effort. We felt it could damage our bid because it offered weak help where strong help was to be expected. I called my friend and member of the Legislative Assembly, Hugh Planche. He arranged an emergency meeting in the premier's southern Alberta office with Peter Trynchy, minister of Recreation and Parks, and Lee Richardson, the premier's assistant. I made it clear to Trynchy that the bid was now in his hands. If we didn't have a strongly supportive letter we would withdraw the Calgary bid. We wouldn't embarrass Calgarians by going forward without the unequivocal support of our own provincial government.

Trynchy took the first letter back and promised to rewrite it. Two weeks before we made our bid to the COA, we received a vigorous letter from Premier Peter Lougheed, stating his solid support for the Games in all ways. It was exactly what we needed. Neither too little nor too late—but almost.

We put together a promotional bid film, something that had never been done before. To keep costs within budget, Bob Niven flew his airplane, photographer Per Asplund literally hung out the door filming the Spray Lakes venue, and Gary Arthur, a local CBC-TV sportscaster we had recruited to help, rummaged through CBC film files to find different shots of various sporting events to be included in our pitch.

Vancouver's bid strategy, in the wake of Montreal's high-cost Olympics, was to emphasize the low cost of its Games plan. Vancouver's financial plan was based on a total budget for the Olympic Winter Games of only $80 million. Having studied the past five Winter Games, we figured that building facilities and hosting the Games would require about three times as much as Vancouver had estimated. We remarked among ourselves that it was ironic that Vancouver's bid team had given each COA director a calculator but had apparently failed to use one for their own budget. We plotted a financial offensive to exploit Vancouver's weakness.

We put together a slide show entitled "Meeting the Standards of the Past," showing the amounts spent historically on Winter Games: Innsbruck, $150 million; Lake Placid, $200 million; Sapporo, $300 million, and so on. We also showed Calgary's proposed budget of $212 million and used our slide presentation to raise serious doubts about Vancouver's readiness to meet Olympic obligations.

Although we felt we had a strong bid, we decided to add something special: we offered, for the first time in Olympic history, a $5-million Olympic development fund for future athletes and the continued use of the facilities after the Games. We hoped the endowment fund would appeal to anyone with an interest in sport. We made ourselves the "legacy" bid. Vancouver became the "cheap" bid. Their message seemed to be, "We want the Games because of the local benefits it will produce." Our theme was, "The Calgary Winter Games will produce a long-term benefit for all athletes, all Canadians, and the Olympic movement."

JOHN EYRE • RICK YOUNG • ELIZABETH SCOTT • STEVE KOSTEN • JUDITH SNYDER • DONALD STEWART • BOYD PAUL • DAVID PUTNAM • MICHELE KEMNA • HOWARD TRIANO • PAUL FRYDL • BRENDA MCDOUGALL • SHARON SANDWELL • SILKEN LAUMANN • GAY MORRIS • LYNN DUFORT • CHRISTA NICHOLSON • MARK KELLY • MARY MOORE • KENT LOWRY • BOB LEFEVER • DAVE YULE • RON NEUMILLER • WAYNE CAMERON • HARTVIG LAURIDSEN • BRETT HOLT • HILDA FRIED • ED WILLIAMS • CATHY MACDONALD • TROND HELGESTAD • DARYL KLITZKE • KATHY FLEISHMAN • KAREN MACLEOD • BARBARA ROCCHIO • KEVIN MCMECHAN • MEL STOTYN • ANDREA ZWACK • CHRISTINE SIMONE •

The Canadian Bid

With our dream in sight we headed east to Montreal, headquarters of the Canadian Olympic Association. Included in the CODA delegation were Alberta Recreation and Parks minister Peter Trynchy, Banff-Canmore MLA Greg Stevens, Calgary MLA Sheila Embury, Calgary Mayor Ross Alger, and the French-speaking chancellor of the University of Calgary, Louis Lebel.

Vancouver had a professional broadcaster at the head of its bid committee, along with former Olympic skier Nancy Greene-Raine and a number of well-known Vancouver businessmen. They were formidable opponents and arrived in Montreal going all out to beat us. They had heard we were making a film and had hastily put one together themselves. We had succeeded again in making them play follow-the-leader.

The night before our Olympic bidding debut, Bob Niven, Jack Wilson, and Gary Arthur, the CBC sportscaster who had assisted with our film, met in my hotel room to review the slides we had chosen as part of our 30-minute presentation. It was immediately clear that the presentation was too long, so I removed several slides from the carousel. Finally I was ready for a dry run, a mock sales pitch to my Calgary colleagues. As I clicked through the slides, a blank unexpectedly appeared where a slide had been removed. "What's that?" I laughed.

"It's not a blank cheque from Peter Lougheed!" quipped Jack Wilson. Wilson had given me a way to send a message with a dash of humor. Some of our detractors were alleging that all our bid had going for it was the big-money backing of the Alberta government. The quip could be used to apply a little reverse psychology. It allowed us to tell our audience that we thought our bid stood on its own merits whether we had the province's backing or not, while at the same time reminding them that the backing was there.

We arose early, feeling intense but relaxed. We handed out white Stetson cowboy hats, to the delight of the COA directors. One of the directors was so taken with his white hat he wrote his name on a piece of paper, stuck it in the headband, and returned every 15 minutes to the coat-check room to make sure the hat hadn't been stolen.

When Calgary's name was called by COA President Dick Pound, I took the podium. I looked out over a small room in Olympic House in Montreal with about 50 people crowded into it. Members of our delegation stood along each side of the room with looks of expectation on their faces. Jack Wilson was beaming confidently, which reinforced my own positive feeling. For the first time I would speak of "the best Games ever."

During the preparation of our bid, we had asked the COA directors to help us, so I opened with:

> I would like to thank each of you for sharing your wisdom and experience with us concerning facilities, venues, and programs.
>
> What you are about to see and hear is a composite of the extensive research and planning done to incorporate these many suggestions and recommendations. The Calgary proposal is a logical blend of an established community need and future Olympic use. We hope you will find our plan imaginative, realistic and complete. We hope that from today on, it will not only be Calgary's plan, but most importantly, Canada's plan for Winter Olympic recognition.
>
> In most sports, it seems you're better off with your head up. Let's not put our head in the sand regarding the cost of the Games. Instead, let's start now to put together aggressive, honest marketing programs to be shared between the COA and the organizing city to help pay for the Games. Then, let's control costs in a proper businesslike manner. The proposal you have received from Calgary is a realistic, heads-up plan for the Olympic Winter Games.
>
> As Canada's Olympic candidate, we guarantee you these things:
>
> 1. First and foremost, to work hard, on your behalf, with you and for you, to achieve the best Games ever held. We'll start tomorrow to build the right team to carry this bid forward internationally. We'll need your help.
> 2. We'll bring the enthusiastic support of a young exciting city—big enough to handle the job, but small enough to have fun doing it.
> 3. The solid support of a stable provincial government with a record of deep commitment to the development of amateur sports facilities.
> 4. Incomparable real winter weather in Calgary. It is reliable weather, plentiful snow, no rain, no fog, and a long, long season—ideal conditions for training of our best athletes.
> 5. A commitment to new Olympic-calibre facilities for every one of the winter sports—permanent facilities—100 per cent owned by the community to guarantee their use after the Games.

6. We'll provide the best athletes' village ever.

7. Add in the largest and most modern media services ever provided for the Olympics.

8. And here's a favorite of ours: a $5-million Olympic Development Fund to guarantee the continuous maintenance and use of Olympic facilities after the Games . . . and to provide ongoing athlete assistance as well.

9. We can provide the assurance of labor peace and no-strike labor agreements.

In short, a well-conceived, well-financed, do-able deal. A chance to expand Canada's amateur sports base which comes once in a lifetime.

The slide show went as planned. The next day the *Calgary Albertan* reported, "King was the glue that held it all together. For instance, during the slide presentation, one frame came up with nothing on the screen. It didn't faze King. Quick on his feet, he simply said, 'And this isn't a blank cheque from Peter Lougheed.' It cracked up the directors." There's nothing like a little off-the-cuff humor.

The key slide in the show was the last one, "Meeting the Standards of the Past." I said everyone in the COA believed Canada was the right place to hold these Games, but as a matter of pride, we could do no less than what others before us had done. I knew we had made our point.

As we took turns making our various parts of the presentation, I realized each of our speakers was taking a little more time than he was supposed to. I was sitting next to Peter Trynchy, who hadn't spoken yet. I whispered to him, "Peter, you're supposed to take three minutes. Do you think you can cut your speech down to one minute?"

Trynchy looked at me in surprise as if to say, "How can I possibly say what I have to say in one minute?"

"Just tell them how much money you've got in the Heritage Trust Fund," I whispered.

And when his turn came, that's exactly what he did. He stood up and said simply, "The chairman has asked me to be very brief, so I really only want to say that the Province of Alberta is very supportive of this bid, and that the Heritage Fund is currently standing at $6.9 billion. We back this bid with all our resources." And he sat down.

It was perfect. No matter what else he could have said, it wouldn't have been as impressive. Not only did we make up our lost time, but we got the message across that Alberta, with its huge resources, was on our side.

When the decision was about to be announced, we were waiting in the lobby in Olympic House for the doors of the COA meeting room to open. Jeanette was there with me. We both realized the decision could change our lives.

The Calgary and Vancouver delegations stood in silent suspense as Dick Pound, president of the COA, emerged from the boardroom, trailed by the COA directors who had selected Canada's seventh candidate to bid for the Olympic Winter Games. From a small podium in the crowded foyer of Olympic House, Pound made short work of thanking both candidate cities and their excellent bid teams. Then Pound announced that Calgary had been selected by a vote of 27 to nine. We were jubilant.

Afterward, there were a few recriminations in Vancouver about Calgary winning the bid. The headlines were CALGARY WINS THE OIL-LYMPICS and VANCOUVER LOSES TO BIG-TICKET GAMES. The fact is that without a proper financial commitment to the Olympics, Canadians would have been in serious trouble with their bid internationally. In retrospect, I believe that if Vancouver had won, the city would have been hard-pressed to bring the Games off for less than $500 million. A major component of that cost would have been the widening and straightening of the road to the Whistler ski area, where half the events were to be held, to bring the road up to Olympic standards.

When the decision was announced, amid the bedlam of cheering and congratulations, I yelled in Jeanette's ear, "You should phone home to tell the boys." Our two youngest children, aged 12 and nine, were waiting anxiously in Calgary to hear the verdict. Our sons had lived with our Olympic involvement for almost a year.

"I can't remember our phone number!" cried Jeanette, tears of happiness streaming down her cheeks.

I gave her our home number and yelled as she ran down the hall, "Remember to tell them it's their mother calling!"

CHAPTER FOUR

The Big League

The difference between ordinary and extraordinary
is that little extra.
AUTHOR UNKNOWN

Round one was over. Round two was an entirely new game, that of convincing members of the International Olympic Committee to choose Calgary over other world cities. The rules, the players, and the league were now very different.

The European Business Model

IOC members are the trustees of the Olympic Games. The Games in turn are the most important means by which the world measures the popularity of the Olympic movement. IOC members must select organizers they can trust with the Games' hundred-year-old legacy. It is no wonder that IOC members seek, first and foremost, organizers who will preserve the Olympic enterprise and build on the traditions that have developed since Pierre de Coubertin revived them in 1894.

As we travelled the world studying the people who ran the Olympic movement, we came to believe that the Olympic

Games, to succeed, must be organized like an established European business venture.

Most successful European businesses are built on three main precepts: the first priority is preservation of the enterprise, the second is reward and recognition for the participants, and the third is good financial results. In North American business the priorities are reversed; usually the bottom line comes first.

If European precepts applied within the Olympic movement, we would have to be careful to present ourselves to the IOC as trustworthy caretakers of the Games. Our hearts told us we should be introducing bold new ideas and solutions to old problems, but our heads told us that might be seen as a risky departure from the proven traditions in which the IOC was anchored. The pace of progress had to be carefully calculated to be comfortable for the IOC. Our bright new ideas would mostly be kept in the closet and trotted out quietly later, one at a time, if the opportunity arose.

We studied the history of the International Olympic Committee, devouring every detail of how this unique organization had survived despite wars, constant political pressures, and assaults from individuals who attempted to use the Olympic platform to advance their own unrelated objectives. We found that many of the "problems" of the Olympic movement were, in fact, products of the success of the Olympic Games rather than fundamental flaws belonging to the Olympics.

As I continued to study the Olympic movement, I began to make speeches about it to Calgary audiences. Speaking to the Calgary Chamber of Commerce in 1981, I drew liberally upon Geoffrey Miller's book *Behind the Olympic Rings* (Lynn, Massachusetts: Zimman, 1979).

> It was said that de Coubertin, one of the great individualists of modern times, disliked organized government, so from the start he was determined to make his Olympic Games independent of governments....
> He formed the International Olympic Committee and filled it with titled men, on the principle that the greater the standing and respect its members enjoyed, the less likely politicians would be to interfere with them. The IOC came into being in 1894, and by 1900, when the second

Olympic Games were held in Paris, de Coubertin, himself a baron, had enlisted princes from Russia and Romania, an Italian duke, a brace of barons from Britain and Switzerland, and numerous counts from all parts of Europe.

From its earliest days, therefore, the IOC was an august assembly, unlikely to be easily challenged by politicians seeking to manipulate the Games for ulterior purposes. De Coubertin and his band of gentlemen sportsmen were as independent as any European baronial family and were free to work untrammelled for the cause of international amateur sport.

The IOC is unlike any other body in the world, and it is understood by few people outside of the Olympic movement. Not many people fully understand that members of the IOC are not selected as representatives of their countries. They have been handpicked, can only join by invitation, and serve as individuals. Their role is to act as the IOC's ambassadors in the country where they live.

The IOC is the supreme authority of the Olympic Games. The IOC created itself and assumed its own authority. It does not answer to the world at large; on the contrary, the organizing committee of each Olympic Games and the National Olympic Committees of 165 countries are answerable finally only to the IOC.

Our mission was to convince this illustrious international group to choose Calgary to host the Games. It was roughly equivalent to convincing the owner of a long-established European family business to trust you to run it for the next four years. You cannot easily accomplish such a thing without first knowing what the owner expects of you, and then establishing high levels of mutual trust and confidence in your ability to pull it off.

But before we could get down to the serious business of putting together our bid for the big league, we had to deal with the immediate realities of life. CODA had no money and we had no place to carry out our daily business, the volume of which was growing rapidly now that we had been chosen to represent Canada.

People Make the Difference

We estimated we would need $1.2 million to finance the bid over the next 23 months, and so we quickly put in place some novel fundraising schemes to produce the juice we needed. We commissioned and sold a Bill Brownridge series of winter sports paintings at $5,000 per set. Charles Weaver, a leading western sculptor, created some extraordinary old-fashioned winter sports bronze figures. We sold the limited-edition series of five figures for $25,000 a set. We sold corporate CODA memberships for $200 each and individual memberships for five dollars an adult and two dollars for seniors and juniors. Those projects produced about $700,000 in cash.

The Royal Bank agreed to lend us expense money as needed, and the province of Alberta advanced $200,000 against its pledge of financial support. Over the whole bid period we never could devote enough time to raise all the money we needed, but we kept replenishing the pot with the help of private donations from Calgarians, whose generosity was remarkable.

We now found it necessary to establish a fully operational business office. Bob Niven acquired space in the penthouse level of the same small office building where he operated his oil company. Jeanette, who was president of the Professional Engineers' Wives' Club, brought a few members and other close friends down to staff the office with volunteer workers. Some of those early volunteers were still working without pay for the Olympics eight years later when the Games were held.

We knew we had to expand our organization to include people who could help us with the international protocol and lobbying required. We needed people with expertise in winter sports as well as knowledge of international customs and fluency in different languages. Our first chance to show our stuff to the IOC was coming up at the Lake Placid Winter Olympics, now just four months away. We would have the opportunity there to study the Winter Games first-hand; we would also have the opportunity, thanks to the fact that Calgary had been the first city to declare itself in the race for the 1988 Winter Games, to get a head start on our unannounced competitors.

The Power of Olympic Persuasion

Before our mission to Lake Placid I had to make a quick business trip to Venezuela and then on to Japan. I decided to take advantage of the opportunity to meet the IOC members of those two countries. For the first time, and accidentally, I became aware of the power of the Olympic movement internationally.

TERRY HRYNIW • GEORGE FLEET • ROLLIE ALLEN • WILLIAM TURNER • BEV PEDE • ED KOSS • STEPHANIE ROBINSON • BARBARA PIATKIEWICZ • NINA MALLORY • DOUG PARSONS • MICHELLE LEBEL • VERLA SHERICK • REG HENDRICKSON • GINA FESTA • JOHN SPARKS • ROMAN PESEK • MARILYN WOODY • MIKE HALPEN • CHUCK BELLIVEAU • ARAFAAT VALIANI • DAVE SMALE • CAROLYN WALDO • ISABEL MARTINS • CHERYL HODGSON • BRIAN PISESKY • JEFFREY JAMIESON • BRIAN FLETCHER • LAURI PENTTINEN • KELLY BORROWMAN • LOTTE VOGRIN • LIZ DEPLEDGE • ANGELA KOKOTT • JUDI MCINTOSH • KIRK BEACOM • MARTIN FAHJE • RUBY WILLMER • CHRISTOPHER

I travelled to Venezuela with my friend and business colleague Julian Romocki, and a representative of the Province of Alberta, Greg White. Shortly after our arrival, Greg questioned the "worker's visa" that my secretary had arranged for me. As he explained it, the worker's visa meant that I would have to pay a special tax called a *solvencia* to get out of the country.

I inquired at the Canadian embassy, where I was given the address of the British-Venezuelan Chamber of Commerce which, they said, would provide my *solvencia* certificate for a small fee.

We hailed a cab and the driver, who spoke no English, took us far out into a seedy district of Caracas. He pulled up in front of a shabby old building that looked suspiciously like a strip joint or low-class dance hall.

We got out of the cab reluctantly, and found a staircase leading up to a long shadowy hallway. We advanced cautiously, our heads swinging from side to side like Wimbledon spectators as we read the names on the frosted glass doors. Near the end of the hall was a door that read British-Venezuelan Chamber of Commerce.

Behind the door was a jovial, British-looking fellow who had been a World War II fighter pilot, as evidenced by the pictures festooning his office walls. When we enquired whether he could arrange our *solvencia* papers, he pulled out an official-looking form and said cheerfully, "No problem, we deal with this sort of thing all the time." He asked us for details on our salaries then assessed us a tax of 10 per cent of one month's salary plus a fee for his services.

Next he asked for our passports, saying he would need them "for a few days."

"No, that's impossible," I said. "We are visiting Venezuelan oil companies every day and we need our passports to get into the office buildings. We can't go anywhere without our passports." Even more important, the next day we were flying to Maracaibo, a city on the Colombian border. We would certainly need our passports at the airport.

"Look," he said, "if you want me to pay the *solvencia*, you must give me your passports."

"Why don't you make a copy of the passports, and we'll keep the originals," I suggested.

"No," he said, "I must keep the passport or no *solvencia*. No *solvencia*, and you don't get out of the country."

I was getting more and more nervous. A passport in a country like Venezuela is like your life. "Are you absolutely sure?" I asked.

"The Canadian government sent you here," he answered impatiently. "You can trust me."

The next day, we approached the Caracas airport security check counter with trepidation and photocopies of our passports. "There's no way we are going to get through here," I said to Julian. But to our surprise nobody asked for our passports and we breezed right through.

On the return trip, however, we weren't so lucky. Standing in line at the Maracaibo airport we saw that passports of all passengers were being carefully checked by armed guards.

"Here we go," I muttered to Julian and Greg. "Let's see if we can talk our way through this."

Greg White went through first because he had his passport and tourist visa. I was next. The guard said, *"Passaporte,"* to which I answered in English, "This is a copy of the front page of my passport," showing him the photocopied page.

"Passaporte!" he demanded huffily, brushing my proffered papers aside.

"I have no *passaporte! Mia passaporte es gone to British-Venezuelan Chamber of Commerce para solvencia,"* I protested. *"No passaporte. Government has mia passaporte."* I was hoping lamely that making English sound like Spanish would make it intelligible to a Spanish-speaker.

"Passaporte! Passaporte!" he shouted. He was not growing friendlier toward me. I began frantically waving to get Greg White to come over and translate for me. By now Julian was caught in the same problem. But Greg was immersed in inspecting the dust on his shoes as if to disassociate himself from the developing scene. He explained later that he wanted to keep out of it so that we would have his help "on the outside" to secure our release when we were detained.

Finally losing his patience, the airport security official blew a whistle, summoning a husky female armed with a machine gun and bullets slung Rambo-fashion over her body.

"Greg! They're taking us away!" I shouted, and finally Greg, apparently having completed his meditation, joined us as we were being led briskly down the hallway.

We were deposited in a small holding room. I could hear someone come marching down the hallway. He came into the room. He appeared to be some sort of commanding officer, a Hitleresque little man, almost a foot shorter than me, wearing a military uniform, boots, and a pistol in a hip holster. He did not look friendly at all.

When I saw him, I believed for a moment that we might never get out. I knew I had to play my cards carefully, so I said to Greg, "Tell him the story of what happened to our passports." He did, but the officer seemed singularly unimpressed. "Then tell him that I am the chief man in the Canadian Olympic movement and that I'm on my way to meet the Canadian ambassador in Caracas. Tell him that if I'm not out of here right away, there will be a big international incident." I pulled out my brand-new Calgary Olympic Development Association card with my title, chairman, to show as proof.

I silently asked God to forgive me for exaggerating my importance in the Olympic movement. Most people in the movement had never heard of me, but at least it was true I had an appointment the next day with Roger Rousseau, Canadian ambassador to Venezuela and former president of the Montreal Olympic Organizing Committee.

Greg dutifully translated what I had said. The commander examined my Xerox of my passport, looking up twice at me, and scrutinized my business card. Then turning on his heel he simply said "*Si*" and walked briskly away, his boots echoing down the hallway.

We were free! Greg White was incredulous, saying, "I don't believe you pulled it off so easily!" He was familiar with local security officials. None of us had anticipated the kind of clout the Olympic movement could carry.

Back in Caracas we had dinner at the home of Roger Rousseau. He chuckled when we described our brush with the security officials and then spent the evening telling us about the IOC personalities we would be dealing with in pursuing our Olympic bid. He set up a meeting with the Venezuelan IOC member, José Baracasa, who was Venezuela's largest shoe manufacturer and an avid basketball promoter. Rousseau lent us his limousine to take us to visit Baracasa at the latter's beautiful central Caracas mansion. We chatted about sport as we walked together through his exquisite garden. He became the first IOC member outside Canada with whom I became friends. He helped us begin to understand the Olympic movement. In spite of diverse and even contradictory backgrounds, people everywhere have a common bond through sport.

A Japanese Joker

Julian and I flew out of Caracas to complete our business in Tokyo. On the airplane I sat next to a Japanese businessman who entertained me for hours with stories about the business customs of Japan. One of the customs he described surprised and delighted me. He told me that most first-class hotels in Japan provide complimentary slippers and a kimono for the guests to take home. I filed the piece of information away, thinking what a nice souvenir an authentic Japanese kimono would make from my first visit to Japan.

While in Japan I could not resist the temptation to visit Sapporo, home of the XIth Olympic Winter Games. Sapporo had beaten Calgary in a previous bid to host the Games, so this place held a special fascination for me. When we arrived at the island of Hokkaido we were provided with a hostess who gave us a tour around the Olympic sites. I learned a great deal in the two days I spent there. To my disappointment, however, I found that many of the Olympic sports venues had been abandoned, leaving nothing but memories for the local citizens. I hardened my resolve not to allow the same to happen in Calgary. At the end of the visit, as our hostess and her fiancé drove us to the Chitosa airport, I said, "You know, one of the really nice customs you have in Japan is the free kimonos you have for customers in your hotels. We don't have that in Canada."

Our hostess cast a puzzled and concerned glance at her companion and there was a short, muffled conversation in Japanese in the front seat. "Julian," I said, "I think we blew it!"

"Let me ask you," I interrupted the hostess, "is it not the accepted custom here to keep the kimonos?"

"No, it isn't," she replied in an apologetic tone. "You are not supposed to keep them."

I told her the story of the Japanese businessman on the airplane, who had apparently been leading us on for obscure reasons of his own. I insisted we pay her for the kimonos so she could reimburse the hotel.

"No," she said, "this will be our gift to you. We will look after it with the hotel." We felt like jerks but to this day we have kimonos as mementos of our visit.

A Japanese Sage

In Tokyo I arranged to meet Prince Takeda, an IOC member, former president of the Japan Olympic Committee and nephew of Emperor Hirohito. He gave us some important advice on how to host successful Games. In succinct Japanese fashion he said, "You must do only two things: first, you must have the support of the people; and second, you must have no problems." No problems! The IOC had been beset by problems almost from day one.

"You must convince the IOC," he explained, "that Calgary will have the *fewest* problems." I took this advice to heart. It was consistent with European business philosophy and also with common sense.

We met two other Olympic notables in Tokyo. One was Masaji Kiyokawa, another IOC member and an influential member of the International Skating Union. Kiyokawa had plenty of helpful hints on how to strengthen our bid. The other was Bobby Hirai, a Japanese Canadian who was born in Japan, had grown up in Toronto, and, when World War II broke out, moved back to Japan. He was an expert in international trade and on the Olympic movement. He became our Olympic consultant and helped us meet Asian IOC members. He also helped us understand the influence of the IOC director,

Madame Monique Berlioux, for whom his sister worked. Our own acquaintance with Berlioux would later confirm what he told us: she wielded power far beyond what her official title would have led us to suspect.

The trip to Venezuela and Japan had been my introduction to Olympic lobbying, and I had enjoyed it. I returned to Calgary full of anticipation for our February 1980 visit to the XIIIth Olympic Winter Games in Lake Placid.

CHAPTER FIVE

Moving in the Right Circles

Many receive advice; only the wise profit from it.
PUBLILIUS SYRUS

W E HAD A CHANCE to put our enthusiasm to work less than four months after our selection as Canada's best bid for the 1988 Winter Games. In February 1980, the XIIIth Olympic Winter Games were held in Lake Placid, New York. This was the CODA bid team's first showing, and we planned to make it an effective one.

Lake Placid is a mountain village of 3,000 people in northern New York State. When the Olympic Winter Games were held there in 1932, only 500 athletes and officials and even fewer media representatives attended. The 1980 Winter Games were a different ballgame. Since television coverage was first introduced at Cortina d'Ampezzo in 1956, the number of events and participants had increased with each new set of Winter Games, straining the accommodation, communication, and transportation systems of the host city. In 1980, 1,283 athletes and an increased interest from the world media were stretching the Adirondack village past its breaking point. The housing facilities and transportation system had been so overloaded they had broken down. One day spectators were stranded at the ski jump for three or four hours after the event ended in –30°C weather before a bus came.

The Friendliest Place in Town

We wanted to send a party of about 30 people to Lake Placid, including our basic bid team plus representatives from the City of Calgary and the Province of Alberta. This was our best chance to meet influential Olympic leaders and to experience all facets of Games organization first-hand.

Our people picked up an option to rent a private five-bedroom bungalow located on the lake quite near the old Lake Placid Club where IOC members would be staying. The rental price for one month—$25,000! Even so, we jumped at the chance, calculating that even if hotel accommodation had been available our costs would have been higher than that when food and entertainment were added in. We were not going to Lake Placid to save money anyway, but to meet IOC members and to learn valuable facts about how to organize the Games. The house gave us a prime location for playing host to officials and for making our way to meetings and events.

We hung a huge sign outside our temporary headquarters announcing "Welcome to Calgary House!" In order to function as both a boarding house and an entertainment centre, Calgary House needed a cook and bottle-washer. We hired a delightful young couple fresh from the local hotel management school.

Our new chef greeted us on the first day. He was about 21 years old, with red curly hair poking out beneath a New York Yankees baseball cap. He was six feet tall, wearing hiking boots that showed signs of never having been laced beyond the midway point. Despite his un-chef-like appearance he cooked beautifully and ran the kitchen well, helped out ably by his girlfriend. Their job was not easy; we had a sellout crowd of guests at Calgary House almost every night. We didn't know who some of the visitors were; they came in off the street because the word was soon out that Calgary House was the friendliest place in town. Our instant popularity wasn't hurt by the fact that Americans were feeling good about all Canadians in the wake of Canadian Ambassador Ken Taylor's rescue of American diplomats from Iran just two weeks before.

Another unexpected asset was Canada's premier skier, Ken Read, whose hopes for a medal had been dashed when his ski came off while he was carving a hard left turn during the first few seconds of the Olympic downhill race. Ken turned out to be a tremendous ambassador for Calgary because of the classy way he conducted himself with the press. Later in the day of his unfortunate Olympic race, he attended a reception hosted by the Government of Canada. Ken, an intelligent, articulate, and handsome young man, was receiving a great deal of attention, especially from the female company present. Surrounded by admirers, he turned to greet me and I said sympathetically, "I guess for you, Ken, the Games are over."

With a devilish look on his face, he winked and said, "No Frank, for me the games have just begun!"

We decided to use Calgary House to put on a luncheon so our bid team could meet the IOC members formally. Jeanette used preprinted invitations and sent them to all 76 IOC members and a few other dignitaries, for lunch with "His Excellency, Edward Schreyer, the Governor-General of Canada." Naturally, we weren't sure how many invited guests would come, but we knew that if they all showed up we would be in some difficulty, since Calgary House could accommodate only about 50 people comfortably.

The CODA wives carefully planned the menu with our gangly red-headed chef, deciding on quiches and salad because the portions could be divided according to the number of guests. The morning of the luncheon, Jeanette was horrified when she noticed that the preprinted invitations had been sent to "you and your guest." This could mean that instead of the 76 guests we thought we had invited, 150 people might shortly be descending on our little bungalow.

IOC members are international diplomats for sport and peace, and like most diplomats, they like to meet government or world leaders to share their views and to broaden the network of Olympic followers. When they got their invitations to lunch with the Queen's representative in Canada, many no doubt felt obliged to attend. At the appointed hour, Calgary House was the scene of a veritable procession of more than a hundred dignitaries. As the cars pulled up one after another we blanched, wondering how we would get all our important guests inside, not to mention how we would feed them. Jeanette quickly instructed the chef to cut the slices of quiche very small and I asked the Calgary people to eat nothing at all. We could have used another miracle of the loaves and the fishes.

Lord Killanin Meets the Guv

Governor-General Ed Schreyer arrived, looking very casual in ski pants and a red wool sweater. He had taken time from outdoor events to attend the luncheon and hardly looked like the vice-regal representative of the Queen the IOC members must have been expecting.

Calgary Mayor Ross Alger, Jeanette, and I greeted each arriving IOC member at the front door. At first Ross seemed a bit dazed, forgetting that he was not at home in Calgary. He greeted Alexandru Siperco, the IOC member from Romania, by saying, "Welcome to Canada. How long have you been here?" Siperco, glancing at him quizzically, said, "I've never been to Canada," and moved on. Ross turned smilingly to greet the next guest. I consoled myself that we couldn't expect to win the support of every IOC member anyway.

Before long Calgary House was filled with the babble of a dozen different languages. I was especially pleased to see Lord Killanin, president of the IOC, pull up in his limousine. Killanin is an Irish aristocrat, cordial but formal, an imposing figure with great ruddy cheeks that quiver when he talks. When I greeted Killanin he indicated in his cultured accent that he was looking forward to making the acquaintance of His Excellency, the Governor-General. I left my position near the doorway to escort Lord Killanin personally, and pushing my way through the overcrowded room I introduced him to Ed Schreyer and his wife, Lily. I left them chatting with a cheerful group of CODA hosts and rejoined Mayor Alger near the door.

By the time the last guests arrived the house was crammed with dignitaries, many of whom had resorted to sitting on stairs or the floor to eat their tiny lunches. It was a mob scene. I decided to fight my way through the crowd again to make sure Lord Killanin was being properly attended to. Eventually I found Killanin in the basement family room, sitting on a soft low chair, balancing his little sliver of quiche on his lap. I was pleased to see he was still with Ed Schreyer, who was sitting cross-legged on the floor at Killanin's feet. The two were chatting together amiably.

When Killanin saw me, he waved me over. We exchanged pleasantries before he asked me the question now clearly weighing on his mind.

"I say," he said, glancing around the crowded room, "where is the Governor-General? When am I going to meet him?"

"This, sir, *is* the Governor-General," said I, pointing to the man dressed in skiwear sitting on the floor at Killanin's feet. Calgary certainly left an impression on Lord Killanin that day, but I'm still not sure what kind.

Establishing White-Hat Diplomacy

Halfway through the Games Jeanette and I moved to a room in the Lake Placid Club, the IOC hotel, to be in greater proximity to IOC members. It was there we learned how to lobby in the lobby and bargain in the bar. Every morning at breakfast we would discreetly line up next to some new IOC members, having memorized their names and faces in advance. Often we'd meet them in hallways or even in elevators. This was how Bob Niven and I first met Madame Berlioux, the IOC dragon lady. As director of the IOC, Berlioux was one of the few senior paid staffers, and Lord Killanin's right hand. She had an imperious and aggressive manner, and we had heard she was someone you'd not care to have as an enemy.

Our first meeting with her was pleasant enough, consisting mostly of admonitions that we respect the proprietary use of the Olympic logos and pictograms. Berlioux, we learned later, took a personal interest in protecting the use of the Olympic symbols, a preoccupation that had not enhanced her popularity.

She had increased her power considerably during Lord Killanin's eight-year tenure. She was just naturally one of those people who soaks up power the way blotting paper soaks up ink. Killanin had made it clear, though, that he would not be seeking an extension to his mandate, leaving the competition open for the election of a new president at the Moscow session of the IOC in July 1980.

Although we were neophytes to Olympic politics, we picked up vibrations that Spanish diplomat and IOC Protocol Chief Juan Antonio Samaranch would be a leading challenger for the non-paying position of president. His main competitor was rumored to be the popular Swiss IOC member, Marc Hodler. Hodler had been president of the International Ski Federation for nearly 30 years and a leading proponent of increasing the stature of the Olympic Winter Games. Jim Worrall from Canada was also giving consideration to becoming a contender for the position of Olympic top banana.

At Lake Placid we handed out white cowboy hats to VIPs, especially those from the IOC. The hats proved as popular among members of the IOC at Lake Placid as they had the year before among directors of the COA in Montreal.

One of my jobs was to meet as many of the eastern-bloc IOC members as possible. At one point, I began to feel that Alexandru Siperco, the member from Romania, was becoming rather friendly toward us. I began hoping that through Romania there might be a way of meeting more IOC members from eastern Europe. Within a few months I would learn how unnecessary it was to worry about finding ways to meet IOC members. Bid cities are not a nuisance to IOC members, but a welcome and essential part of the process. I have since seen the great effort IOC members make to hear out stories of hope from bid-city organizers.

One night, as we left a hockey game in the Lake Placid arena, I noticed Siperco smile and wave to me. This seemed to confirm my feeling that he was becoming our friend. As we walked back to the old Lake Placid Club, Siperco, walking briskly, began overtaking us from behind. I whispered "slow down" to Jeanette. Siperco caught up, and then I realized with chagrin that he only wanted to remind me I had promised him my white hat as a souvenir! We did part friends and have remained so over the years since. White hats have the power to break down imaginary barriers between strangers. I made a mental note then and there to make white hats a signature of our bid team.

We returned home after Lake Placid exhausted but pleased. We had made many friends and had been overwhelmed with the complexity of the operation. We had also launched our bid. It remained for us to promote it around the world.

Horsing Around

Right after the Lake Placid Games, in April 1980, we made our first report to the Canadian Olympic Association in Montreal. We were in high spirits after our successful experience in Lake Placid and decided to make an impression by sharing some western humor with the COA. I sent Doug Kowel, our PR man on loan from Molson's, to Montreal in advance with instructions to rent a horse and a glitzy costume something like the one the Electric Horseman wore in the Robert Redford film. Jack Wilson had agreed to ride the horse right into the dining room of the hotel during my after-dinner report to the COA.

"This isn't going to work," Doug told me when I arrived in Montreal. "I can get a horse, but the hotel manager refuses to allow a horse in the building. For one thing, the dining room is on the sixth floor, and the only way to get a horse in there is up the food elevator. Not only that, if the horse damages the carpets, we will have to pay for it, and it could cost $3,000."

"Doug," I said, "Let's just go for it. By the time they find out what we've done, it'll be too late for anyone to complain."

On the night of the COA banquet we were ready to make our first report as Canada's bid committee. Doug had arranged for the horse to be delivered to a special door in the back lane behind the hotel. He waited nervously by the appointed place. When the horse and trailer arrived, however, the driver took it to a different door and spoke to a surprised hotel employee. Not knowing what to do, the employee decided to call Dick Pound, president of the COA. He said, "There's a fellow in the back lane says he's got a horse for the Olympic committee. Where would you like me to put it?" Pound must have smiled victoriously as he struck a blow for eastern conservatism and said, "Tell them to take the damn horse away. We don't want it."

In the meantime, Doug Kowel was calling my room in a panic, saying "Frank, the horse didn't arrive!"

"Okay," I said. "We'll go with Plan B." We had devised a backup plan just in case the horse stunt didn't work. Up in the COA banquet hall I stepped up to the podium, saying, "The lighting of the Olympic cauldron is one of the most significant events of the Olympic Games. Even though there are eight years left to go, and we haven't even won the Games, we have been practising our own unusual Olympic torch ceremony. As a treat, we're going to show you a trial run." A murmur of approval and expectation ran through the crowd. "It's not perfect yet, so please bear with me," I cautioned.

Doug Kowel jogged into the grand hall in bare feet and shorts, wearing a T-shirt that was small enough for his generous belly to stick out beneath it. He looked like some sort of grotesque imp. He had a mop of curly hair, was smoking a cigar, and was carrying a torch. The torch consisted of a plumber's helper wrapped in aluminum foil. The upraised cup of the helper contained a small amount of flaming fondue oil.

Doug ran about huffing and puffing, pausing here and there to kiss the ladies. He came up to the front of the room. A magician we had hired waited for Doug to arrive before he removed the lid from a huge cauldron, three feet in diameter. Doug paused, acknowledged the audience, and in a moment of low drama lit the cauldron. Everyone laughed and applauded. Then the magician put the lid back on the cauldron, extinguishing the flame. With a flourish he removed the lid again and six live pigeons flew out into the hotel dining room.

The place went crazy. It wasn't quite as good as the electric horseman would have been, but it did leave the impression Calgary would be different.

I watched the look on the face of Thelma Wright, a former great Canadian middle-distance runner and a member of the COA. A few hours earlier Jack Wilson and I had joined Thelma in a run to the top of Mount Royal, where a pigeon had dropped its load, hitting me squarely on the forehead. I had cursed my bad luck and spent the rest of the run emphasizing that the only thing I didn't like about the Olympics was the need for doves or pigeons and the tendency for them to use my sparsely thatched head as a target. When the pigeons were released into the COA banquet hall, Thelma watched me duck as the birds flew around me. She led the cheers and laughter.

Facing the Odds

As we immersed ourselves in international lobbying, we quickly recognized a few of the complex forces that would bear on the outcome. No European city bid for the 1988 Summer Games, but in 1980 two European cities announced they were bidding against us for the Winter Games: Cortina d'Ampezzo, Italy, and Falun-Are, Sweden. We checked the Olympic records and found that in every year except 1932 at least one of the two Games had been held in Europe, which is still the centre of gravity of the Olympic movement. Adding to speculation about Calgary's poor chances was the fact that our competitors had most of the required facilities in place, while Calgary had none. Cortina had held the Olympic Winter Games in 1956, and Falun was a sports centre for Sweden's consistently good winter sporting events.

During the Lake Placid Winter Games, President Carter unexpectedly announced a U.S. boycott of the Moscow Games because of the U.S.S.R. troop occupation of Afghanistan. In the spring of 1980, the Canadian government sacrificed our Olympic athletes and our perfect Olympic attendance record to politics as Canada joined the Olympic boycott. By then, Sweden and Italy had announced their bids for 1988 and confirmed their intention to send a full team to Moscow. We watched the fruitless efforts of the COA to resist the federal position. The COA then reluctantly yielded to the threat of loss of government funding. It was a major setback for us. It was clear now why de Coubertin didn't want to rely on governments to finance his Olympic dream. Governments have their own agendas.

The odds were now stacked against us, since the Soviet bloc would be unable to support a Canadian-backed bid from Calgary because of the Olympic boycott. My emotions ranged from shock to anger and then to empathy for our athletes whose once-in-a-lifetime opportunity had been snatched away. They were pawns in a different kind of game.

The Magic Words

Now more than ever we had to learn how an underdog could win. We got busy asking the people who were going to be voting to share with us their visions of how to make the best-ever Olympic Winter Games happen. We travelled about two million kilometres to talk to each and every IOC member. About one-third of them came to Calgary to see this promise of a greater future about which we spoke so passionately. We asked a lot of questions and we listened carefully. We often used the magic words, "We need your help."

"You are the trustees of Olympic ideals," we said. "Please help us understand every detail of what the Games should be." We told the members of the IOC that Canada was fertile ground on which to sow Olympic seeds. Our geography, our climate, our youth, and our need to support growing numbers of people from other lands were all to our advantage. We found that IOC members were not necessarily willing to commit their support to Calgary, but they were eager to offer us advice. We were far behind our competitors. We did need the help of the IOC members and they knew it. Gradually we built a vision of the Games, one that closely duplicated the input we received.

In July 1980 Bob Niven and I went to the IOC session in Moscow as the guests of Canadian IOC members Dick Pound and Jim Worrall. We spent our days visiting Soviet organizers, touring facilities, and examining operational services. Each evening we waited dutifully in the IOC hotel lobby for IOC members emerging from their daily meetings. This was our second or third meeting with some of them.

I stepped into the IOC hotel one afternoon to find Peter Ueberroth, president of the Los Angeles 1984 Organizing Committee, already there. He was in Moscow to present his report to the IOC.

"Hello, I'm Frank King, chairman of the Calgary Olympic bid committee," I opened before trying the magic words one more time. "I'd really appreciate your help if you can spare a few minutes."

"I'm sorry, Frank, my time is pretty tight. Why don't you come down to Los Angeles and I'll give you all the help you want."

My time was pretty tight too and I didn't relish another long-distance trek to see a man already standing right beside me, so I tried a different approach. "Peter, I know you're president of the Young Presidents' Organization, and I'm a member of YPO too." The Young Presidents' Organization is a closely knit worldwide network of young business entrepreneurs who are organized for self-help and self-education. Peter smiled, looked at his watch, and said, "Why don't you come up to my room in 15 minutes. I can give you half an hour before I leave."

Bob Niven and I spent more than an hour with Peter Ueberroth, learning all we could about the inner workings of the Olympic movement from his point of view. Peter is a strong leader and a good businessman, but his autocratic style often led to strained relationships with the IOC. Peter's advice to me reflected his aggressive do-it-yourself style, which has made him successful in business. Because Los Angeles had been the only city willing to organize the 1984 Games, Ueberroth and his colleagues had been able to demand novel conditions of the IOC. While this left some IOC members uncomfortable, Ueberroth may have had no tenable alternative, given the lack of substantial support from any level of government. The unique set of circumstances in L.A. probably helped the IOC develop its own financial autonomy in later years.

As the rumors had predicted, Lord Killanin decided not to seek a second term as president of the IOC. Four IOC members sought to replace him, including Willi Daume, organizer of the 1972 Munich Games; Marc Hodler, president of the *Fédération Internationale de Ski* (FIS); Juan Antonio Samaranch, a former politician, banker, industrialist, and Spanish ambassador to the Soviet Union; and Jim Worrall, the "friendly giant" from Canada. The election of Killanin's successor took place at the Moscow session, and we were there to watch.

The early odds favoring Samaranch were borne out; he easily beat his three opponents. Samaranch was known as an efficient, no-nonsense organizer who had plans to unify, strengthen, and expand an Olympic movement that was facing doubts about its future, given that almost 40 per cent of the 1980 Olympians were not attending the Moscow Games.

First Impressions

We were particularly anxious to connect with Samaranch because we suspected he might already personally favor the rival bid that was being launched by Cortina d'Ampezzo, Italy. Niven and I arranged for a personal meeting with Samaranch in his room the day after his election as president. He was cordial and encouraged Calgary to go for the bid in spite of "a few problems." Samaranch displayed one of the characteristics of a great leader: he responded positively. He undoubtedly had personal preferences, but he made certain to leave us with the impression that the new leader of the IOC welcomed all bidders as ad hoc members of the Olympic family.

We asked Samaranch about his goals for the Olympic movement. Learning that he was interested in building good relationships with governments in all Olympic countries, we decided to try to arrange a personal invitation to him from Pierre Trudeau, then prime minister of Canada. I contacted Jim Coutts, the prime minister's chief aide and an old acquaintance from my university days. Through him we organized an invitation by the prime minister to the president of the IOC. Samaranch accepted a meeting set for April 1981. It would be our first opportunity to build a rapport with the IOC president.

A Tacky Gift

Bob Niven and I had carried a briefcase full of low-value gifts to be used if appropriate in our Moscow greetings to IOC members and sports federations. For some strange reason we had included in our gift inventory dozens of samples of Alberta tar sands, beautifully packaged but utterly inappropriate as a memento of Calgary for the international sports world. I will never forget the look of total surprise on Madame Berlioux's face when these fresh-faced oilmen from Calgary presented her with a sample of Alberta tar sands as we departed. This was literally a tacky gift. Not surprisingly we still had virtually all of our tar sands samples at the end of our stay in Moscow.

When we arrived at Moscow's international airport, our Olympic hostess helped Bob Niven check his luggage at the departure lounge for Aeroflot, the Soviet national airline. His bags, which had arrived with no problem, were assessed a $300 (U.S.) overweight penalty. The hostess argued that the charge was excessive, but we lost the argument and had to pay the tax. Having witnessed this debacle, my hostess said, "You must do everything possible to lighten your luggage." Normally that's an impossible task, but I realized I might accomplish it by dumping my unused tar sands samples. It must have been quite a sight for passersby to see a foreigner with his suitcase open at the curbside, depositing packages of black sand and Olympic brochures into the wire wastebaskets there.

My luggage was also overweight, by Soviet standards, but my hostess was persistent and convinced airport officials it was close enough.

Advice From the Shoemaker

In October 1980 Bob Niven, Bill Warren, and I went to a conference of the General Assembly of International Sports Federations in Monte Carlo. The general assembly is comprised of all the international sports federations, some of which, including the International Ice Hockey Federation, the International Skating Union, and the International Ski Federation, would have a great deal of influence in the final selection process.

Horst Dassler, president of the Adidas shoe empire and son of the original founder, Adi Dassler (hence the name Adidas), was at the Monte Carlo meeting, and Bill Warren and I seized the chance to get the advice of one of the most important and influential men in the world of sport. We introduced ourselves and, after a brief chat about our Olympic ambitions, said that we would appreciate his input into our bid. His response was precise and very German. He said, "You have little chance of winning but I like you, so I will help you."

We were surprised at his perception that we had little chance of winning, and discussed it with him at length. Dassler felt the sport and political connections of our two rivals, Cortina and Falun, were too strong to overcome. Dassler did not imply that the final decision had been pre-ordained but that, realistically, the odds were stacked against us. Canadians had not achieved as much as Europeans in the Olympic movement in spite of our enthusiastic participation from the beginning. We learned from Dassler that we would have to work hard to build personal rapport with IOC members and sports federations to compensate for the long-standing trust that existed between the IOC and our competitors. We appreciated Dassler's realistic appraisal of our challenge. Knowing what problems we faced was half the battle. Doing something about it was the other half.

We had been told that Canada simply doesn't have the right connections in sport administration; we don't get our officials elected to high places. The list of key figures in the international winter sports federations includes leaders from Germany, Austria, Switzerland, and Norway. And although the situation is beginning to improve, it is still unusual for

Canadians to be among the movers and shakers of the Olympic movement. Two exceptions are Canadian IOC member Dick Pound's influence on the IOC's approach to the administration of its business affairs, and Jim Worrall's long-standing contribution to the development of a revision of the Olympic Charter. Worrall was also the first Canadian ever to be elected to the IOC executive board and the first to offer his name to stand for the office of president of the IOC. Pound has followed in Jim Worrall's giant footsteps, serving as a member of the executive board and a close adviser to President Samaranch. Pound is now expected to be a candidate to replace Samaranch when he steps down.

We asked Dassler what we had to do in order to win. Among other things, he suggested we focus on winning the African votes. Dassler offered to introduce us to Colonel Hasine Hamouda, his colleague and a very influential man in African sport. Hamouda is the editor of *Champion d'Afrique,* Africa's equivalent of *Sports Illustrated.* The publication is owned and sponsored by Adidas, which puts a great deal of effort into promoting sport in Africa. Colonel Hamouda had connections in Africa to IOC members and national leaders that would be invaluable to us.

We were by now not quite so naïve as to assume that Dassler was helping only us. In fact, it was clear he was also helping at least Cortina, and, we believed, Falun as well. By contributing advice to all three candidates, he could be happy with every possible outcome. If Dassler was helping others, it didn't bother us at all. The important thing was that he was helping us. We felt we might be able to win on our own, but with help, we could do it for sure. Dassler and Hamouda introduced us to IOC members and that was crucial, especially in Africa.

During our visit to Monte Carlo I called Chris Elekes, my secretary at Turbo, to check for any important business calls. She said, "Guess what? Ralph Klein was elected mayor last night."

I said, "C'mon Chris, don't try to pull that on me." She wasn't kidding. Ross Alger had been soundly whipped by a new people's mayor—an investigative TV journalist who had often been Mayor Alger's chief critic.

Ralph the Mayor

I wanted to get our new mayor, whom everyone seemed to call "Ralph," involved in the Olympic project as soon as possible. We met frequently and decided his international Olympic debut would be a trip to Europe in February 1981.

We set up a normal busy itinerary, including visits to the World Ski Championships at Schladming, Austria, and to the European Figure Skating Championships in Innsbruck.

Innsbruck, a city of about 250,000 people, is snuggled in a tight valley in the Austrian Alps south of Munich. It is a city with strong Olympic traditions and is a popular meeting place for Europe's sports fraternity. It was an ideal opportunity to introduce our new Calgary mayor to the international sports media.

I arrived in Austria a day earlier than the mayor, made a speech in phonetic German to the international media in Schladming, then took the train to meet Ralph and Rod Love, his bright young executive assistant, in Innsbruck. I had hoped the visit, including the arrival of the mayor, would be seen as an important gesture from the City of Calgary.

Without my knowledge, the mayor had brought an expensive silver-clad western saddle to present as a gift to Innsbruck Mayor Lugger, or Olympic Louie, as people affectionately knew him. Olympic Louie had presided as mayor over the Olympic Winter Games of 1964 and 1976 in Innsbruck. We liked the notion of Ralph and Louie becoming friends and ultimately both Olympic host-city mayors.

At a large reception taking place as part of the European Figure Skating Championships the mayor and I found a perfect forum for our Calgary pitch. I gave the deputy mayor of Innsbruck a white cowboy hat and I, in turn, received an Austrian alpine hat, which I plunked on Ralph's head. He looked great in it. But Mayor Lugger was absent, so the personally engraved silver saddle could not be presented. In fact, Ralph's extravagant silver saddle was never picked up by Lugger, and Klein ended up hauling it back to Munich, where he stashed it in the hotel lost-and-found for pick-up. It was years before the $2,500 silver saddle was recovered by

Klein's staff from the hotel storage area and delivered to Olympic Louie.

We toured the 1976 Olympic venues and somehow I talked Ralph into taking a ride down the Olympic bobsleigh run at Igls. I think what turned him on was that I told him he might well be the first Canadian mayor to do a bobsleigh run. Ralph likes being first. It was my first bobsleigh run too, and it hooked me on the thrills and chills of yet another winter sport.

The President Meets the Prime Minister

The stakes in our bidding game were raised significantly when Pierre Trudeau agreed to invite Samaranch for a private meeting in Ottawa in the spring of 1981. There was some risk the two men might not hit it off and Calgary would find itself in deeper trouble. We knew Samaranch was concerned about the fact that the Government of Canada had refused accredited Taiwan athletes entry to the Montreal Games in 1976. At that time Canada had just opened diplomatic relations with mainland China, and Taiwan refused to come to the Games if the mainland Chinese were also coming under the name of China. The diplomatic row over nomenclature had ended with Trudeau's government refusing entry to the Taiwanese.

That unilateral action by the Canadian government violated an agreement between Montreal and the IOC that had guaranteed the free entry of all fully accredited Olympic athletes. Before Samaranch's visit, we briefed the prime minister's office on the sensitive aspects of the issue. At the same time, we advised Samaranch that it would be helpful if he could extract from the prime minister a guarantee that all accredited athletes would have free entry to attend the Calgary Winter Games in 1988. If Samaranch was successful in obtaining a personal guarantee from Trudeau, it would save us some difficult negotiating later. We figured Samaranch pulled more weight than we did. If Trudeau refused, however, it would add another significant obstacle to our success.

Before Samaranch's visit to Ottawa, we dropped in at Olympic House in Montreal to host a ceremony to make

Samaranch an honorary chief of the Blackfoot Nation. Through Ralph Klein we arranged for several Natives from the Blackfoot Nation, including Chief Leo Pretty Young Man, to bestow the honor on Samaranch and to include a more modest ceremony for IOC Director Monique Berlioux.

Mayor Klein and I had agreed that we would share a cab to Olympic House on the morning of the ceremony. Ralph, however, didn't appear at the appointed time. After pacing for 10 minutes I called his room and, when there wasn't any answer, ran up and knocked on the door. Still no answer. I became worried because time was evaporating on us. I raced through the hallways to find a chambermaid with a master key to open the mayor's room. To my surprise we found the mayor sound asleep in a bathtub full of water. As we tried to retreat gracefully, he awoke with a start. I called to him that we had just come to remind him what time it was. Scrambling out of the tub he said, "I'll be with you in just a minute." Sure enough, in a few minutes he appeared, freshly scrubbed, unfazed, and ready for the day's activity.

After we had greeted President Samaranch and Madame Berlioux, who had arrived at Olympic House ahead of us, the Native ceremony began. President Samaranch sat cross-legged on the floor and then Chief Pretty Young Man, chanting a traditional Blackfoot song, danced around the president of the IOC, smeared his face with Indian facepaints, and finished by placing a magnificent headdress on his head.

The ceremony was followed by a dance in which the dancers used several rings like hula hoops. They held the rings up flat in front of them, the edges touching, in patterns strongly reminiscent of the Olympic symbol. I thought to myself that if I'd known what the dance was like, I could have got the dancers to include the Olympic symbol in their traditional performance.

In the ceremony honoring her, Madame Berlioux, an ample lady, sat on a chair in the middle of the front row in a crowd of 40 or 50 people while the dancers whirled around her and then painted her face. It was quite a sight to see this formidable lady with an imperious look on her face as our Native dancers daubed red streaks down her cheeks with their thumbs. It would have made a great photo, but we missed it.

That night Dick and Julie Pound invited Juan Antonio Samaranch, Jim Worrall, Ralph Klein, Monique Berlioux, Louis Guirandou n'Diaye, the Ivory Coast's ambassador to Canada and a member of the IOC, and myself to a dinner in their Montreal home. Several handsome children were around the house, and Julie was a relaxed hostess, spending most of the evening chatting with her guests while her maid efficiently delivered a four-course gourmet meal from the kitchen.

President Samaranch is an interesting dinner conversationalist but he makes a practice of rising from the table promptly at 10 p.m. to return to his hotel. After he left, Dick and Julie said, "Let's take our shoes off, put our feet up, and have a nightcap." The maid brought in a round of cognac for everyone and then to my amazement slipped out of her shoes, put her feet up, lifted a tiny glass, smiled, and said "Cheers." The "maid" that evening had been Julie's friend and neighbor, Di Chapman. It seemed she and Julie had a great time serving guests in each other's homes, and they both fit the same perky maid's uniform. They said they appreciated the fun of overhearing dinner conversations when playing the maid!

We chartered a small private airplane to fly President Samaranch and Madame Berlioux to Ottawa for the meeting with the prime minister.

It was the first time that I had been to 24 Sussex Drive. We were greeted at the door by the prime minister himself, who showed us into his famous house and then out onto the back lawn. He showed us his swimming pool, which had been the cause of a lot of furor, having been constructed for his family at the expense of undisclosed donors within the Liberal party. His sons were there playing in the pool.

After having a cocktail in the back garden and enjoying the view out over the river, we went into the house to the dining room. I sat next to the prime minister, who sat next to President Samaranch. Next to Samaranch were Madame Berlioux and Dick Pound. Across the table were Jim Worrall,

Ralph Klein, and Louis Guirandou n'Diaye. We chatted about things of no importance in the beginning, but it didn't take long for the two intellectuals, Samaranch and Trudeau, to get onto some interesting subjects.

At the time Samaranch had only been president of the IOC for a few months, and it had been one of his early projects to see if he could gain support for the idea of a universal passport for all Olympic officials and athletes. The IOC hoped all countries would agree that athletes and officials of the Olympic movement could travel without constraint throughout the world with an identity card. It was an ambitious idea in keeping with the Olympic spirit of internationalism, and something that had never been tried before. Trudeau listened attentively as Samaranch described his plan in some detail. I watched the polite but unconvinced expression on Trudeau's face with interest. I tried to predict how he was going to respond to this unique proposal of Samaranch's.

"Mr. President," Trudeau replied, "I think the idea has a great deal of merit. I think it should be done. It would be good for our world if we could all agree on such an idea. I will tell you this. When all the other countries of the Olympic movement have signed such an agreement, Canada will also sign." I think Samaranch was disappointed, but the prime minister's answer had been astute. He had said no in a way that did not offend. Samaranch's idea never gained the support it needed.

Then the discussion turned to whether Canada was prepared to guarantee the entry of all accredited athletes. The prime minister made short work of this question by simply saying that Canada would, of course, observe the IOC Charter. He said, however, "You must recognize that in certain matters, even the IOC Charter could not prevail over the security of a nation or over any other matter of urgent national interest." But he added that the times when such an urgent matter would arise would be very infrequent, and therefore pledged his absolute guarantee that the people of Canada would honor the Olympic Charter and allow all athletes with Olympic accreditation to enter. Our advance briefing had paid dividends. The response Samaranch had elicited was exactly what we had hoped for.

Then it was Trudeau's turn to do a selling job. "You know, Mr. President," he said, "it would be a great honor for us if the IOC would consider once again awarding the Games to Canada. In 1976 we had the Summer Games in Montreal, a city with a predominantly French culture. Our country is large and diverse, much like the Olympic movement itself. Wouldn't it be perfect if we could then have the Winter Games in Calgary, a place where English culture is predominant?"

It was a meeting that could have failed if one of the leaders had offended the other, but as it turned out, both leaders played their roles perfectly and parted friends. Calgary's chances of winning the bid rose a notch.

Momentum Builds in Calgary

Back home we spent a great deal of time convincing Calgarians to support the bid. There were always a few people who found reasons to oppose our undertaking, but by and large the public response was enthusiastic. I received many speaking invitations around town, and I used the occasions whenever possible to generate excitement and win support. Each speech included a promise of great achievement and a request for help:

> Once in a lifetime an opportunity comes to do something great like this—to be the best in the world. The history books are full of great achievers. The Olympic Games provide cities with a chance to take their place in history.
>
> I love this country and I love this city, as I'm sure you do, and I believe that great good can come to us as it has to others who have had the Olympic experience.
>
> Thousands of volunteers and spirited supporters will be required to make Calgary's Olympic Winter Games a success. After the Games, the city will assume its role of being an integral part of the world community, and our identity will be expanded beyond cowboys and oil barons to include sportsmen and sportswomen.
>
> The Games will leave a legacy: the knowledge that this city has the talent and potential to do just about anything it puts its mind to: a shot in the arm for amateur sport and physical fitness and millions of dollars worth of new facilities for future generations.

LANGRIDGE · JAKE LONGMORE · PATRICIA LANGLEY · SHIRLEY NEUFELD-WONG · ALLEN CHURCH · FRANK BOUCHER · CONNIE DU BERGER · ROSS BEST · LEONARD LAURENDEAU · BILL MARGACH · EARL OLSON · MICHAEL SHEPPARD · JOE CUILLIERRIER · JANE HARCHE · IRENE STRONKS · BILL RANSON · KEVIN BLEACKLEY · KATHERINE ANDERSON · GARRY GERMSCHEID · NORANNE DICKIN · JOHN MCGUFFIN · REGINA SACHELI · JOHN RICHELS · CONSTANTINE NIKITIUK · KIM VERHEGGE · JEAN CLAUDE NADEAU · PAT LOEWEN · DENNIS WILSON · GERT MILLER · DAVE BOTKIN · JEANNIE TRACH · BILL BROOKS · MICHELLE GOTZEAMAN · CATHERINE SHUBERT · KELLY

> If sport has taught us anything, it is that you've got to have a goal and you've got to believe in yourself if you're going to succeed.
>
> If Calgary is your home and you'd like to make it an even better place to raise your children, then help us. Don't just wish us well and hope that we do the job. Help us to stretch to meet the challenge. Help us to push all the positive buttons and join us. Then one day soon, Calgary will have become that better place because we had a dream . . . and because we believed in ourselves.

Calgarians responded. Support from the private sector— in time, services, and money—was substantial. Labatt's breweries agreed to sponsor our bid film. Air Canada donated airline passes. The Royal Bank gave us financing. Businesses throughout the city helped by giving us favorable rates, or by contributing the services of their key employees. Engineers volunteered their time and skills to complete the technical studies required. Members of the media were generous with their coverage of the CODA story.

The public response shaped our identity and breathed life into our organization. This support of the people was precisely the evidence of commitment sought by the international Olympic establishment.

Covering All the Bases

In the spring of 1981 Jeanette and I went to a week-long seminar of the Young Presidents' Organization in Singapore. We decided to combine the Singapore trip with a visit to a number of other countries in the Far East that were not winter countries but nevertheless had IOC members. We took two or three days' vacation on the beautiful green island of Bali before arriving in Djakarta, Indonesia, where we were picked up by the Canadian ambassador's limousine to be delivered to the embassy for a briefing. We went through a routine we repeated in five other countries. We had cocktails or a lunch with the local IOC member, met the national Olympic committee leaders, and then held a press conference to talk about Calgary and support for Calgary's bid in the international Olympic movement.

The reaction we met in Indonesia and elsewhere was incredulity: "Why are you here? We don't have any skiers or

KAUR · DOROTHY SPRIGGS · CRAIG LEHTO · JOHN DOYLE · ROBERT FRENCH · HELEN THOMPSON · BRIAN NORFORD · RON WHITEWAY · BERTO PEGORARO · CLAUDIA MORIARTY · MAUREEN O'KEEFE WEST · CARMEN MCCLENNON · BRIAN SCHEIRMAN · LISE ROMPRE · JOANNE HANSEN · JANE WILSON · LISA SPAVOR · GREGG ELLIOT · SHERYL BLACKIE · KAY PRINGLE · KIM FRIPP · GREG GARNETT · JOYCE HISEY · GWYNETH DE VRIES · GEOFF CREGO · SHERRY STARKE · RETA JENKEN · BONNIE NAHORNICK · PAUL KELLY · ROGER JEHLE · KELLY KRYCZKA IRWIN · MAC BENDER · BARB PETERSON · MARK LEBLANC · WILL GASKARTH · DONALD SMILLIE · DAVID BOUTILLIER · PAT

skaters." And our answer was always the same: "We all belong to the Olympic family and we need the advice of the sports leaders who live here in order to understand your vision of the future. We want to hear about what has gone right and what has gone wrong in previous Games, because our goal is to have better Games than have ever been held before."

I found out later that our approach was novel. Other bid committees seemed to feel that only the winter sporting nations counted when voting for Winter Games. That is incorrect. All members of the IOC vote and go to the Winter Games, and they all have views on how things should be done. I believe our conscious effort to cover all bases thoroughly was one of the reasons we ultimately won. It's a lesson in commitment to detail that I'll continue to use in business.

From Indonesia we continued on our whirlwind trip, travelling to Thailand, Malaysia, Hong Kong, Korea, and Japan, all within nine days of our leaving Singapore. We learned a little bit about each of the countries, and I felt that members of the Olympic Family were appreciative that we had come so far to talk to them. We had begun to build support in the Far East.

Se Habla Español

With all our travelling, it became necessary to hire a general manager to run the CODA office and control its finances. Our group still largely consisted of volunteers, although we had by now hired a general administrator, Don Siler, a former quarterback from the University of Calgary Dinosaurs football team and a graduate in sports administration. We had also hired two former secretaries from the mayor's office, Sylvia Moir and Theresa Konkin, both of whom had been fired by the mayor's office shortly after Klein had been elected. Sylvia Moir was employed by the Olympic organization longer than anyone—a total of nearly eight years. I often referred to her as our mother because she looked after everyone so well as secretary, receptionist, and office manager.

We were looking for more than a run-of-the-mill general manager. Everyone in CODA had to be a promoter of the Calgary bid. We were weak in the Latin countries, and we realized that with Samaranch as the new president of the IOC we had to find someone who could speak Spanish fluently and who could tell our story in Latin America.

Bob Brinkerhoff, a young Calgary oilman and a member of our committee, introduced me to Steve Corbett, a headhunter who would locate executives for a fee. At our first luncheon meeting Corbett volunteered his services to find us a general manager who had the persuasiveness of a salesman and the manners of a diplomat, and who also spoke fluent Spanish. Corbett agreed to find us our new person in time for a big meeting I had in Mexico with Mario Vazquez Rana, president of the Association of National Olympic Committees and of the Pan American Sports Organization, and an influential person in the Olympic community. Vazquez Rana owned a chain of Mexican newspapers and later, for a period, owned the UPI wire service operations.

Time, like money, was a scarce resource around CODA. Only three days before the important trip to Mexico, Steve Corbett called to report, "It's been difficult, but I have a short list of candidates to show you." There were 10 people on Steve's list, but it was clear not one was close to being the right person. "Steve," I said, "I'm really disappointed. I can't accept any of these people. They are totally out of the question."

"I was afraid that would be your reaction," he replied. "I'm sorry. I did my best, but I just can't find anybody with the qualifications you need. You're looking for too much in one person."

"Nonsense," I chided. "There's an obvious answer. You're the person we're looking for. I'm leaving in three days for Mexico and I'd like you to be on the plane with me."

Steve spoke excellent Spanish and was an entrepreneur with management moxie. He was naturally outgoing and had a sense of humor. I had been impressed with him from the first. That's why the list of others seemed so inadequate by comparison.

"Okay," he said, "I'll go on the trip with you and I'll talk it over with my partners and my wife after the trip. I'll see how you operate and then decide what it's like to be in this job."

On the way to Mexico I spent hours briefing Steve about our project, and on the way back he said, "Count me in. There's no way I couldn't do it." Like the rest of us, he had fallen in love with the Olympic challenge and a chance to go for the gold.

Steve was perfect for the job. He became our full-time general manager, looking after most of the business affairs of CODA. We also asked him to get the support of the IOC members in all the Spanish-speaking countries. There's no doubt he won over most of them, and without them we could not have won the bid. There were many forks in the road that led to Calgary in 1988. This was one of the junctures where our choice was the right one.

A Promise Reaffirmed

The Trudeau government was returned to office in March 1980, and Gerry Regan, the former premier of Nova Scotia, was sworn in as the new sports minister, replacing Steve Paproski. Regan and I quickly became friends. He intuitively understood what we at CODA were doing and he dedicated a lot of his time to helping us make it happen.

In July 1981 Gerry travelled all the way to Caracas, Venezuela, to help Steve Corbett, Dick Pound, and me present Calgary's plans to the Pan American Sports Organization. A conversation I had with him in Caracas turned out to be a financial turning point. During a walk one evening in the hotel garden, Regan agreed to provide our Games with the full $200 million originally promised by Iona Campagnolo. I told him we had started with a commitment of $200 million from non-tax sources. Paproski had never fully understood our insistence on this, but Regan did. "Can you find enough non-tax dollars?" I wanted to know.

"I thought you'd never ask," he replied, explaining the Tories had given the national lottery away and the Olympics would be his ticket to get it back.

"I will get you your $200 million," he said, "but in return you must promise your support for some new plans I have to raise money for sport."

"How you get the money's your call," I said. "We'll support you, but if the plans don't work out, you answer politically for it. We'll give you good Games."

Seoul Mates

Caracas was the first place we met the Koreans, who were bidding for the 1988 Summer Games. I especially remember Sang Jin Chyung, their protocol chief, a man who never stopped smiling. He later thanked me for helping Korea win the Games. Initially he didn't know many IOC members and was shy about approaching them. In Caracas Chyung stood quietly on the sidelines while we were buzzing around, shaking hands and engaging actively in conversation. He looked like he could use a friend so we took him under our wing, introduced him to all the IOC members that we knew, and invited him to our gatherings. We urged him to become a little more aggressive in getting to know IOC members, assuring him they didn't bite.

In Caracas Dick Pound made his maiden speech on behalf of the Calgary bid, and it was a beauty. Together with Regan's persuasive personality and high profile, and Steve Corbett's silver-tongued Spanish, we made more friends and progressed toward our goal.

I remember meeting Bill Simon, president of the United States Olympic Committee, at the meeting of the Pan American Sports Organization in Caracas. When Simon was U.S. secretary of the treasury his name appeared in print on all U.S. dollar bills. Now he had a stack of crisp new one-dollar bills with his name on them and he was autographing them and giving them away for his own amusement. I approached him to get one for myself and asked if he had a couple of hundred more for my friends back in Calgary. He said he didn't.

Getting to Know You

CODA, rapidly increasing in size in preparation for the bid to the IOC in September 1981, now had an executive of nine volunteers, five full-time employees, and about 50 other volunteers. Our 23-person board of directors included past and present heads of the Calgary Stampede Board, former mayor Ross Alger, and an old friend of mine, Justice Joe Kryczka, a former head of the Canadian Amateur Hockey Association.

By now Iona Campagnolo had also joined our team. She had left politics, having lost her seat when the Conservatives gained power in 1979. She was interested in helping, and we felt that having the former sports minister aboard was a real asset, the more so when her French-language skills were taken into account.

We divided up our lobbying task. Iona and Roger Jackson took Africa; Bill Warren and Jack Wilson took Western Europe; Steve Corbett had South America; Bob Niven took India, Pakistan, the European countries bordering on the Mediterranean, and the Middle East; and I took the Soviet bloc and the Far East.

Our assessment of Iona Campagnolo was correct. She and Roger Jackson met me in Paris on their way back from a major whirlwind trip in Africa that had been arranged for us by Horst Dassler and Colonel Hamouda. Their trip had been very promising, and it was clear that Iona had played a major part in making it a success.

That night in Paris, Horst Dassler invited Roger, Iona, and me to a European Cup soccer match. At a VIP reception at half-time, we met half a dozen senior people in the Olympic movement, including João Havelange, president of FIFA, the International football (that is, soccer) federation, and Franco Carraro, vice-president of FIFA and chairman of Cortina's bid committee.

I noticed Iona in animated conversation with a little group that included Franco Carraro. As I joined their circle I gathered that verbal missiles were about to be launched between the two. Iona was describing her trip through Africa and explaining why she thought Calgary would make such a wonderful host city. Carraro, however, looked aloof and unimpressed and was not buying Iona's sales pitch. He bluntly dismissed our choice of a mountain skiing site, saying,

"Your ski hill is simply too far away. It's totally unacceptable for Olympic Winter Games."

Iona rose to the challenge as though it had been an insult thrown by the opposition during Question Period back in her days on Parliament Hill. "Our ski hill may be further away than yours," she replied sweetly, "but at least we arrive without our kneecaps being shot off!" At the time a popular practice among terrorists and mobsters in Italy was to maim their victims by shattering their kneecaps with a gunshot.

Carraro turned and walked stiffly away as I swallowed an hors d'œuvre, toothpick and all. Iona, laying her hand on my arm, looked at me as if to inquire if she had taken her point too far. I whispered, "You certainly got his attention." After the trip to Africa and the debate with Carraro, our bid began to be treated more seriously, by Cortina at least.

To make up for our lack of established connections, we continued to meet as many IOC members as possible. We had decided on a plan to make contact with each IOC member at least three times, including once in their home town and once in ours. We set up a map with different-colored pins, showing the locations and voting preferences of IOC members, as far as we were able to determine them. If any IOC members indicated a preference for one of our competitors we would meet with them, saying we understood not all members could pick Calgary first and asking for consideration in the second-round vote. This was a gentle way of keeping full contact and building trust even with those members who favored one of our competitors. For this reason I felt it was important to set up a private meeting with João Havelange. We had tried to see Havelange on several occasions, but he was always busy and hard to reach. Suddenly one Saturday I got a telex from him saying he would be free to meet me the following Tuesday—in Paris. I had no choice but to drop all business, hop on a plane, meet him in Paris, then fly home the following day. Dick Pound joined me for the trip. Havelange was friendly and helpful and careful not to indicate his preference. I asked for second-round support.

At home we began entertaining a parade of IOC members and representatives from the international sports federations who took us up on our offer to visit Calgary. It was important that some IOC members see what Calgary had to offer first-hand. In August of 1980 Marc Hodler, head of the *Fédération Internationale de Ski* and spokesman for the six winter sports federations, visited Calgary to inspect and endorse our sites. I had shared with Hodler my concern over a few of the mistakes we had made in lobbying the winter sports federations. His response: "Never regret those things you've done, only those things you have not done." We took his advice and stepped up our attention to every detail required to get the support of the winter sports experts.

By the time we went to Baden-Baden to present our final bid to the IOC, representatives of all six international winter sports federations—biathlon, bobsleigh, hockey, luge, skating, and skiing—endorsed Calgary's bid. It was, to our knowledge, the first time a city had received the unanimous endorsement of the international federations prior to the final bid.

We continued the Calgary style of (as we put it) "listening naïvely to our customers" that had served us so well at numerous dinner parties in the homes of CODA executives. That way people were more open with us.

Getting to know IOC members on a more personal basis allowed them gradually to assess us and to build their confidence in us. Many of them were impressed by the size of the city, having assumed that Calgary was just a little alpine village like Banff or Lake Placid. They were surprised to find a booming city of 640,000 people, with amenities and infrastructure already in place. After the mammoth transportation problems of Lake Placid, they were reassured that Calgary's size and well-developed public transit system would prevent similar problems here. That was a big plus, considering Calgary still had to build all the sports facilities needed for the Games.

The dinner parties at our home included, where possible, our sons David and Stephen, then aged 15 and 12. In many cases having our boys present contributed to the relaxed and personal touch of the evening, and the boys made many international friends. It was a tremendous opportunity for kids their age. Later, when they accompanied us to Sarajevo for the 1984 Winter Games, Jeanette and I were delighted to see IOC members come up to them in the hotel lobby and shake their hands.

At one Calgary dinner party for several IOC members, Ahmed Touny from Egypt, the father of seven or eight children, amused our boys for several hours by making paper cutouts and doing parlor tricks. Lance Cross, the IOC member from New Zealand, after touring the Calgary Zoo, shared a dip in our whirlpool spa at home with our family. Other CODA families helped out by bringing contributions to the many IOC dinner parties—Margie Niven's spinach salads, Jack Wilson's salmon, Peggy Warren's desserts. Everyone pitched in to ease the load.

On Mother's Day in 1981, we shared a family dinner in our home with Louis Guirandou n'Diaye, IOC member and ambassador to Canada from the Ivory Coast. He and his wife Simone were accompanied by their personal valet, an elegant man named Samba who always wore white gloves. Louis and his wife are both tall, with an elegant, even regal, bearing. We often joked with Louis that Canada was the only country with three IOC members because although Louis was the IOC member for the Ivory Coast, he lived in Ottawa at the time. Mr. and Mrs. Reggie Alexander from Kenya also came to dinner at our house. Mrs. Alexander, who is a petite lady with a very British accent, asked Jeanette, "And how large a staff have you?" At home in Kenya Mrs. Alexander was used to having several cooks and housekeepers.

Jeanette smiled and said, "Well, the boys sometimes help with the dishes, and my husband pours the wine when we have guests." Jeanette hadn't thought of inviting her neighbor in to serve our guests, as Julie Pound and Di Chapman did.

Bob Niven, after hosting the IOC member from Turkey, 71-year-old Suat Erler, was rushing his guest back to the airport when another driver blocked his exit from the hotel parking lot. In his frustration, Bob hollered out the window, "Get out of the way, you turkey!" The words escaped before Bob remembered that he had the IOC member from Turkey in the back seat of his car! A stunned silence followed, after which a red-faced Bob tried in vain to explain the meaning of the expression to his distinguished Turkish guest.

In June 1981 I went to see Jean, Grand Duke of Luxembourg, the IOC member for Luxembourg. I wanted to bring him a gift, but it was almost literally a question of what to give a man who has everything. I picked out an Indian tomahawk made in the style of tomahawks of old.

As I entered the palace carrying this awkward-looking package under my arm I was met by the chief of security and protocol. When he noticed my package he enquired what it was.

"It's a personal gift for the Grand Duke," I explained.

"Of course it's not a weapon of any sort?" he probed.

"Oh no, of course not," I answered. "I would never dream of bringing a weapon into the palace." With that, he ushered me in.

When I was received by the Grand Duke in his drawing room, I said I would like to present a gift that already had an interesting story attached to it. As he examined the weapon, I told him what it was and related the conversation with his chief of security. The Grand Duke had a laugh over the incident, and our meeting marked the beginning of a friendship. I hope I didn't cost the security chief his job.

People Power

Returning home from world travels, we had to feed the constant demand for funds to pay our bills. CODA had already begun to borrow money from the bank without any personal guarantees. The Royal Bank was generous in its support, but we couldn't afford to overlook the need for funds, so in May 1981 we launched another of our unique fundraising efforts. This time it was to be a celebrity dinner. It was a pretty posh affair—we had decided to charge $1,000 per plate, making it the highest-priced dinner in Canadian history. We invited Prime Minister Trudeau, who had not been to Calgary for years. His energy policies had been unpopular with the oil industry, giving him all the reason he could have needed for staying away.

I asked his aide, Jim Coutts, whether it would be appropriate to provide a female guest to dine with Trudeau, who was then separated from his wife Margaret. We agreed to invite Calgarian Donna Rupert, a recent Miss Canada, to dine with the PM. We phoned Donna in Los Angeles, where she was a model, and she said she would be delighted to come and be part of the official party.

Our dinner was a massive success; more than 600 people paid $1,000 each to attend. The cream of Calgary high society, and some of the cream of Canada's business community, were there. The meal consisted of nine elaborate courses, including reindeer consommé, duck pâté, and veal tenderloin. Anne Murray provided the entertainment. We shared the evening with a number of young champion athletes, as well as two tables of Calgary's pioneer citizens. Two IOC members were also present. We hoped they would take the message back to their colleagues that Calgarians were solidly behind their bid team and one hundred per cent committed to getting the Games.

Everyone who came to our celebrity dinner received a special gold-colored commemorative CODA pin. These gold-colored pins later became hot collectors' items even though they had cost us less than the cloisonné red pins we normally sold to new CODA members for five dollars.

The gross revenues of the dinner were around $600,000, the net about $425,000. The event had temporarily bailed us out of our bid-financing problems, but there was a constant cash call on our meagre reserves nonetheless. We were still travelling all over the world looking for support from IOC members and trying to encourage them to visit Calgary. Our strategy was working, but we were still without the financial resources to do what we were telling the world we were capable of doing.

A few months before we went to Baden-Baden, we launched a final membership blitz. Steve Corbett organized a group of volunteers who went door-to-door canvassing for memberships in CODA. We found we had severely underestimated public interest in the Olympic bid. Volunteer canvassers would return to CODA's office 10 minutes after they had left, saying, "I sold all my pins at the first three houses."

We sent the canvassers back out with bigger and bigger boxes of pins. To this day, we don't know exactly how many memberships were sold, since accurate records weren't kept. Based on cash received, the number could have been as high as 83,000, which was the number we used in our presentations to the IOC.

While all our lobbying and fundraising efforts were going on, Bob Niven was busy finalizing the technical aspects of the bid, most notably selecting our venues and estimating costs.

Our plan for construction of the major facilities was simple: our government partners would oversee the construction, freeing the organizing committee from being accountable for spending taxpayers' money. Governments would be happy to take credit for constructing shiny new facilities, and the organizing committee could confine its attention to the running of the Games themselves.

When the Saddledome project later became the subject of controversy, we were pleased that we had left the expenditure of taxpayer dollars to City Council, even though aldermen were not prepared for the heat you often catch when you play near the Olympic flame.

By the time we set out for Baden-Baden, West Germany, where the IOC would decide our Olympic future, we felt confident our plans for facilities and operations were without any serious problems. We had come to know and respect the members of the IOC. They didn't know it yet, but they had virtually written our bid book for us. Most of all, as Prince Takeda had recommended two years earlier, we had won the support of the people of Calgary.

CHAPTER SIX

Baden-Baden

The future depends on you.
PIERRE DE COUBERTIN

OUR PRESENTATION TO THE IOC Congress was to take place in September 1981. Our bid books had been delivered to all 83 IOC members and each of the six sports federations by March. Even though the bid books met the minimum requirements of the IOC, we devoted ourselves to putting together an additional technical book describing in detail every venue and several alternate possibilities we had selected. The two books were packed with background information, statistics, glossy pictures, and technical drawings, and were likely among the most complete such books ever produced for an Olympic bid. We didn't want to leave room for failure.

Now, at last, we were gaining confidence in our long-range funding situation. By September 1981 we had calculated a $415-million balanced budget, consisting of $200 million from the federal government, $70 million from the provincial government, $25 million from the city, and $120 million from

FERN CORRAINI • SHAWN RANAHAN • CAROLYN HYNDMAN • STAN SPARLING SOLBERG • TURI SLETNER • JEAN LARSON • TERESA BELKIE • GORD RUTHERFORD • ILENE SCHMALTZ • SIMON BARRETT • JOHN ASHBOURNE • CATHY MORAN-BAKER • SIGI ZIMMERMANN • PETER LOEWEN • GRACE CRESPO • JOHN LINSTER • LIZ KANE-AKERLEY • CARLA MILLIGAN • BOB MONILAWS • EMILE VERSAEVEL • SANDI SPEAR • CONNIE MILLER • DIANA FOLK • JONATHAN BLAINE • MILES PALMER • DAN ROUTLY • PATRICIA ELASZ • CARL SCHWARZER • JAY PRINGLE • MICHAEL PALKA • MICHAEL DYER • DEANNA ZEYHA • LLOYD DRAPER • MONA KNUDSLIEN • BETTY MILLER • PHIL BUCKINGHAM • NELSON

television rights, tickets, sponsorships, and marketing programs. CODA was the first group to have such a complete funding package worked out in detail before winning the right to host the Games.

"Come Together" Is Born

With a solid foundation under us, we turned to how we would present the personality of our bid to the IOC. We had received an offer from Warren Miller, the American producer of popular ski and travel films, to produce a bid movie for Baden-Baden. But we wanted these Games to be made in Canada, so we hired a Vancouver company called Creative House to produce an inspirational slide show—including a new song—to capture the spirit of the people of Calgary.

CODA's senior people passed on to the people at Creative House some of the most popular comments that we had picked up from IOC members, together with some phrases and ideas of our own. The people at Creative House then distilled what we had given them into a theme for our slide show. The theme we settled on was international co-operation. It was the same idea that was inspiring IOC President Juan Antonio Samaranch in his efforts to make the Olympic movement the world's leading social movement by the end of the century. Calgary was in a new part of the world, a city unfettered by the past and looking toward the future. We believed that the Games in Calgary should serve as a bridge to allow people to—and this became our motto—"come together."

As with the bid books, we spent hours poring over every word in the text of the slide show to be sure nothing important was left out and nothing unimportant left in. We waited anxiously for the day when the themesong, "Come Together in Calgary," would be presented to us. We had agreed that the finished version would be sung in part by a children's choir. The CODA bid team gathered at a party at our house to preview the first tapes of the song. At the end of the first playing our small group of CODA workers clapped, whistled, and cheered. The themesong expressed exactly the Olympic message we wanted. We were delighted and it boosted our confidence.

The song "Come Together in Calgary" had the durability of a great themesong, helping to win the bid for the city. We also used it later in films to tell the story of the Calgary Olympic Winter Games, and, of course, we played it at the opening and closing ceremonies of the Games themselves.

It was gratifying, during our travels, that people, hearing about the progress of our preparations for the Games, would often say, "It's really coming together, isn't it?" The words "come together" served not only as our invitation to Canada and the rest of the world, but as a slogan for making our plans a reality.

Creative House also produced what was, at that time, the largest computer-synchronized slide presentation ever made in Canada. Using 11 projectors and an enormous 20-foot-by-40-foot screen, it was to be the centrepiece of our bid presentation, an attempt to win the IOC members over by grabbing them emotionally. The CODA presentation show won a Gold Quill award in New York for business presentations—sort of like an Academy Award for advertising.

Preparing to Win

Fred Wuotila, one of our most capable volunteers, was sent to Baden-Baden to find a hotel for us and iron out other details before our arrival. Fred was the perfect advance man for a job requiring attention to detail and an ability to acquire goods and services at no or next to no cost. Fred's ability in the latter department was so great that we often called him Fred the Scrounger. He rented a beautiful 85-room spa-type hotel, the Quisisana, for our delegation's headquarters. We had learned our lesson from Lake Placid. The other bid delegations, from Falun and Cortina, arrived later than Calgary to make their arrangements, and ended up with inferior accommodation.

Fred found the toilet paper in Germany a little rough for a country gentleman like himself, so he shipped over two cases of our own toilet paper, a fact that was headlined with amusement in the *Calgary Herald*. He also purchased and shipped all the supplies we would need for entertaining, icluding two 44-pound bags of pancake mix for a Calgary-style pancake breakfast.

John Pickett, on loan to CODA from the Canadian Olympic Association, made arrangements with BMW for us to borrow five new cars. When we added uniformed drivers from the Canadian Armed Forces base in Baden-Solingen, we were the best-equipped team in town. Fred scouted out the old train station, which was to be the exhibition hall, and selected the best site for our bid display, alongside our competitors, and the cities of Seoul, South Korea, and Nagoya, Japan, which were bidding for the summer Games. He saw to the erection of the the giant screen for our slide presentation.

We took note that the Queen of Sweden, a former hostess in the Olympic Winter Games, was actively supporting the Falun bid. We tried to offset this powerful asset of Sweden's by selecting some of the other favorite Olympic protocol hostesses for dealing with IOC members. John Pickett had introduced us to Dr. Emmy Schwabe of Innsbruck, Austria. Emmy had been the Chief of Protocol for two previous Olympic Games and had become well-known for her ability in training young women to be VIP hostesses. Queen Sylvia had been one of her protégées. We asked her to help us select five or six of the best-trained Olympic hostesses in Europe, based on their knowledge of protocol, language skills, and experience with Olympic people and procedures. The assistance of our European hostesses was important to our bid. IOC members felt more comfortable dealing with Calgary when they saw friendly faces from Games of the past.

The IOC session in 1981 received special media attention because it was held in conjunction with the 10th Olympic Congress. Olympic Congresses are held only when major issues or changes to the Olympic Charter are discussed, and thus they guarantee heightened interest and attendance from IOC members and the media alike. At the Baden-Baden congress there were 83 IOC members, together with representatives of 142 national Olympic committees and 46 international sports federations. In total 700 delegates, 450 support staff, and 500 media representatives were in Baden-Baden. It was an Olympic summit meeting. We would soon see if we had learned to play the summit game.

JAN ELLIOTT · FRED COX · HARRY H. HIGGINS · REIDUN MOE · GLORIA O'NEILL · SHIRLEY MACARTHUR · SHARON GOODFELLOW · KIMI RUTZ · SHIRLEY MACNEIL · BRENDA CHRISTIE · SHELLEY SWITZER · RICK TINGMAN · MARK LIM · RHEA TIMMERMAN · RICK MULLAN · KEITH WOOD · ALBERT GATES · ERIC WALKER · JAMIE BEATSON · TIM ELLAM · RONALD STOREY · BRIGITTE BACHMANN · GARVIN SIROIS · DONNA GELLNER · DAVID DICK · PAUL TRAPTOW · ROBERT FISHER · RUTH SCHURCH · HEATHER SHEPPARD · LORETTA NG · PETE KENNEY · MARIANNE METZGER · STEW SCOTT · CAROLE PEARSON · WILF LANGEVIN · PAUL KRIZAN · CHARLES MILLS · MARK HERMAN ·

The Sports Pool

Sixteen days before our final bid presentation, Gerry Regan announced the Canadian government's plan for raising its funding for the Games: a new national sports pool. The pool, patterned after European soccer pools, was to be a system of public betting on the outcomes of professional baseball games. It was Regan's way of re-entering the national lottery business, which the previous government had ceded to the provinces. But the provinces greeted the plan with hostility because it horned in on their new jurisdiction, and the public greeted the plan with a giant collective yawn. It soon became evident this might not be the popular vehicle for funding the Games that Regan had hoped it would be.

Just prior to going to Baden-Baden we were pushing hard to finalize the federal government's commitment of $200 million for the Games. We were surprised with the wording sent to us by Gerry Regan's staff on the draft agreement. The document said the federal government would pay "up to $200 million." We asked them to eliminate the words "up to," since we were counting on the entire amount and not a penny less.

"Don't worry about that," the federal bureaucrats said. "That's standard government wording. We all agree that you will be getting the whole $200 million, but this is the way we prefer to write the Cabinet document."

"Bullshit!" I responded. "If we all agree then let's use the exact words that describe our agreement." We stuck to our guns and eventually got the wording the way we wanted it. Our persistence on this point during the hectic days before our trip to Baden-Baden preserved full federal participation in the Games. As events unfolded in later years it became evident some of the most competitive games would be played not in the public eye by amateur athletes but behind the scenes by federal bureaucrats . . . and on this very issue.

Last-Minute Panic

The day before we left for Baden-Baden, I got a phone call from Fred Wuotila, our advance man. "Frank," he said in a panic, "our display is simply not good enough. We are not even in the same league as the other guys. You should see their displays!"

We had spent most of our limited budget on the bid books and the slide show because the public displays didn't necessarily influence anybody but the media. I told Fred not to panic; when we arrived the next day, we would take a look at it and see what needed to be done.

So at last the trip to Baden-Baden was on. The feeling in Calgary as we left was one of hope, but not necessarily of expectation. The world media had cast us in the role of underdog, having already determined that the real fight was between Falun and Cortina. We didn't mind that position, because we felt the IOC members would not appreciate the media deciding in advance how they would vote. I later learned that Lars Eggertz, the chairman of the Falun bid committee, believed that Calgary had been the favorite choice of the IOC going in. There is always self-doubt about where you stand when the competition is so intense.

Our delegation included an official group of about 25 people. With spouses, our team swelled to about 50 people. Former mayor Ross Alger joined us, flying over at his own expense. We were met at the Frankfurt airport by a small bus that took us through the Black Forest to the health-spa resort of Baden-Baden. It was a strangely silent bus ride. We had worked hard for three years on this bid, and the realization that all our efforts were now on the line was both frightening and inspiring. Still, our team cheered as the bus wheeled off the German autobahn into town.

On arrival Jeanette and I went immediately to the train station to see the other Olympic displays and to soothe Fred Wuotila's frazzled nerves. It wasn't easy. Cortina's display was a giant Styrofoam model of the whole Dolomite Valley, with replicas of the mountains and all the little villages and facilities, right down to tiny hotels and chairlifts. It was impressive, filling a room of roughly 100 square metres. Fred had climbed up behind the Cortina mountain from the Calgary side and planted a tiny Canadian flag at the summit, which remained unnoticed for most of the display period.

The Swedes had also outdone Calgary. They had built a full-size, $200,000 log house with built-in bars, videotaped messages, and beautiful hostesses in costume serving Swedish food and drink. The cities of Nagoya and Seoul had bid displays that were at least as impressive. By contrast our display was modest, consisting only of posters, banners, pictures, a chuckwagon and a small table-top model of the Spray Lakes Valley and another of the proposed new Olympic Saddledome. Our display looked quite anaemic, sandwiched between our two European competitors and the two Oriental summer sites.

We went to work making minor adjustments. We bought some green plants, hung the banners differently, and improved the traffic flow among the display tables. We could do little more. I gave the team a pep talk, because many of them were growing fearful and despondent, fearing we had really blown it. It was clear that although we had worked hard to be the best at everything we did, we just didn't have the best display.

"Our display," I said to them, "is not a fancy one made of bricks and mortar; our display is our people. Our people will make the difference and we'll win this bid. We have excellent bid books and a great slide presentation. What we have to do now is show our Calgary personality. We can only offer who we are."

Our CODA team was dressed in what we referred to as "dignified western" attire: blue sports jackets with a western cut, grey slacks, white shirts, and navy striped ties. Blue jeans were discouraged, but denim skirts for the ladies were considered appropriate. In addition to our CODA team, we had brought with us two Mounted Police officers in full scarlet-and-blue uniforms, together with Lambert and Yvonne Fox, a Native chief and his wife from the Blood tribe in Southern Alberta. Two musical groups, the Gary Buck Calgary Western Band and the Canadian Brass, completed the entourage.

As the critical days of the bid unfolded, the hope that our strength was our people proved right. Our Mounties were a big hit. They gave out thousands of autographed photos. And when Chief Fox and his wife danced to the beat of Native tomtoms, people crowded into our area, leaving the other bid displays virtually empty. We learned that our unique western heritage is interesting to people from other parts of the world.

When the Italians saw how warmly our performers were being received, they upped the ante by bringing in 40 male singers from La Scala opera in Milan. We prepared our own counteroffensive. As soon as the Italian choir started to sing, we would turn up our recorded Indian drum music to full volume. Lambert and Yvonne Fox danced magnificently, singing their distinctive Native chants. A few lines of opera were enough to send most IOC members and the public away from the La Scala singers and over to watch our Native dancers and red-coated Mounties.

Calgary Mayor Ralph Klein arrived at Baden-Baden four days after we did. He brought with him three aldermen—Stan Nelson, Don Hartman, and Larry Gilchrist—as well as his executive assistant, Rod Love. There had been quite a bit of squabbling in City Council about which aldermen would get the freebie trip to holiday in Europe. At one time the mayor proposed to take nine members of council with him, at our expense. We reminded him that CODA didn't even have enough money to pay the airfares of people who had already worked without pay for three years to make the bid possible. We were adamant the city delegation be kept small. Most aldermen had done little to help CODA during the bid and were not familiar with the bid process or the IOC members. But under pressure from City Council, Klein decided to bring three of his colleagues along at city taxpayers' expense.

This Town Ain't Big Enough for the Both of Us

Right after his arrival in Baden-Baden, Ralph Klein asked for a private meeting with me. He presented me with a letter he had signed on the mayor's official stationery. The letter contained an unbelievable demand. In exchange for the support being offered by Calgary City Council at Baden-Baden, CODA would have to guarantee that the City of Calgary would have a majority on the board of directors of the Olympic organizing committee.

"This is absolutely impossible," I said. "I would never consider such a request presented here at the eleventh hour. But anyway, we see the Games as a community project run by volunteers, not by government. In Montreal we saw an example of what happens when a city government tries to run the Games. People try to take from the Games rather than contribute to them. We need your co-operation, not more government control. The people will run these Games. It is fundamental to our success."

Ralph expressed his concern about the city's responsibility for Olympic-related costs. I reminded him that we had presented a complete plan for financing the Games to City Council. Other levels of government had already committed themselves to paying the major costs, and City Council had approved the arrangements as fair. Besides, many of the venues were not even in the city of Calgary.

"If you do not agree to the terms of my letter," he countered, "I must tell you that I am prepared to withdraw City Council's support for this bid here and now."

I could not believe that City Council would undermine our efforts at this late date, nor that the people of Calgary would be happy with the prospect of taxpayers taking all the risk of financing the Games, as they had in Montreal. Furthermore, a move by the city to control the Games would surely result in a loss of federal and provincial support.

"Has City Council passed some new motion while I was away?" I asked. Ralph indicated that it had not. "Then I'm sorry, Your Worship, but I must rely on the motion from City Council authorizing CODA to proceed with the bid. I suggest you take your letter back and forget about this very bad idea." But Ralph pressed the point again.

"I'll make you an offer," I said. "If you are serious about this demand, I'll step down as chairman of CODA right now and let you and the aldermen present the bid to the IOC. There is no middle ground." I handed the letter back to the mayor and left.

That afternoon Premier Peter Lougheed arrived, and I reported what had happened. "I hope you agree with my stand," I said.

"To have done anything different," he replied, "would have been a disaster."

Ralph Klein didn't withdraw city support, and he never spoke about the letter again. But his first attempt to gain more control over our group was a warning of more trouble to come.

Klein was not the only fellow who tried to improve his position at Baden-Baden. Captain John Morrison also tried. About eight months earlier an unexpected visitor to my office had introduced himself as "Captain John Morrison of Air Canada," saying that Doug Port had asked him to help with whatever arrangements were required. Port, western regional manager for Air Canada, was an important member of our CODA committee. I spent half an hour chatting with the gentleman, trying in vain to figure out why he had come to see me. I never did.

I had long forgotten Captain John Morrison by the time we got to Baden-Baden, until I got a call from John Pickett saying my Air Canada friend had arrived and had taken the premier's room in our hotel, as well as receiving accreditation as part of the Calgary team.

"That's impossible," I said. "He's not my friend—I don't even know the guy." John Pickett and I hustled over to the accreditation office and asked if somebody called John Morrison had received a Calgary accreditation pass. Saying he was my friend, he had taken the pass reserved for Eric Morse, a legitimate member of our team, claiming it was a simple case of his surname having been misspelled on the documentation.

When I called Doug Port back in Calgary, I was surprised to find out he had never heard of Captain John Morrison either. "Morrison" was a nut or a con man, someone who had simply decided to help himself to a position on our bid team if he could. Half an hour later our smooth-talking imposter was stripped of his accreditation, removed from the hotel and sent packing, never to be heard from again.

The New Kids and the Bloc

On the plane to Baden-Baden, Bill Warren and I had stayed up all night talking to Aggie Kuklowicz, a former NHL player who had been a Russian interpreter and negotiator for the 1972 Canada Cup hockey series. Aggie worked for Air Canada and was along to assist as our Russian translator. Aggie invited us up to the first-class section and we spent several hours winging through the night discussing how we were going to deal with the bad feelings of the Soviets resulting from Canada's decision to boycott the Moscow Games.

Aggie said, "You must meet the Soviet sports minister and somehow convince him that the interests of sport will be poorly served if it is seen that the Soviet bloc is ganging up on Calgary. You should remind him that the Soviets rely on the hard currency that comes from the Canada Cup international hockey series. Remind him that the Soviets could lose a great deal if the Canadian sports minister or the premier of Alberta is offended by the whole Eastern bloc voting as a unit."

We had little to lose, so we asked Aggie to set up a meeting with the Soviet sports minister and president of the Soviet Olympic Committee, Sergei Pavlov, for 3 p.m. the following day. I organized my schedule and prepared myself accordingly, but at 1 p.m. the sports minister's assistant called Aggie to reschedule the meeting to 11 a.m. the next day, saying the sports minister was required to give a presentation to the IOC.

Aggie was immediately suspicious that the Soviets were playing games. He advised me not to show up to a meeting unless all the conditions were right. The next day Aggie went alone to the meeting to be sure that Pavlov was really coming. At 10:50 a.m., Aggie phoned back: "Don't bother coming, the meeting is off. They want to see you tomorrow night at the COA reception."

We upped the stakes by saying Premier Peter Lougheed would be coming with me to bring greetings from the people of Alberta in addition to those of the Calgary bid committee.

We went to the COA reception without high hopes, feeling sure the Soviets were playing more games. Aggie moved dutifully ahead into the private room to check if the sports minister was there, and found instead only a junior official.

"I don't think you should go in," said Aggie, and I agreed. Instead, Dick Pound, as host of the occasion, moved to clear up the impasse.

He met the Soviet official, telling him the chairman of the bid committee was disappointed the Soviet sports minister had failed to show up for three meetings. He said he thought the chairman and the premier of Alberta would likely ask the Canadian sports minister to speak to the Soviet sports minister about his apparent breach of etiquette.

When Gerry Regan arrived in Baden-Baden he met with his Soviet counterpart to convey his expectation that Eastern Europe would not vote as a bloc against Calgary. He cautioned the Soviets to avoid anything negative that could affect international relations in sports. In the end the Swedes claimed the Soviet bloc did vote against Calgary, but because Calgary won anyway our relationship with the Soviets was not ultimately affected.

Touching All the Bases

Gerry Regan worked tirelessly in Baden-Baden for the bid. He came for a few days and helped us during the high-energy phase of the lobbying process. When business called him to Halifax, he flew back to Canada on the Concorde jet, and then returned to Baden-Baden just in time for our presentation. We were grateful that he had chosen to become actively involved in helping us.

Every morning at 7 a.m. we held meetings of the key players on the bid committee so that we could all report on how we were faring with our assignments. At first Ralph Klein, known for catching a few zees well into the mid-morning, did not attend. After Alderman Don Hartman complained to the Calgary press that the CODA people weren't keeping their mayor informed, however, Ralph started showing up.

The CODA bid team had reached agreement on strategy. After assessing our position each morning we would plan for the day's activities. We continued to survey delegates attending the congress for any sign that Calgary's Olympic campaign might be faltering. When a weakness in our campaign appeared we would assign our people to check it out. Negative rumors had to be quelled and problems fixed by the team members most familiar with the issues. Other team members arranged invitations for visits to our hotel during breaks in the IOC programs.

BARRY DAVIS · MAUREEN CAREY · GORDON MISKOW · PETER AINSWORTH-COTTON · JOSEPH AVERBUKH · JANE ANDERSON · BLAKE SPRINGER · KATHLEEN DICKSON · ANNE MADDEN · MARINA PERERA · DON YOUNG · ROB FLEGG · ANNE GREEN · JOHN ALEXANDER · DAVID TETTENSOR · ROBERT BRESCIA · DAVE HORODEZKY · PAMELA OSTICK · TERRY MERRITT · KAREN OHREEN · ANDRE HARPE · HELEN HUTTON · CARON JOHNSON · DENNIS TOEWS · BILL HINTZE · RUSS BRASSOR · KAREN DUKE · SHARON FITZNER · CHERYL FLIEGER · JANIS DUNNING · LESLIE PARSONS · NORM ASMUNDSON · DOROTHY MAILER · LAURA PATRICK · ERIC COX · ARLENE BILLSTEN

Like many conventions, the IOC session had a social program to keep the spouses of delegates entertained. At that time, all the delegates were male; that has since changed. Some of the Calgary wives took part in the social program, and in doing so, socialized with IOC wives in an effort to improve our chances of generating positive pillow-talk about Calgary.

We tried to cover all bases, being careful not to pressure people, but trying to be present wherever we could to act as hosts. Everyone took turns working at the Calgary Olympic display booth down at the old train station.

Jeanette and I developed a liking for most IOC members we met. Jeanette had also established a rapport with several IOC members' wives who had visited our home. Among them was Jeannette Peper, wife of the IOC member from Argentina. Long before, when I first met Roberto Peper, to my great embarrassment I had inadvertently called him "Dr. Pepper," even though he was neither a doctor nor a soft drink. My slip had been forgiven, however, and we had become good friends.

In contrast to our low-key lobbying of IOC members, we took the town of Baden-Baden by storm. The Canadian Brass, wearing tuxedos and cowboy hats, drew huge crowds wherever they played. We hosted an event downtown especially for children, featuring the Mounties, the Native dancers, and the western band we had brought along with us. The fact that we went to the trouble to stage a cultural event for youth was appreciated by many IOC members, who felt far too much attention was being focused on themselves. We gave out red-and-white jelly beans in little jars marked "How sweet it is—Calgary 1988." People loved it.

The Hunt Dinner

The hunt dinner was a regular weekly feature of the Quisisana Hotel, at which fresh game was served to guests there. One evening we invited a few IOC members to the dinner, and it turned out to be the highlight of the events we organized. The hotel staff decided that since everyone there spoke English either as a first or second language, they would present the dinner menu in English rather than German. Rotund, rosy-cheeked gentlemen in caps, breeches, and scarlet tunics blew horns to announce each of the courses. They attempted to say what each course was in English even though they didn't speak any. Their mangled pronunciation added to the festive mood. Course after lavish course was brought out with increasing revelry. The beer flowed.

Near the end of the night two police officers, dressed in the uniforms of the local police with capes, breeches, caps, and high leather boots, interrupted our festivities, shouting, "Vee are zee Polizei! Vee are here to schtop zis vild drinkingk und partyingk. Zis drunken karousingk must schtop or vee vill arrest you! Or you can share zee beer mit us and vee vill al enchoy it!"

It was not the local police—it was our two Canadian Mounties, who had been spending the evening tipping lagers with the Baden-Baden police. They had traded their red Mountie uniforms for the green and red German uniforms of their new-found friends. Word spread back to the IOC through the two or three members who had attended the dinner that, as the voting approached, the Calgary folks were confident and in good spirits.

We rented an old castle in Baden-Baden to hold a western pancake breakfast for the European media. The international press was remarkably favorable. The headline of an article in the Baden-Baden newspaper written after the children's day and western day that we had sponsored proclaimed: CALGARY AND SEOUL: THE CITIES WITH HEART AND SOUL.

The Final Crunch

About halfway through our time in Baden-Baden the second-in-command of the Cortina bid committee came up to me as Jeanette and I were entering the back door of the old train station en route to work at our display booth. "I want to talk to you now," he said gruffly. "Privately."

Much to Jeanette's consternation, the grim little black-suited man and I retreated to the deserted back lane. Once we were alone he leaned close to me and said, "We know what you are doing, and if you don't stop, we will put a stop to it!"

"What is it exactly that we are doing that seems to bother you?" I asked.

"You are influencing the newspapers," he said. "You are paying the newspapers to write these good stories about you. We have more friends in newspapers than you will ever have, and we will put a stop to this if that is the kind of game you are going to play. The press are friends of Cortina. You must stop this immediately!"

"I hate to disappoint you," I said, "but we haven't asked the press to do anything for Calgary and we certainly haven't used any pay-offs. I'm surprised at your accusation, but perhaps that is the type of tactic you would use."

"All right," he said. "If you won't stop, then I promise you we will put a stop to it."

"Fine," I replied. "You do whatever you like." I walked back to rejoin Jeanette, who was waiting apprehensively at our display booth. I assured her my kneecaps were intact.

Because of their mounting fear that they were no longer the front runner, the Italians were beginning to make mistakes. They were hosting numerous breakfasts, lunches, and dinners, many of which were poorly attended. They were realizing as they went around to collect votes that the votes weren't there, and they were starting to panic.

As the time for voting neared, we often discussed at our early-morning meetings whether we should react to the pressure being exerted by the competition and change our bid strategy. Up to now we had been doing a soft sell, but for the final crunch we considered switching to a hard sell. Both Cortina and Falun were running around aggressively chasing votes, making whatever promises or threats they could in hopes of garnering them. But we decided there would be nothing for us to gain by changing our plan. Rather than start pushing the panic button we decided to keep pushing the positive button.

In spite of some doubts, we reminded ourselves that we were Canadians and if we tried to emulate either the Swedes or Italians we would no longer be originals, only cheap copies. Even though every day we faced another crisis where an IOC member's vote was thought lost, we stuck with our original plan.

"We may have lost one here, but we've gained another one there," we told ourselves. "We'll redouble our effort to talk to everyone to see if our proposal has anything wrong with it. Let's be sure every IOC member has no doubts about our bid."

Our lobbying often went on until the early hours of the morning. We were all operating on nervous energy and little sleep. We were fortunate to have arranged chauffeured cars, because as it happened there was a bus strike in Baden-Baden at the time, and the IOC members were happy to be driven around by our radio-equipped BMWs with uniformed drivers and hostesses speaking their native languages. It rained lightly almost every day, so we timed our radio-dispatched cars and drivers to be available to whisk IOC members to their destination as soon as they emerged from their congress meetings. We even drove members to meetings with our competition. Our five cars were always buzzing around, and aside from the obvious advantage of giving us a chance to chat with IOC members, it demonstrated how well-organized we were. We had the best transportation and hotel arrangements even though we had travelled the farthest.

In view of the aggressive competition for the Games, we were concerned somebody might try to sabotage our elaborate slide show. Before we left for Baden-Baden we had told the media we were bringing the slide show on the airplane with us. We did bring a copy with us but the real high-quality original was brought separately by Robin Lecky from Creative House, who didn't let it out of his possession. Once in Baden-Baden he set the show up in the Canadian Armed Forces base in Baden-Solingen to test it, and then arranged to have it guarded 24 hours a day until we needed it.

The IOC session continued to occupy the main presentation hall at the Grand Casino until the evening before the bids, so our team had to work until 2 a.m. to set up our elaborate computerized equipment. Fred Wuotila had managed the logistics of our mission beautifully so far, and was so concerned about protecting the show from sabotage that he brought a sleeping bag and slept that night right on the stage of the Grand Casino convention hall, intending to guard the slide show personally. During the night, however, Fred got up to use the bathroom, missed the stairs in the dark, and fell off the stage, injuring his neck. He appeared the next morning wearing a cervical collar and looking very much like a wounded footsoldier—which, in a manner of speaking, he was. In order to meet IOC dress standards for the presentation, Fred painted a natty tie on his cervical collar, and carried on as if nothing had happened.

The Seventh Bid

We had accreditation for only six members of our delegation to sit on the stage during the presentation, and it was a tough job to choose who the six should be, since so many people had played an important part in the bid.

We decided our official delegation would consist of Bob Niven, Jack Wilson, Roger Jackson, Ralph Klein, Dick Pound, and myself. The rest of the accredited members of our team, including Steve Corbett, Don Siler, Bill Warren, John Pickett, Brian Murphy, Ross Alger, and Fred Wuotila, got seats in the main part of the hall of the opulent, glittering Grand Casino. Jeanette and the other wives were refused entry by Madame Berlioux and her staff, but eventually they slipped past them into the upper balcony, where they were joined by Peter Lougheed and Gerry Regan. The IOC had assembled to hear final presentations from Calgary, Falun, and Cortina.

As a result of a random draw of names, Calgary was selected to go first. When the members of our team were seated, I stood at the podium in front of the IOC session and introduced them. I sat down as they each made their speeches. Dick Pound spoke first, claiming Calgary was probably the best-prepared city ever to bid for the Olympic Winter Games. Ralph Klein handed over to the members of the executive a thick list of thousands of people who had paid money to join CODA, saying Calgarians were ready and willing to welcome the world. Roger Jackson outlined the proposed new sports facilities and the endowment funds to ensure they would continue to be used after the Games. Everyone spoke well; everything went as planned.

It was my turn, time to make the most important sales presentation of my life. I was mindful of our 30-minute time limit as I summed up the key ingredients of our bid.

> Over the last three years, you have shared with us on many occasions your vision of what the Olympic Winter Games should be. We've been strongly influenced by your advice. It's been an important part of developing a strong bid for us.
>
> In preparing my comments for today, there was a temptation to recite to you all of the many important features of our bid which you have helped us develop. I believe that most of you know us well enough to know that excellent facilities are available, our financing is arranged, and all our plans are complete for 1988.
>
> So rather than risk boring you with the traditional recitation extolling the virtues of Calgary as an Olympic host city, I have decided to share my thoughts on only two features which make Calgary's bid unique.
>
> The first is that the Games of 1988 must be problem-free. We learned this from you. Some of you have expressed surprise at the extent of the preparations our committee has already made. We have worked hard to provide solutions, not problems.
>
> We've worked hard, with the help of international winter sports federations, to select the best sites for the future of winter sports.
>
> We've worked hard to keep the cost of the Games in line with the needs of our growing city.
>
> We have avoided grandiose expenditures for facilities which would not be used regularly after the Games.
>
> Many of you are familiar with Calgary and you know that.
>
> There will be no problems with comfort and safety for members of the Olympic family. And there will be no problems with housing and transportation.
>
> And it is certain that we can arrange special charter flights to keep the cost down of bringing athletes to Calgary.
>
> We have received full and enthusiastic support from all levels of government. And, of course, we have the overwhelming support of the people of Calgary. The mayor has told you just how eager the people of Calgary are to succeed with this bid. We have all watched our city catch Olympic fever.
>
> In short, the Winter Games must be problem-free. In Calgary, they will be problem-free.

The second important point which we learned from you is our mutual desire to hold the Games in different parts of the world to help spread and strengthen the Olympic movement. I've seen the positive power of Olympism at work in Calgary already. I've seen the way my own children speak with pride about Calgary's Olympic dream. Like thousands of other young people, they have become committed to our goal.

I've seen the tears on the cheeks of my fellow workers often when we've achieved even the smallest success along the way.

I've seen a city get behind this project and get things done without a complaint like never before in our history.

Canada has always been a solid partner in developing winter sports. We share the dream of spreading the Olympic movement. What better time than now to bring the Games from Europe in 1984 to Canada in 1988, where the Winter Games have never been held.

By choosing Calgary, you will encourage other new cities to step forward and to bid for future Games. We will be mindful of our responsibility to share our experience generously with those who follow after 1988.

We've enjoyed this competition. We respect the excellent bids of our competitors. So much, that we've doubled our effort to earn your respect and your confidence.

Over the last three years you have encouraged us. You have supported us. You have inspired us. And we are grateful.

I know Calgary will organize Games with no problems. I know Calgary is a place where the world can come together in friendship and peace. And I look forward to co-operating with each of you in the years ahead as we watch Olympism grow in promising new regions of the world.

You have a great gift in your hands. It's a gift of trust and friendship. It's a gift of pride and accomplishment. It's a gift which only a few cities have had the honor of receiving.

Along with all Calgarians and all Canadians, we await your important decision.

And now please accept this special invitation from the people of Calgary.

With these words the great hall was cast into darkness and the slide show lit up the gigantic rear-projection screen, shining down on all the IOC members in the amphitheatre. We held our breath for an instant until the words and music of "Come Together in Calgary" filled the hall, accompanying almost 1,100 computer-synchronized slides over the 11-minute show. The slides showed Calgary and its mountains, Canadian

Olympic champions from the past, and Canada's stars of the future training for their chance to earn Olympic gold. The show was stunning. It ended a quote from de Coubertin: *"L'avenir dépend de vous."* The future depends on you.

During the show Roger Jackson reached over and patted me twice on the knee. That was his signal he thought we had won it. I felt butterflies in my stomach and tingles on the back of my neck as I thought, "Roger, you just may be right."

To conclude our presentation Dick Pound addressed his colleagues in the IOC as president of the Canadian Olympic Association. We had decided to face the issue of the Moscow Games boycott head on. Pound made an eloquent plea to his IOC colleagues to separate the issue of the boycott from the decision of who should host the 1988 Olympic Winter Games.

He said that when the boycott was announced by U.S. President Carter, the IOC had taken a vote, and every IOC member, not just the Eastern bloc, had condemned the government of the U.S. for taking a political action that unfairly hurt athletes and supporters of sport around the world. To not vote for Calgary would be to punish the supporters of sport in Calgary for a political decision that was clearly not theirs. In light of the blanket condemnation of the American boycott, a bloc protest against Calgary on political grounds would be hypocritical. It would be an admission that the work of politicians had influenced the actions of the Olympic movement. Pound's argument was compelling. His presentation was perfect.

We had been told in advance not to expect anything more than polite applause after our presentation, that it was not the IOC's practice to show any sign of open preference or encouragement. We were surprised, therefore, to hear what seemed to us to be loud applause as we walked out. We were ecstatic: there had been no flaws, everyone spoke well. We felt sure our message had come across.

But how could we be sure the others were not equally convincing? Bob Niven and I managed to sneak back in for part of the Cortina bid, and were amazed to see they showed a 45-minute film that was like a travelogue of tourism in the

ANDERSON • KAY KUWAHARA • BARRY NYE • MARK BEACOM • SUSAN RENTON • BARBARA KATHOL • ROMA BROWN • DARLENE DENARD • MARILYN COOPER • SANDRA GIBEAU • KELLY BARCA • RUEDI SETZ • STANLEY KOTEK • RON PHILLIPS • GREG FOLK • WILL KING • ANN PHILLIPS • STEVEN BECKER • MICHAEL GELDERT • GEORDIE MCCONNELL • SHERRI ARMSTRONG • DONALD CHARLTON • CLIVE LLEWELLYN • GARY REAVIE • DIANE MACCORMACK • MATT WOOFTER • ESTHER TERRI • LYNN SEAR • ROBERT ACKERMAN • LARRY CRAIG • HARALD NESET • ELAINE SMITH • MONTY MONTABONE • RICHARD CONES • FRANCES GARDIPPIE • DAVID BEE • KRISTIE HEHR • INGE

Dolomites. And then the film stopped dead halfway through! There was a 10-minute wait before they could get it going again. We had been concerned that our plans would suffer a similar fate, but this day was reserved for us.

I saw parts of the Swedish bid as well. They used Queen Sylvia and King Carl Gustaf, great young supporters of sport who are very popular with the IOC. Queen Sylvia, the lovely IOC hostess who had worked under Dr. Emmy Schwabe in 1964, had met the handsome young King of Sweden at the Olympic Winter Games, and her fairytale story of romance and royalty had come true when the king asked her to be his bride.

Soon the presentations were over, but the voting wasn't to take place until the next day. That night the NBC television people put on a party attended by several CODA members at which IOC members were greeting and hugging us. Everywhere we went we received hearty congratulations from old friends. The bid delegation from Cortina was also there, as always dressed in black. They were standing alone against the side wall, talking quietly with each other, not mixing with IOC members at all. The Italians looked like they were going to a funeral. I hoped it wasn't anyone I knew.

As we arrived Joe Kryczka came up to me with a serious look on his face. He told me we might have a problem with Gunther Sabetski, the German president of the International Ice Hockey Federation. Joe said that Gunther, who owned a newspaper wire service, was putting out strong messages in favor of Calgary and that some IOC members were beginning to feel the promotion of Calgary through the media had gone too far.

Earlier in the week, Gunther had come to our hotel for dinner, and had spent most of the evening teaching Jeanette how to say knife, fork, thank-you, and other words in German. He had also taken pains to teach us how to propose a toast the European way. "You must look directly into the eyes when you drink, otherwise it is not proper," he had explained seriously. "This is very important."

We had gotten along quite well with Gunther but unfortunately, without any encouragement from us, he had phoned his wire service to put out yet another positive story about Calgary on the eve of voting. It might do us more harm than good.

I pulled Gunther out of a group conversation and asked him to pull his wire stories. He stiffened his back and his face reddened. His top lip drew back until it was barely visible and he said, "*Ja,* it vill be done!" It was clear he was chagrined. He had done all he could to help Calgary and now was being asked to stop promoting us.

As we were leaving the NBC party, I caught the eye of the head of the Cortina delegation. I raised my champagne class as a toast to him, and remembering Sabetski's instructions, looked him straight in the eye as I nodded and smiled.

His face changed color. "You smiled!" he sneered. "You smiled! How dare you smile?" I walked right on past, looking into his eyes and smiling all the way. Afterwards I had trouble convincing Jeanette we were competitors but not enemies, and that they were not going to kneecap me at dawn.

September 30th, 1981

The next morning I woke up sniffling, feeling like a cold was coming on. I asked Jeanette whether we had any vitamin C.

"Yes," she answered, "they're on the shelf of the medicine cabinet. Take four of them." Sure enough there was a little bottle of tablets, so I shook out four, popped them down, and went for a bite to eat.

Bob Niven and I left promptly at 8:45 a.m. to make a final appearance before the IOC Executive Board to answer any questions before the voting took place. By the time we reached the conference centre, I was beginning to feel really terrible.

Bob looked at me and said, "You look awful. Are you feeling O.K.?"

"I feel weak," I replied. "I don't know what's wrong with me."

"Would you like a cup of coffee?" he offered. "You should be sharp for these questions."

By the time Bob returned from the coffee machine, I was sound asleep in my chair. He shook me awake and I said drowsily, "I don't know what is the matter with me." I gulped down the coffee, but sat there in a stupor until finally Madame Berlioux popped her head out from behind the giant wooden door and said, "No questions for Calgary. You may go."

I got up numbly and walked out of the hotel with Bob. "Thank God for that," I said. "I'm going back to lie down for a while to see if I can shake this off." We walked together for 10 minutes travelling through a park and up the hill to our hotel. The whole time we walked I didn't say a word.

I went immediately to my room, hit the pillow, and was gone. Three hours later Jeanette came up to find me still co-matose in bed. At 2 p.m. she returned with a sandwich and a bowl of soup and woke me up, asking if I would like some lunch. I couldn't believe how tired I felt.

It didn't take long to put two and two together. Instead of vitamin C tablets, I had swallowed four sleeping pills Jeanette had brought along in case one of us was unable to sleep on the plane.

I did get out of bed, and by the time our team walked back down the hill to hear the results of the voting, I was beginning to feel all right again. By then I'd had a good night's rest plus another four hours of forced sleep, and that was more than I'd had the previous three nights put together. Even better, I didn't have a cold any more. The "vitamins" had worked.

We walked to the Grand Casino, full of excitement and op-timism. Somehow I knew we had won. Unfortunately our wives had to wait in another building a few blocks away to see the announcement on TV. I felt badly about them being ex-cluded; it seemed unfair that so many officials whose contribution had been far less substantial were allowed in, while some really hard-working people were shunted into the background. The IOC has since improved access for spouses, the media, and others to its major announcements and press conferences.

We had agreed that if we were announced the winners, we would simply stand and acknowledge our victory in a quiet and dignified way. The decision on the Summer Games was announced first, and the Koreans stood politely and bowed.

At 3:57 p.m. on September 30th, 1981, Juan Antonio Samaranch announced that *"la ville de—Calgary"* had won. Despite our best intentions we all leapt uncontrollably from our seats and shouted with delight, hugging each other in celebration. After we settled down, Mayor Ralph Klein, Dick Pound, and I went onto the stage to sign the agreement. We quaffed champagne and made a small toast on stage. I remembered to look directly into the eyes of our host.

The formal part was now over, and President Samaranch disbanded the IOC session. Our wives joined us and the real party started. The Canadian Brass burst through the crowd playing a lively rendition of "When the Saints Come Marching In." They completely drowned out the IOC's lovely string quartet which, recognizing superior odds, quietly got up and went home. Then "the Saints" really got marching as Jeanette, having picked up the Olympic flag, started a conga line, which weaved its way around the Grand Casino hall to the astonishment of our more conservative European friends.

Only 20 minutes after its decision, the IOC may have begun to have second thoughts about its choice of winter city, because the whole thing turned into a party Calgary-style. The staid Grand Casino in Baden-Baden may never again see such an outpouring of pure joy. The Canadian media were swarming all over, doing interviews with every CODA member and especially Gerry Regan, Peter Lougheed, and Ralph Klein. It was bedlam. It was great!

In the midst of the excitement Steve Corbett came up to me and said, "Frank, you're due at the press conference. You're already late." I'd forgotten all about it. I had been asked to leave right after the announcement, to represent Calgary at the international press conference about two blocks away.

I sprinted over, arriving dishevelled and panting, 20 minutes late. I had in me four sleeping pills, a glass of champagne, and the best news of my life. The IOC press people were sitting up straight and I was aware there was a reasonable chance they would be annoyed. The first question was from the French press and it was: "Mr. King, we consider the fact that you are 20 minutes late for the news conference to be very rude. I hope this isn't some indication of how you are going to organize the Games."

Feeling unbelievably elated, I said, "First of all, I must apologize to everyone. We were so excited I didn't realize the time. But I'll make it up to you—we'll start the opening ceremonies in 1988 20 minutes early!"

By 5 p.m. our little Quisisana Hotel was mobbed with people. Some of our men stood at the entrance to turn away any more people arriving to celebrate with us. The hotel kitchen couldn't keep up with the food and drinks, so a few of the wives pitched in and helped, often being mistaken for the staff.

The Swedish sports minister and the head of the Falun bid committee did a traditional Swedish bear dance. Grabbing each other's ankles, one man standing rightside up and the other upside down so that each man's face was between the other's knees, they cart-wheeled through the hotel. I couldn't believe it! One of the Swedes was about 75 years old. Our western band played and Ralph Klein, Don Siler, and I linked arms and warbled, "Oh Lord, it's hard to be humble"—proving conclusively that we were not "perfect in every way."

The only people not there were the men from Cortina. Jeanette didn't complain.

Later we learned in some detail how the IOC voting had gone. It was obvious Cortina's last-minute tactics had cost them dearly, for they ended up third on the first ballot with 18 votes. Calgary got 35 and Falun 25. On the second ballot Cortina dropped off, and Calgary beat Falun 48 to 31. Our campaign for second-round support had paid off.

On the way home to Calgary, our Western band led the whole plane in a sing-along version of "Alberta Bound." When we arrived at the airport we had been almost 48 hours without proper sleep. As we emerged from customs we were greeted by a crowd of several thousand people. A band played and people cheered as we were led onto a small stage with a podium. Our sons, David and Stephen, had talked their way past officials into the customs area and hugged us heartily when they saw us for the first time in more than two weeks. My sister, her husband, and many close friends were also there to greet us. We were tired but happy. Our whole team attempted to stand together on the tiny stage.

As I stood at the podium flanked by my family and our bid committee, and facing our friends, the words that came to me were simple: "When enough people believe, a dream can come true."

CHAPTER SEVEN

Rough Roads

The price of greatness is responsibility.
WINSTON CHURCHILL

O N SEPTEMBER 30TH, 1981, the City of Calgary was selected to host the 1988 Olympic Winter Games.
Within hours, encyclopedias and maps all over the
world were being opened to see where this unknown place—
Calgary, Canada—was. Maria Theresa Samaranch told me the
mayor of Cagliari (pronounced *Cal-ee-air-ee*), the capital of
Sardinia, in Italy, received several telegrams after Calgary
won the Games, congratulating him for his city's great
achievement. He must have been surprised.

When we stepped back into our humble offices at the
Calgary Olympic Development Association, we were greeted
by a huge bouquet of flowers arranged in the shape of the
Calgary Olympic snowflake symbol, with a note:
"Congratulations and all my love—Anne Murray." The whole
city, meanwhile, was erupting with cheers and tears.

My first speech to Calgarians, though, was cautious. It was
entitled "To Whom It May Concern." I said the Olympic Winter

Games were a priceless gift entrusted to Calgary because of the spirit of our people. We now had to decide how to accept this gift and treat it properly. Like a piece of fine crystal, if we abused it, or tried to take it away from each other like spoiled children, it could fall and shatter at our feet. But if it was handled carefully, it had value we could continue to appreciate for generations to come. The choice, I said, was ours.

OCO'88 Is Born

It was time to begin setting up the Olympic organizing committee. First we had to find a suitable name by which the public could identify us. Los Angeles had become the Los Angeles Olympic Organizing Committee, or LAOOC (pronounced *lay-ock*). But we couldn't become the Calgary Olympic Organizing Committee because the acronym would be COOC—although "kook" might have been appropriate on certain days. We thought we could fix that problem by adding "Winter Games" to the name, but that became COWGOC, and "cow jock" was just not something we wanted to be saddled with. We eventually agreed on OCO'88, the acronym for Olympiques Calgary Olympics '88, a name suggested by Frances Jackson-Dover, then our manager of communications. OCO'88 was born early in January 1982. We set up a 12-person volunteer board of directors, of which I became chairman and Bob Niven vice-chairman.

Each member of the board was given a specific area of responsibility, such as finance, marketing, or communications. There were complaints from Ralph Klein, who felt representation from the city was inadequate, so we added a second seat on the board for the city. That seat went to Bob Holmes, a senior member of the city planning department. It was agreed that the best people to run OCO'88's executive board were those responsible for the CODA bid, plus the two Canadian IOC members, three COA representatives, and one member from each level of government.

Although many of the same individuals were involved, OCO'88 was quite a different organization from CODA. CODA had been a loosely-knit organization of a few volunteers, and OCO'88 was quickly developing into a large, multifaceted business operation. As such, OCO'88 would quickly need a president, someone to be in charge of the day-to-day operations of the whole $1-billion enterprise on a full-time basis.

The president would be OCO'88's chief operating officer, while I, as chairman, would remain the chief executive officer. The president would be a full-time paid employee; I would remain a volunteer. For the moment, however, while we searched for a president, I would have to act as chief operating officer as well.

Our search began in 1981 and carried on into 1982. While it brought out almost 100 applicants, not a single one was properly qualified, so we began a private search. We wanted a good business person, a hands-on, project-oriented administrator with good communications and diplomatic skills, and probably somebody who could speak French. We also wanted someone with an established interest in sport and culture, and who was a well-known leader in the community.

David Leighton, then the president of the Banff Centre, a prestigious arts and business school, had many of the characteristics we wanted. My first thought was that with his profile in the community and his high position with the Banff Centre, there was little chance he would be interested in taking a four-year leave to become president of OCO'88. Nevertheless I called Leighton and told him we were looking for a president and that I would be pleased if he would let his name stand for consideration. Within a day or two he confirmed he was interested. He provided me with his résumé and other information, and we arranged for interviews with the executive committee.

Our First Choice

David Leighton won the contest for president of OCO'88 and was announced as our choice in March 1982. By then we had established an office on the third floor of the Mobil Tower in downtown Calgary, with a staff of about 15 people. He began his duties as president of OCO'88 in May 1982.

Bob Niven and I spent the first few months transferring to Leighton the ideas, concepts, and principles of both the bid committee and the new organizing committee, so that he would be able to implement the many plans and promises we had made. The early months with Leighton were pleasant. He seemed amicable and there were no real differences in approach. He proceeded with hiring people who would serve OCO'88 in several senior positions. Included in those hired were Ron Collie, a well-known Calgary engineer, and Bill Wardle, former president of Laura Secord. Collie would handle facility development plans, and Wardle marketing.

The first sign of difficulties appeared in the summer of 1982 when I began working with Leighton on our first detailed financial plan. The board of directors wanted a complete budget for the final five years of the Olympic countdown period. During the bidding process Bob Niven and I had prepared preliminary budgets, often working together at home on the kitchen table, sweating over the major elements that would shape our Games. It was now Leighton's task to convert those rough numbers into a detailed five-year plan, which we called the Olympic Games Plan.

Feeling the need for assurance, I frequently asked Leighton how the budget was coming. The typical response was, "It's coming fine, we're getting the full co-operation of all the staff, including the volunteer chairmen." After several weeks of hearing how well it was going, I wanted to see the actual budget so I could give him my input.

"When the time is appropriate," he said, "I will let you know." But soon it seemed to me as if the "appropriate" time had already passed, so I insisted we set up a budget-review meeting for the week following.

One week later, to my disappointment, Leighton told me the budget was still not quite ready. I agreed to allow him one more week, but insisted I then wanted to see whatever he had, whatever shape it was in. In the meantime, I asked Bob Niven to find out from members of the staff how they thought the budget was coming. The feedback he got was unencouraging.

When Bob and I finally saw Leighton's work one week later there was little to be pleased about. Even the preliminary work was weak and incomplete. The budget simply wasn't done, and what was done reflected a lack of understanding of the complexity and scope of the task ahead.

I told David Leighton I was very disappointed, indicating that Bob Niven and I would be quite prepared to assist with the budget preparation. Leighton was indignant, saying he was a mature businessman and it was an insult to suggest he would need help from younger, less experienced men like Bob Niven or myself.

Leighton's first meeting with the board of directors was not successful. He left early to attend a wedding anniversary party, leaving the board with many unanswered questions. I could sense the dissatisfaction with Leighton, and the members of the board left nothing to my imagination. It was clear Leighton would have to improve quickly or face a palace revolution.

Leighton and I talked frequently about the tremendous obligation to perform that we all faced, and about how nothing short of the best would be tolerated. Finally a meaningful budget started to take shape, although it was rejected by the board on several occasions before it was approved. It was under the experienced guidance of board member John Lecky that the Finance and Budget Committee finally extracted a useful budget from Leighton.

The Board Provides Direction

Roger Jackson and I travelled to Ottawa for COA meetings in April 1982. On the plane Roger revealed to me an idea he had begun to develop to build the world's first covered speed-skating oval at the University of Calgary. Not only would it serve the Olympic movement well, but it could also become a field house for the Booster Club. I loved the idea. After all, the idea to bid for the Olympics in the first place had sprung from our desire to build a field house. Although that objective had long been eclipsed, it was still worthwhile. The idea went on the shelf for a bit, though, because neither Roger nor I had the time to develop it.

In early 1983, Brian Murphy of our sports department discovered that the Paskapoo ski resort, on the western edge of

1983

Calgary, was for sale. Sometime around June, he together with Ron Collie in engineering proposed to the board that ski jumping, bobsleigh, and luge be held at Paskapoo instead of Bragg Creek. It was one of those *Eureka!* ideas that instantly grab you.

The question remained where speed skating should take place. Murphy and Collie prepared studies that argued for Paskapoo; Jackson and the University of Calgary did studies of their own, which concluded the university site would be better. Both proposals found support on the board, and both developed through healthy debate. The original proposal for Paskapoo was for an outdoor oval, but it was soon agreed that wherever the facility was built, it would have to be covered to protect against the vagaries of Calgary weather.

Leighton liked the Paskapoo proposal, but after several months of deliberation, the board rejected the Paskapoo site in favor of the university one. Leighton's disappointment showed, but he said nothing, the board's decision on the matter having been made.

Leighton's silence, however, did not mean he had acquiesced to the board's decision. He and OCO'88 Vice-President Ron Collie flew to Edmonton in an attempt to convince the Province of Alberta to build the oval at Paskapoo. Leighton was either poorly advised or poorly prepared, because the Province of Alberta, more than anyone else, wanted the new facility at the University of Calgary, which the province owned. Leighton had painted himself into a corner. The province rejected the attempt to circumvent the board decision and immediately expressed concern to me about the actions of our president.

Peter Ueberroth had been of the opinion that the L.A. Olympic organizing committee's board of directors were just a bunch of grip-and-grin guys, not to be taken seriously. Leighton had visited Ueberroth in L.A., and might have picked up that point of view from him. Regardless of Ueberroth's perspective, however, Leighton would soon find out that he could only ignore this board at his peril.

Matters went from bad to worse when we found Leighton had committed OCO'88 to paying the University of Calgary an unusual amount of money for its co-operation in providing facilities. While the commitment he had made could have been overturned, it would have been a matter of some embarrassment to have told the university that the president of OCO'88 did not have the confidence of the board in this matter. So the board reluctantly supported Leighton, granting a $7-million windfall to the university for parking lots and various other projects.

The board consisted entirely of businessmen, and they were becoming concerned about Leighton's performance. The mayor of the city was complaining, as were the two IOC members on the board. While I certainly didn't discourage discussions about Leighton's performance, as chairman I often defended him because I wanted him to have a chance to adapt to the job. It became increasingly obvious to me, however, that he was floundering under the enormous burden assigned to him. An Olympic organization is much more complex than a single business; it is one of the most difficult management challenges anywhere.

While there was growing unrest from some volunteers, many of the staff, some of whom he'd hired, were loyal to Leighton.

Concern among board members reached its peak when, at the December 1982 board meeting, Leighton again performed far beneath the expectation of many. The board decided that some action must finally be taken. Leighton had left the meeting directly for a Christmas vacation in Barbados, setting aside the priority of closing the gap that was opening between him and the board. On December 30th we convened an emergency meeting of the board with our western members present in person and our eastern members present by telephone. A unanimous decision was reached to terminate David Leighton in his position as president of OCO'88 before year's end. It was my job to tell him of the decision.

It is totally contrary to my nature to fire someone by telephone, but the options of having Leighton fly back from Barbados or flying down there myself to terminate his employment seemed impractical. So I made the best of a bad mess and decided to phone David Leighton with the news.

I reached him at his hotel after several failed attempts, so it was nearly 7 p.m. on New Year's Eve when I finally spoke to him. Roger Jackson was with me as we spoke to Leighton on a speaker phone. I came directly to the point, reporting about the emergency meeting of the board of directors the day before at which a unanimous decision had been reached to relieve him of his duties effective immediately.

This was a low moment, not only for David Leighton, but also for me. Leighton was understandably shocked and said he couldn't believe what he was hearing and would fly back as soon as he could. He asked me to reconsider and to discuss it with him when he got back.

I told him I would be pleased to meet with him as soon as he returned, but that reinstating him was not an option. I met Leighton for the last time on January 18th, 1983, with David Tavender present as his legal adviser.

After several hours of discussion we agreed on a final settlement. David Leighton left the OCO'88 offices walking briskly, pushing past a media scrum waiting in the lobby for an announcement which they had somehow got wind of. It was not the first time the media had gotten hold of something before we had made it public. We had a leak somewhere in our organization.

When I emerged I simply told the media that we had management difficulties which we thought could not be patched over, and that because Leighton and the board had different philosophies about how OCO'88 should be run, we had decided to terminate him as president. (In plain English, "different philosophies" basically meant we were not seeing eye-to-eye.) I said that a temporary executive team, chaired by myself, would be put together until we could find a new president.

David Leighton accused me and others of seeking a more powerful position within OCO'88. He also explained the conflict by saying his management style was to employ professionals and we had disagreed over my strong volunteer-oriented approach to organizing the Games. I had never heard that argument from Leighton before, but now that he mentioned it, there was no question in my mind that these would be volunteer Games.

In spite of the difficulties, David Leighton had made important contributions to our committee. One was to hire Bill Wardle as vice-president of marketing. Wardle turned out to be one of the key players on the OCO'88 management team. On the day Leighton was discharged, I had a discussion with Wardle about whether he would stay in his position or whether his loyalty to Leighton was such that he could not continue. Even though he still maintained a great respect for David Leighton, Bill understood the board's reasons for firing him and committed himself to OCO'88 regardless of our decision. I reaffirmed my confidence in Wardle and we shook hands. Although we worked together closely for six years after that, we never discussed the matter again.

Looking Again

At this point some thought was given to choosing Wardle to replace Leighton. Strangely, one of the things that went against him was that we felt it was crucial he be maintained in his position in marketing, rather than taking him into the more general management position of president. We were relying heavily on revenues from the private sector through the sale of TV rights and sponsorships, and Wardle was already setting his sights on that challenge.

For the winter of 1983, a volunteer Internal Review Committee of Niven, Warren, Jackson, Lecky, and myself worked with the staff to prepare, without benefit of a president, the first Olympic Games Plan. A search for a successor to Leighton started immediately, and we set a deadline of June 1983 for having a new president on board. Headhunters were sent out, and a long list of potential candidates was reviewed and shortened until we had only four candidates left.

Included on the final list were Art Froese, president and director of the Calgary Olympic Coliseum Society; Harold Millican, on assignment with the Northern Pipeline Company; Doug Mitchell, a well-known Calgary lawyer; and Bill Pratt, the project manager of the Olympic Saddledome.

Mitchell subsequently withdrew from the competition to become commissioner of the Canadian Football League. We had earlier made some mistakes in defining what we wanted in a president and what we wanted the president's job description to be. This time we wanted a hard-nosed, hands-on business manager. Bill Pratt was clearly our man.

Even before his work on the Saddledome, Bill Pratt was the man behind construction projects that today are landmarks in Calgary. The son of a senior Ottawa bureaucrat, Bill made his way west as a young man looking for opportunity. He found work building roads and bridges with the legendary construction kings Red Dutton and Reg Jennings. He worked his way up through their organization and then left to become the general manager of Calgary's Exhibition and Stampede.

His record shows his influence in building Calgary's largest shopping centre, Chinook Centre, and Calgary's old-west museum and theme park, Heritage Park. During his 10-year term presiding over the Calgary Exhibition and Stampede, he expanded Stampede Park and built the new racetrack grandstand. He was the controversial project manager for the first Olympic facility, the Olympic Saddledome. Later, he indirectly oversaw the building of all the other Olympic facilities, which were all completed on time and within budget.

Bill Pratt is a short, bull-chested man with a broad face, heavy eyebrows framing intense eyes, and a quick, bright smile. Controversy has been a regular companion for him. His management style depends, to a significant degree, on loyalty and respect for authority from his subordinates, probably a trait he learned from Red Dutton. He often has a "gut feel" for what to do, and he's usually right. He tends to rely on himself to such a degree that the people beneath him sometimes feel frustrated or even intimidated. His decisions are virtually unshakeable.

Bill's strength has, at the same time, been his weakness. He will not suffer fools gladly. He'd rather fix it himself than let a less competent person try and fail. He has no time at all for the media.

On most important issues, Bill Pratt and I did not disagree, but when we did it usually resulted in fireworks. On a number of occasions I demanded that Bill take action to correct obvious deficiencies, or that he listen when our major partners—sponsors, TV people, and governments—were speaking about problems ahead. In dealing with Pratt in these kinds of matters I often had to use velvet gloves and a baseball bat: velvet gloves because Bill is a man with great pride in his accomplishments; the baseball bat because he's not always a good listener.

Having worked beside him for five years, I think his dogmatic style has robbed him of the public recognition he deserves for what he has done. But in time, his style will be given less importance and the focus will shift to the reality of what he has accomplished for his community.

As our interviews for the position of president of OCO'88 progressed, other board members besides myself became convinced that Pratt's pragmatic approach could be an asset to OCO'88, given that we had others more skilled in diplomacy. Mayor Ralph Klein, however, had raised immediate storm warnings about Bill's candidacy. Klein made perfectly clear that he wanted someone other than Pratt to get the job. The two had had run-ins before, starting back when Klein was an investigative reporter and Pratt worked for the Calgary Exhibition and Stampede.

Just before decision time I received a call from Don Hartman, who was also no fan of Pratt's. Hartman called at 8 a.m., just before I left for the meeting at which we were to consider the nominating committee's recommendations. Hartman had worked for years with Pratt on the Stampede Board, and he told me that if we elected Pratt as president he would strongly oppose us, and we would live to regret the decision.

"Don, I appreciate the phone call and the warning, and I will pass along your comments," I said, "but the decision is for the OCO'88 board of directors to make." Within an hour the board confirmed the appointment of Bill Pratt as president. Even as we introduced our new president, however, a controversy about the Saddledome was about to erupt.

A Burr Under the Saddle

I had asked Bill Pratt during our interview if there was anything about the Olympic Saddledome project we should know that would influence our decision in selecting him as president. He had said he knew of nothing. It was a project of which he was proud, and he said he felt his performance on the project was part of the reason why he should be chosen. His knowledge of the facility and its uses was considerable.

I had double-checked with Bill Dickie, chairman of the Calgary Olympic Coliseum Society, regarding Pratt's performance and suitability. His reaction had been favorable. Dickie did tell me, however, that the Saddledome project was facing a possible cost overrun of about $9 million. He had sought my advice as to how the extra money should be found and how the need for it should be explained to the public.

I had suggested Dickie approach the two government partners and call on them for additional funds to cover the overrun. As far as explaining it to the public, I thought it was quite obvious what the reasons were. The members of the Calgary Olympic Coliseum Society had decided to reduce the original budget by $10 million without reducing the scope of the work. In order to get the arena built in time for the 1983 hockey season, they had also decided to fast-track the project by beginning to build before the designs were complete. Along the way they had decided to add expensive nice-to-have features into the project. All these were legitimate explanations of the cost increase now worrying Dickie. I argued that they should be explained to the public as soon as possible.

Dickie, however, felt the public would not easily accept a $9-million cost overrun on a $60-million project. I countered that anything less than early public disclosure would be construed as embarrassment on the part of management and the board of directors. With open disclosure there was no need for such embarrassment. Virtually every other public project in Calgary at the time was experiencing much worse cost overruns.

Just before the media announcement of Bill Pratt's appointment as president of OCO'88, I discussed Dickie's concern with Bill Warren. I shuffled Warren away from the crowd of reporters to a quiet corner of the room where we would not be overheard. As I described the facts surrounding the $9-million overrun to him, I turned, and there to my surprise was Crosbie Cotton, the *Herald* Olympic reporter, standing quietly eavesdropping.

In less than two weeks the headline in the *Calgary Herald* forecast a Saddledome overrun of $9 million. The Saddledome crisis had begun.

Clearly it was not a question of the Saddledome being a bad deal for the people of Calgary, nor of the costs being unjustified given the quality of the facility. This story was a classic tempest in a teapot. The main media assumption was that the public had been misled about the real costs of the building. Both Don Hartman and Art Froese represented the city on the board of directors of the Calgary Olympic Coliseum Society. But they ducked any responsibility by claiming little or no knowledge of an overrun. The implication was that if they didn't know, and the board of directors didn't know, Bill Pratt had either misled the board or didn't know either.

Bill was a perfect scapegoat, not only because he was now the president of OCO'88 and was going to be in this highly visible position for the next five years, but also because he was under a contractual gag order from the Calgary Olympic Coliseum Society, which prevented him from saying anything to the media without the express permission of the society. That prevented him speaking out to clear himself. He received legal advice that he shouldn't violate the gag order without permission, and he couldn't get permission. He was between a rock and a hard place.

The media had a heyday with the story. The more the subject was reported, the more the public became angry and concerned. Rumors surfaced that in fact the overrun was much larger than $9 million. Eventually, a figure of $16 million was reported and widely believed by the general public.

Auditors were called in as the media howled with indignation. I felt like a useless bystander in a process that could damage public confidence in our organization. I decided to set the cat among the pigeons with a calculated comment to the media. "If the whole story of the Olympic Saddledome cost overrun were told," I said, "it might affect the outcome of the next election." It was the fall of 1983, and a civic election was coming up.

I had in mind that the reporters would start sniffing about and might flush some comments out of Alderman Don Hartman. Hartman was on the Saddledome board of directors. He had agreed to reduce the Saddledome budget without reducing the scope of the project—in fact, he had even pushed for extras without allowing extra money to pay for them.

I was surprised when, instead of flushing out Hartman, the media went after Klein, who was also up for re-election. At the height of pressure from the media pack, Klein took the Saddledome files in his possession and threw them into the hallway outside his office for reporters to study. "This is every paper I have," he declared. "If you want to go through them you are welcome." Of course the reporters thumbed through the papers briefly and then gave up, because it was too much work to go through all the paperwork on such a complex project. Klein's theatrical gesture served nicely to deflect blame away from himself. Of course, he wouldn't have had to bother if I had kept my mouth shut.

The provincial government came under media attack next for not revealing all it knew about the project. The suspicion of cover-up grew to paranoia among reporters and eventually among the public. Still no explanation came from the board of the Saddledome project.

The Sky Is Falling

The question also remained of who was to pay for the overrun. The federal government, which did not have any responsibility for managing the project, did not want to help pay. OCO'88 had no such responsibility either; we had played no part in the construction and had not even been represented on the society's board of directors. Nonetheless the city and the province asked us to pay one-third of the extra cost. We

PLATE 1 Calgary House, the friendliest place in town and CODA's headquarters at the Lake Placid Olympics (1980).

◀ PLATE 2 Canadian IOC member Dick Pound chatting with Calgary Mayor Ross Alger at Calgary House.

PLATE 3 From left to right, Jack Wilson, Sim Laing, IOC President Lord Killanin, and me at Calgary House. ▼

PLATE 4 IOC Director Madame Monique Berlioux and IOC President Juan Antonio Samaranch at Blackfoot induction ceremony, Olympic House, Montreal (1980).

PLATE 5 From left to right: myself; Louis Guirandou n'Diaye, IOC member from the Ivory Coast; Prime Minister Pierre Elliot Trudeau; and Samaranch in the garden at 24 Sussex Drive (1980).

PLATE 6 Here I am receiving a five-dollar CODA-membership payment from Pierre Trudeau at our $1,000-a-plate fund raising dinner (1981).

PLATE 7 Bob Niven and I at Baden-Baden, being carefully watched by Franco Carraro, leader of the Cortina bid committee. Calgary was selected to present its bid first (1981).

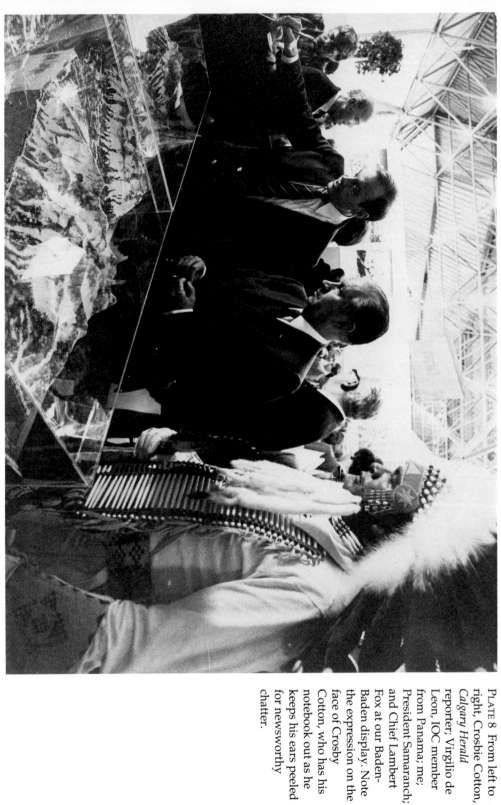

PLATE 8 From left to right, Crosbie Cotton, *Calgary Herald* reporter; Virgilio de Leon, IOC member from Panama; me; President Samaranch; and Chief Lambert Fox at our Baden-Baden display. Note the expression on the face of Crosby Cotton, who has his notebook out as he keeps his ears peeled for newsworthy chatter.

PLATE 9 Our Baden-Baden bid team standing quietly and bowing in a dignified manner as the winner is announced.

PLATE 10 Our RCMP representatives at the CODA Hunt Dinner, Rich Nekoniuk and Hart Eichmann. *"Vee ahr enchoyink it!"*

PLATE 11 Myself, Don Siler, and Mayor Ralph Klein singing "Oh Lord It's Hard to Be Humble," at the Quisisana Hotel after winning the bid at Baden-Baden.

PLATE 12 Back row left to right: Louis Guirandou n'Diaye; Sir Lance Cross, IOC member from New Zealand; Alexandru Siperco, IOC member from Romania; Ashwini Kumar, IOC member from India; Virgilio de Leon, IOC member from Panama. Front row: Dick Pound, IOC member from Canada; Madame Monique Berlioux, IOC Director; Maurice Allan, Secretary-General of the COA; and me, the one with the grin on his face, signing the Olympic agreement at Baden-Baden.

PLATE 13 The saints come marching in, led by the Canadian Brass and the CODA delegation at Baden-Baden. Fred Wuotila, at extreme right, is wearing a cervical collar with a tie painted on it. He is talking to Alderman Stan Nelson.

PLATE 14 At centre, Jeanette King carrying the Olympic flag and leading the CODA conga line at the Baden-Baden victory party.

▶

PLATE 15 From left to right, Premier Peter Lougheed, Colleen Klein, and Mayor Ralph Klein, celebrating Calgary's victory.

▼

PLATE 16 David Leighton, the first President of OCO'88, at a press conference on July 16th, 1982, announcing his appointment.

PLATE 17 The first board of directors of OCO'88 gathered for this photo on March 4, 1983. Back row, left to right: Bob Niven, Dick Pound, James Worrall, John Lecky, Maurice Allan, Bill Warren, and Bob Holmes. Front row, left to right: Anita Slazak, Ralph Klein, me, Roger Jackson, and George de Rappard.

PLATE 18 Getting the thumbs-up from Dennis Swanson, vice-president of sports, ABC television, at Canada Olympic Park.

PLATE 19 Children in Calgary schools participating in the Olympic Education Program.

PLATE 20 From left to right, Senator Bud Olson; me; and the Honorable Jacques Olivier, federal sports minister, arriving at Canada Olympic Park to sign the federal assistance agreement.

◀

PLATE 21 From left to right, the Honorable Céline Hervieux-Payette, federal sports minister; Premier Peter Lougheed; and Mayor Ralph Klein, cutting the ribbon at the opening of the Olympic Saddledome, 1983. ▼

PLATE 22 At the opening ceremonies at Sarajevo, 1984. From left to right: Margie Niven; behind her Jennifer Niven; and behind her Bob Niven; centre foreground, Jeanne and Peter Lougheed, Jackie de Rappard, and Bill Pratt.

PLATE 23 From left to right: Jeanette King, Ken Read, and Prince Albert of Monaco at a pre-Olympic Red Cross children's luncheon.

PLATE 24 Bill Wardle and the three bears at the announcement of Kodak's sponsorship of OCO'88.

PLATE 25 Children enjoying winter play with Hidy, the first-ever female Olympic mascot. Hidy struck a blow for the emancipation of mascots everywhere.

PLATE 26 Capturing the fire of the sun at Olympia, Greece, November 1987.

PLATE 27 From left to right, Bill Pratt; Bob Niven, carrying torch; André Bombardier; Dave Thompson; me; Roger Jackson; Mayor Ralph Klein; the Honorable Otto Jelinek, federal sports minister; Jerry Joynt; and Sylvie Bernier, Olympic gold medalist in diving, at St. John's, Newfoundland, on the arrival of the Olympic flame. The flame is being carried in the miner's lamp held at centre.

PLATE 28 The Right Honorable Brian Mulroney lighting the Olympic cauldron at St. John's, Newfoundland.

PLATE 29 Former Olympians Ferd Hayward and Barbara Anne Scott King, with Brian Mulroney, about to receive the first Olympic torch at St. John's, Newfoundland, November, 1987. The Calgary Olympic Torch Relay was the longest in history.

PLATE 30 On the road in southeastern British Columbia with the Olympic torch. From left to right: Mark Tomlin, Steve King, Jon Rule, me, and David King.

reluctantly agreed under the condition that OCO'88 immediately be granted representation on the Saddledome board.

In an attempt to quell public concern over the Saddledome affair, the Province of Alberta appointed a commission headed by David Tavender. Tavender's commission interviewed all the people who had anything to do with the Saddledome project, and, after many months and several hundreds of thousands of dollars, Tavender came out with a report accusing the Coliseum society directors and Bill Pratt of not fully understanding the cost consequences of decisions made during construction of the Saddledome. At the same time he exonerated everyone, and particularly Bill Pratt, of personal wrongdoing.

One of the main implications of the Tavender report was that Bill Pratt ought to have known better. He should have been able to forecast the cost implications of his board's decisions and should have warned the board members. The report put Bill in a bad light, and by implication raised an ugly question about OCO'88: if Pratt ought to have known better regarding the costs of the Olympic Saddledome, then wasn't OCO'88 headed for a disaster with the same man heading a much bigger, more complex project—the Games themselves?

The Calgary media certainly raised the spectre of Montreal's financial debacle in the minds of many Calgarians. It was the beginning of a silly season of horror stories that the sky was falling on almost all Olympic projects. Fear is a four-letter word. In the case of Calgary's media, "fear" stood for False Evidence Appearing Real.

The Saddledome project was not a bungled construction job; it was a bungled communication job. In its time of high construction costs, it came in closer to budget than virtually any other city-managed project. But the media and the public thought they were being misled. If the proper facts had been conveyed to the public from within the Coliseum society at the beginning, the outcry would have been averted. It was never clear who had been responsible for communicating those facts, but the bungle had been theirs.

Moving Mountains

The selection of our various sports venues was one of the early events in which the public participated. Aided by newspaper editorials and abetted by the public statements of environmental and other self-interest groups, the local populace tried to find a position they could support.

The main controversy centred around the premier alpine skiing event, the men's downhill. It was up to us to choose the turf for the Olympic Winter Games, and it was never in doubt that we would do it with an eye to giving our team home advantage. The Crazy Canucks had established Canadian credibility in the downhill, and built their reputation on their ability to ski technically difficult courses. The course we chose had to be a challenging one. Some said this obviously meant Lake Louise, but we stuck to our position that the events would not be staged in a national park.

There were other criteria that had to be met as well. Practical matters such as accessibility, cost, and after-use were as important as the challenging alpine terrain the skiers required. Although the weather conditions were a factor, once we had decided to move out of the park we were committed to a fairly small region of the mountains, and that region generally receives pretty much the same weather throughout.

We chose Mount Allan as the sole site for alpine skiing, and a protest group called Ski Action Alberta sprung out of nowhere to challenge our plans. We had rejected our own first choice of Mount Sparrowhawk (immediately west of Mount Allan) because the cost of new roads into the Spray Lakes valley and additional facilities would have been at least $100 million greater than for Mount Allan. Ski Action Alberta was a group of avid skiers and environmentalists who believed that other sites south and west of Mount Allan were better choices for the alpine events. The media gave Ski Action Alberta's story big play, and the public sentiment against our Mount Allan choice grew. Matters weren't helped any when Nancy Greene-Raine pronounced Mount Allan a mickey-mouse hill and even Ken Read expressed reservations about the venue.

MARGARET MILNE • STUART YORK • JAYDEN STEPHENS • JEAN GREIG • DENIS GRADY • JANET FEHR • SAM WONG • DAN LUSSIER • MARLENE GUKERT • MARGARET TIBBO • MARIKA DERHAK • STEVE RADIN • MERTIE BEATTY • JACK ROOME • JANIE DALKE • ELAINE SCOBIE • TRUDIE TURNER • KERRI SCHMIDT • WILLIAM HALL • RYAN JORGENSON • TYRON TIEFENTHALER • KEVIN NYHOFF • KATHY SAWYER • JIM YOUNG • AUDREY COUTTS • BETTES STRATTON • DOREEN SZUCH • LARISSA HASS • PATTI THIELEN • MICHAEL COLLINS • OLGA WOHLGEMUTH • JENS KOLBJORNSRUD • BRENT YASUDA • MARY JANE BOWIE • HARRY WIEBUSCH • EVA MCLAUGHLAN • LINDA

Inside OCO'88 we had reviewed the options and were confident that Mount Allan was the best choice. Our attention turned to how we could convince the public we were right. We decided the best way was to get our chief opponents, Ski Action Alberta, to do the job for us.

We asked Ski Action Alberta if they agreed that challenging new ski slopes must be developed outside the national parks to meet our Olympic commitments. They said they did. We asked them whether they were simply opposed to Mount Allan or whether they had an alternative in mind. They replied that they could easily find an alternative, but they lacked the financial resources to conduct feasibility studies. We asked them how much funding they would need in order to come up with a recommendation, assuming we gave them access to all our files on competitive skiing criteria. They named a figure of $30,000 and we gave it to them. We added one stipulation: that they agree ahead of time to hold a press conference when they had reached a conclusion.

They were incredulous. We were insisting they make their results public, something they intended to do in any case. Of course they would agree to that, they said. But they had no experience setting up press conferences. "No problem," we told them. "We'll set it up for you." They left our offices ecstatic that they had received a chance to develop their plan.

Six weeks later we had Ski Action Alberta's comprehensive plan for the ideal Winter Games alpine skiing venues. The group was happy to fulfill its promise to hold a press conference, which we arranged. They announced a plan to put the Olympic alpine events in two different locations, one of which was Mount Sparrowhawk. Their proposal had many of the attributes that had been part of our original Olympic bid proposal. It also had many of the practical flaws.

The press conference by Ski Action Alberta was one of those turning points in the creation of a plan. If there had been any doubt in our own camp about Mount Allan before this event, there remained none afterward. After Ski Action Alberta presented their proposal, the barrage of questions from reporters began. The first was a bullet right to the heart of the

MACMILLAN-ROGERS • SHEILA STINSON • TAMMY DRASKOCZI • MARGARET NAYLOR • JOHN BUHLER • APRIL SPRAGG • SYLVIA MERTEN • NICOLA TORRINGTON • MARGARET SHELTON • JILL NIELSEN • HENRY HOFFMANN • OLGA KREUTZER • KATHERINE MACMILLAN • AUDREY TAYLOR • SHARON LEMECHA • DANIELE BLACKETT • CATHERINE CLAKE • JOAN BOURASSA • BRUCE LOUNSBURY • ALLAN PETRIE • BILL WILSON • ARTHUR MCCULLOCH • ARCTON LANCASTER • LINDA WALTERS • SHARRON BURY • KEN THOMPSON • JOHN FISHER • SHIRLEY SEDGEWICK • ALAN AYERS • SUSANNE MIKKELSEN • IAN MACLEOD • JOHN MACKASEY • KEN RODGERS • BRIAN GRANT • SARA CASSETTI •

issue: "Have you estimated the cost of this scheme?" asked Gary Bobrovitz of CFAC television.

They said it would cost about $200 million if you included all the new roads and infrastructure. Their plan, like our original plan for Mount Sparrowhawk, necessitated widening and paving perhaps 50 kilometres of the Smith-Dorrien highway south of Canmore, building two lodges instead of one, and constructing a new athletes' village. For comparison, the estimated cost of developing Mount Allan was about $25 million.

"Where do you expect to get $200 million?" Bobrovitz asked Ski Action Alberta.

"That's not our concern," they replied. "It's up to the organizing committee to find the money." And that was that. Nothing more was heard of the protesters or their plan. We went ahead with Mount Allan—the only practical choice.

Mount Allan became the first mountain in Olympic history to host all men's and women's alpine events. The savings in pageantry, security, media infrastructure, and public facilities were enormous. Those savings are now at work in the endowment funds of the Calgary Olympic Development Association.

Ken Read had been in love with the Sparrowhawk idea. Most men's downhills are about two minutes long; the one at Sparrowhawk could have taken three minutes. One stretch of the course, which Ken had helped design, was called Read's Ridge. But now we needed to design the best possible downhill for Mount Allan, so we got Ken to help us.

During the Games the question of whether the ski area on Mount Allan, which we named Nakiska (a Cree word for meeting place), would be steep enough for alpine skiers was answered by the athletes themselves. Almost one-third of the male downhill skiers who came to compete refused to do so when they inspected the course before the Games. The precipitous headwalls on the upper section were demanding for even the best, and too tough for the so-called "Olympic tourist" athletes who hoped to be able just to point their skis downhill and coast.

CHAPTER EIGHT

Poor No More

Sweet are the uses of adversity.
WILLIAM SHAKESPEARE

IN LATE 1983, OCO'88 was less concerned with the Saddle-dome media sideshow playing in town than with the pressing need to fund the Olympics. From the moment CODA won the bid in Baden-Baden, our financial options had begun to narrow. The National Energy Program of the Trudeau government had pounded the stuffing out of the Western Canadian economy. Massive new energy-resource taxes removed billions of dollars from Alberta and caused numerous business failures and unprecedented unemployment in Calgary. Until 1982 Calgary had chalked up five consecutive years of more than $1 billion in construction activity, a record in Canadian history. But now the good times were over. Suddenly 40,000 Calgarians were unemployed.

Following the euphoria of Baden-Baden we tried to be publicly optimistic about the Olympics, but privately we were concerned about financing them. As time went on serious public concerns were raised about Calgary's ability to afford them. Many people felt we had bitten off more than we could chew given the state of the economy. One red-faced gentleman, for instance, came up to me after one of my gung-ho speeches and said, "I don't know how you can remain so positive under these terrible circumstances. Don't you know there is a recession?" I replied with equanimity, "Yes, I know there's a recession but I've decided not to participate."

Brave words! CODA was $500,000 in debt, the economy was collapsing, financial commitments from governments were still uncertain, and we knew little as yet about sponsorships or ticket revenues. We took a hard look at our options, and decided to focus on the best financial hope we had—television rights.

We had some obvious advantages for television. We were close to the world's biggest commercial TV market, the United States. We spoke the same language and had the same technology. Costs would be low and time zones would be perfect for major viewer events. Calgary's recession forced us to expend greater effort to realize maximum TV revenues. It would be our first major challenge.

My experience with the Olympics has convinced me that one of the keys to management success is to have a series of challenges that continually test the strength and character of the team. Successful managers always respond positively, whereas weak ones develop "loser's limp" and find a reason to fold under adversity. During those early years our small team was tested frequently.

We realized that although many of us had extensive sales and marketing backgrounds, practically no one in our organization knew anything about selling television rights. We did the only thing we could: we hired an expert to analyze the U.S. market and to give us a crash course on U.S. television network business economics. We wanted to know everything we could. We wanted historical details on advertising and rights revenues from all major American sporting events, including football, baseball, basketball, and previous Olympic Games.

MARY KROCHENSKI • DEBBIE HARRIS • MIKE DAVIS • SYED KIDWAI • STEVE CASTLE • IKBAL DAMANI • TERRY BRENNAN • STUART PATTERSON • RUTH HENDERSON • GINNIE STEWART • LEN BRODY • DEANNE KONDRAT • DANIEL WEGG • LINDA HARMON • TROY HERTER • BARRY STEVELMAN • SANDRA LEBLANC • JEAN ANN MURRAY • JOHN TERRY • JILL GRANT • FRANCO LOMBARDO • OWEN CARNEY • RUTH LUOMA • MARK WOOD • ALOIS VOITCHOVSKY • ROBERT CONNOLLY • HILDA VAN CAMP • ANGIE REED • WALLY CRESSMAN • BRENT NESS • ROO RABEL • DENNIS HARLEY • SUE HILL • LOYCE CLARKE • KARIN NEILSON • JOHN DAVIES • MARLENE SWINTON • DIANE DAVEY • MARK

We preferred not to study Olympic TV revenues in isolation because the financial precedents were not inspiring. The first Winter Games to be televised were those in Cortina in 1956, and they created virtually no television revenues at all. The U.S. television rights to the 1960 Squaw Valley Games had sold for $50,000, the 1964 Innsbruck Games about $600,000, the 1968 Grenoble Games $4.5 million, the 1972 Sapporo Games $5.4 million, the 1976 Innsbruck Games $10 million, the 1980 Lake Placid Games $15.5 million, and the 1984 Sarajevo Games $91.5 million. While it was obvious the trend was favorable, we intended to raise far more money from TV rights than had ever been raised before. Our preliminary estimates had already been ambitious; we had hoped to get $150 million U.S. Now we had increased our estimates to at least $200 million.

Our consultant carried out a survey of U.S. homes that revealed some interesting results. I was particularly attracted to responses to the question, "What is your favorite sport on television?" As might be expected, the men of America split their answers among football, baseball, and basketball. The women, however, who represent 51 per cent of the population, voted 72 per cent in favor of one sport—figure skating. The male population also listed figure skating reasonably high on the scale. We cranked out a marketing strategy designed to convince television networks we actually had a television product approaching the value of the Summer Games, emphasizing that half the people in the U.S. would choose to watch figure skating over other television sports.

We were on the right track but we needed more inside knowledge of how our customers operated their business, so we hired Trans World International, the sports marketing firm of Mark McCormack, the world's leading sports-marketing guru. TWI's Barry Frank had formerly worked as president of sports for the CBS television network, and had been involved in several Olympic TV negotiations from the network side. His advice on building a marketing strategy for TV rights was an important step in the right direction.

The Concept of Value

Our marketing plan was simple. We would ask our customers what they wanted most, then give it to them. Olympic organizers in the past had often told the networks what was being offered and if it wasn't what they wanted, too bad. The organizers had gotten paid accordingly. Value has a way of finding its own level.

When we started talks with the U.S. television networks, we used the same strategy of "listening naïvely" that we had used with the IOC. "We don't know much about U.S. television," we said, "but it's hard for us to understand why you have traditionally paid so little for TV rights to cover Olympic Games. The Olympics should be a special TV event, but your previous best offers don't reflect a very high value."

Our admission of ignorance created an impression of naïveté that caused the networks to let their guards down. We did our best to act like the fresh fuzzy-cheeked cowboys from Calgary that they expected us to be. They were only too happy to educate us.

"Let us tell you why we never pay more for Olympic rights," they offered. "We never know in advance who the host broadcaster is or even where the events are going to be held. The Games are held at the wrong time of year and there is not enough TV prime time overall. You do not know the camera positions, you do not even know specific dates and times events are going to be held." The list went on and on.

"Let's get it straight," we said. "Do you mean that if we had more prime time, defined the host broadcaster and the camera positions, told you where the venues were, and had more sporting events of the kind the public likes to see, that we could get considerably more revenue from television?"

"Absolutely," they said. "But you won't, because it's never been done, not even in Los Angeles." What we had heard was that the fundamental concept of giving higher value to produce higher rewards had never been the focus of Olympic TV marketing.

We formed a television rights committee. It was headed by Dick Pound and Monique Berlioux, both representing the IOC, and included Bill Wardle, Bill Pratt, Bill Warren, and myself. The committee set the strategy for selling TV rights for the Games.

A Better Mousetrap

In view of what we'd heard from the three U.S. television networks, we decided to make dramatic changes probably never thought of before in the Winter Games. We analyzed each event and identified which events were most popular. We continued our studies of the American television system to understand why and when advertisers would pay the most. We learned that during the last two weeks of February 1988 the "TV sweeps" would be held in the U.S. The sweeps are a time when audience ratings determine the competitive rankings of the networks and establish the value of future advertising rates. If networks are rated high in the sweeps they can charge more for advertising. Our original dates for the Games had been the last week in February and the first week in March, those days having been picked as a result of meteorological studies. We now looked again at the weather charts and found there would be practically no weather disadvantage if we moved the Games a little bit earlier to coincide with the U.S. sweeps in February.

We also decided to build a better mousetrap by improving and expanding the sports program. To do that, it was necessary to extend the Games to 16 days from the 12 days that had been used for 60 years. This was an important idea not just for better television coverage but for better competitions as well. We had noticed that the Olympic hockey tournament in Sarajevo could not be held in the 12 days allotted for the Games. Canada played its first hockey game against the United States before the Games had officially opened. Canada's victory ruined the U.S. team's chances of winning a medal even before they carried the American flag into the stadium for the opening ceremonies. By extending the Games to 16 days, we could reorganize the sports schedule to be better for spectators, better for athletes, and—with three weekends included—much better for television, because more events would be in prime time.

A longer schedule also allowed greater flexibility if there were postponements due to weather or other things beyond our control. This was critical because revenues from television rights depend on what you deliver, not on what you promise. As it turned out, our decision to hold the first 16-day Olympic Winter Games saved our bacon, because freaky weather during the Olympics did create numerous schedule changes. We were glad then that we had covered one of the major threats to the business success of the Games with extra days of insurance.

Our extended timetable allowed us to look at some other attractive options for presenting the games. For example, for 60 years the Olympic hockey tournament had not been designed to dramatic advantage. Historically, 12 teams played in the tournament, but only four teams advanced to the medal-round finals. Canada didn't make the finals in Lake Placid because it played one poor game against the Finns. The defending gold-medal U.S. hockey team didn't make the finals in Sarajevo.

Remembering how popular figure-skating competitions were to TV viewers, we also spread out the best figure-skating events over three weekends so that greater public anticipation could be developed. Spreading events out also made for better ticket sales, and the athletes received greater individual recognition with star billing on the weekend marquee.

Our plans for bigger and better Olympics also included adding more events, such as team ski jumping and team cross-country skiing. Of course, we realized that we would have to persuade the international sports federations and the IOC to agree to any program changes. We also wanted to add an exciting new demonstration spectator sport, freestyle skiing, that had never been held before in the Winter Olympics. Curling, popular in North America and Western Europe, and short-track speed skating, described by some as "roller derby on ice," would also be demonstration sports. All these additions to the program added to the value of the TV package, while helping the new sports gain recognition and fans.

For the first time the Winter Games were being packaged as a marketable product. We developed clear specifications for what we were offering. We added every possible feature so that the networks would bid higher than ever before.

The Impact of Television

There are some who believe athletic competitions should not be staged for television, but in the modern world sport and television are best friends. Sport creates some of television's biggest audiences, and TV revenues are vital to the future development of sport.

A large television audience has two major effects. It provides unparalleled recognition for athletes and for the sports they represent, and it produces money to build sport even more in the future. Olympic television revenues are not shot off into space, or shelled into an enemy encampment; they go directly into sport, and into the promotion of world peace through sport. The complaints of commercialism usually come from countries where only public funds (taxes) are used to promote sport.

In a free-enterprise economy like Canada's, the government isn't needed to act as a laundry service for revenues that are used for sport. Businesses that want to support sport and the Olympic aims can do so efficiently by dealing directly with the National Olympic committees, the international sports federations, or the Games organizers of their choice. The alternative is to fund Games by increasing taxation, which affects everyone, including those who don't want their money spent on sport. The Olympic movement is able to offer direct sponsorship of sport to those who are interested. Private sponsorship of the Olympic Games worked well in Calgary and Los Angeles, establishing successful models for others to follow. The IOC can let governments stick to taxing their citizens to meet their own domestic political agendas.

And yet organizers of the Olympics have so far been able to resist the temptation to exploit the Games' full potential value to corporate sponsors. The Olympic Games are one of the few major sporting events where venues and athletes' uniforms are not used as commercial billboards. This is an elegant distinction.

We set out to finance at least two-thirds of the cost of the Games, including a complete set of new world-class facilities, from Olympic TV revenue generated from our single 16-day event. I know of no other event in the world where such high value is generated and shared so generously with the sportsmen of the world, and particularly with the citizens of the host city.

We went to bid early to select our host broadcaster. The host broadcaster is responsible for installing complex broadcast facilities and producing video footage of all Olympic events. When TV rights are sold, it is the right to transmit those TV images to their home country that broadcasters buy. The rights holder in a given country may add its own material, but the footage of the sporting events themselves is provided by the host broadcaster.

Canada had only two networks capable of becoming the host broadcaster. CTV won the contract, competing against CBC-TV. CTV's costs were lower, and the network convinced us it had all the necessary expertise, based on its affiliation with ABC and Wide World of Sports. It was interesting to compare the difference in approach between the two networks. CBC, a Crown corporation, bid like a bureaucratic bully, telling us what we had to do, while CTV, a privately owned network, listened to what we wanted and responded. The result was that CBC watched from the sidelines while CTV was paid approximately $50 million to build and equip the International Broadcast Centre and to perform the host-broadcaster service for the world.

CTV also paid us $4.5 million for the Canadian rights to televise the Olympics, so it became both the host broadcaster and the Canadian rights holder.

• MARION MCDOUGALL • JACQUIE DENTON • ROSANNE PISESKY • KRYSTYNA KROWICKI • JOHN GINGLES • HELEN MILES • MARK SHERRINGTON • SYLVAIN LOYER • STUART BANKS • ARLENE ROWAN • MYLES SHERIDAN • DEBBY GILLIES • LES WATSON • ANN STEEVES • DANIELLE JOLIVET • SANDY SHENHER • CARSTEN STANJECK • RODNEY DAROZA • SUSAN WARRINER • ABE HIRANI • KEVIN HEMPEL • HEATHER CASWELL • HOPE SMITH • KIM STEVENS • DOUG GODDARD • GEORGE HARRISON • TERESA SHOCK • JUDY BROOKBANKS • MARY ANNE SMITH • FLORENCE WHITROW(TRAPTOW) • LYNN BECKER • CLAIRE MALCOLM • ALAN BRYANT • MARLENE BALDWIN • NEIL WATSON •

We worked like beavers to be in a position to approach the U.S. networks with a host broadcaster, a full set of broadcast specifications, a 16-day schedule, a revised hockey tournament, more events, and more prime-time material.

After we gave each U.S. network the new-look bid package, we held meetings with each of them, at which they presented their best dog-and-pony shows and answered our questions. At the end of our evaluation, we came to the conclusion that any of the three U.S. networks, ABC, NBC, or CBS, was capable of carrying the 1988 Olympic Winter Games to the full American market. The final choice would be strictly a matter of price.

This decision was a great disappointment to ABC, which had broadcast eight previous Olympic Games. ABC felt its excellent track record indeed gave it a technical advantage. ABC was probably right, but we figured any of the three networks was capable of doing the job, so we did not want to disqualify them.

NBC, for its part, offered to pay us a substantial cash bonus if we would negotiate unilaterally with it. In view of our empty treasury we might have been wise to accept NBC's offer, but we rejected the proposal. We had decided to play for big stakes.

Always Make Your Bets on the First Tee

Each network received a thick legal document that was to be completed, signed and sealed with a $5-million deposit of good faith. If the successful bidder decided not to proceed with the contract, the $5 million would be forfeited and the rights would go to the next-highest bidder.

In having each TV network sign the agreement in advance we were trying to avoid the kind of problems that had occurred in Los Angeles and other Olympic cities. L.A. negotiated the best price first and finalized the contract later. Once the price had been agreed upon it became the ceiling. As the details were worked out ABC negotiated tougher and tougher terms, eroding bottom-line value to Los Angeles. ABC and the other networks could get away with this because it was their business and they knew exactly what they were doing. In contrast, our

Olympic organizing committee was playing a game it only partly understood in those early years. We were true amateurs, negotiating from weakness with capable professionals. Few organizations face a hundred-million-dollar negotiation without any previous experience.

This set-up is an advantage to the networks and other suppliers who know their business and, unlike the organizing committee, intend to remain in business long after the Olympic flame goes out. Our only advantage was that we were highly motivated because our organization was so poor the health of the whole venture depended on a successful deal. We had a clearly defined goal—stay alive or face the alternative!

We structured the TV rights agreement to accentuate our strengths and minimize our weaknesses. But the networks wanted none of it. We were breaking rules they had invented and that had always been to their benefit. When they saw our proposed agreement, they each said in turn, "You've got to be kidding! We don't do business by signing blank contracts. We won't play by your rules."

"Well, that's really unfortunate," we said. "We are going to miss you in Calgary in 1988." But each network made a similar speech and walked out, leaving us worried and wondering whether we had pushed them too far. We had relied heavily on the concept of giving the networks a high-value package, and now, when it came time for us to reap our expected high rewards, the tough approach looked like it had maybe proven disastrous.

A week later, though, whether thanks to our negotiating skill or dumb luck, after a few telexes back and forth all three contracts arrived, each signed and accompanied by a certified cheque for $5 million U.S. deposited in trust with the IOC. None of the big U.S. networks felt it could afford to be left out of Calgary's Olympics. We were relieved. Our concern now was to clinch a good deal.

Staging Our First Event

We decided to hold the TV bidding in Lausanne, Switzerland, to remove the umbilical cord connecting the bidders with their New York head-office people who might say, "Don't bid more." Ours was a simple and proven game-playing strategy: we wanted to play on our home courts, using our rules, with us keeping score. And since we were already holding each network's contract signed in advance, we had removed any real need to have their lawyers present, a negotiating coup on any occasion.

By coming to Switzerland, each network demonstrated its commitment to the bid. Going in, each one knew it had only serious players up against it. The psychology of the position favored us.

It was already the end of 1983. The Sarajevo Games were only two months away and our consultant, Barry Frank, was urging us to wait until after those Games to take bids for the TV rights, to capitalize on American enthusiasm for the impending Los Angeles Games.

While we were pondering our timing options, IOC President Samaranch, a wise man, had been doing his homework. "You must bid the TV rights before Sarajevo," he said. "If you do not agree I will insist you guarantee to the IOC that the fee will not be less than $200 million." He felt sure the American pre-Games hype was overblown, and the American hockey and ski teams would not do well in Sarajevo. He said, "If there are disappointments, the TV ratings will be down and we will get far less for our television rights."

We listened carefully to what he had to say and decided to follow his advice. There were other factors that supported our decision. ABC, which was likely to bid the most, had extra motivation to win the Calgary bid because it had successfully won the rights to broadcast either the summer or winter Olympic Games each time for the last two decades. ABC had worked for four years to get ready for Sarajevo and was sending over a team of more than a thousand people. We felt ABC would vastly prefer Calgary to Seoul, because of the monumental problems and extra costs of broadcasting the Summer Olympics from South Korea. The Seoul time zone is 12 to 14 hours away from the big U.S. market. In addition, the political, linguistic, and technical situation in nearby Calgary offered clear advantages to the U.S. networks. We guessed ABC wouldn't want to tell its Sarajevo broadcast team it wouldn't be doing the Olympics again until 1992, so that made Calgary top priority to keep the ABC Olympic broadcasting record alive.

Of course, this same logic applied in reverse for ABC's competitors; if it was good for ABC to have the Calgary Games, it would be good for ABC's competitors to take the Games away from them.

We were also better off if we held bidding before Seoul did. By holding bidding first, we would be dealing with all three networks while their treasuries were still full. If we let Seoul beat us to the punch, we would have one weak bidder that had already satisfied its Olympic appetite. Our success depended on getting off the mark early. And we had yet another important reason to bid early: we needed the money.

We suspected the IOC had similar reasons for wanting TV rights awarded early. Going into the 1984 Games the IOC treasury was running dangerously low, and Samaranch was driven by urgency to replenish the coffers with the IOC share of the Calgary TV rights contract. The importance of the Calgary TV rights bid could not be overestimated. It would provide the principal source of funding for our Games. We had almost all of our eggs in this one basket.

At the same time, however, all of our radical new plans for restructuring the Winter Games format still had not been approved by the IOC. Approval would have to be obtained at the IOC session in Sarajevo two months hence. If we accepted U.S. television rights bids before we had IOC approval we were out on a limb. We decided to go for it. We believed the new Games format was a logical and practical direction for future Winter Games to take. We felt confident the IOC would support our plan. Nonetheless, we had performed major surgery on the Olympic status quo, and, if the IOC turned us down after we had selected a U.S. network, we could face a costly renegotiation of the whole TV deal.

Bill Pratt, Bill Wardle, Bill Warren, and I went to Lausanne for the bid in late January 1984. We were joined by three representatives of the IOC: Madame Berlioux, Dick Pound, and Danny Russell, one of the IOC lawyers seconded from the CODA bid team. Barry Frank and Betsy Goff from Trans World International rounded out our delegation. All three networks sent executive vice-presidents or presidents of their sports departments. Roone Arledge represented ABC, Arthur Watson represented NBC, and Neil Pilsen represented CBS.

The Divine Rights

Lausanne is a university city in southern Switzerland, perched on the shore of Lake Geneva. It is the site of the IOC's permanent headquarters. We rented a conference room in the Lausanne Palace Hotel overlooking the city. From there we orchestrated a business auction with all the elements of a high-stakes poker game. The events of the day would have made a good TV movie.

"We will set the minimum acceptable bid for each round," Pound told the representatives of the three networks. "You will have one hour to prepare your bid. You can decide to drop out, meet the minimum, or bid more than the minimum. If any bidder needs more time a one-hour extension will be granted once for each round.

"We will not tell you what the other networks are bidding, and we will not stop the bidding until there is only one network left. Thank you for coming and good luck."

At the appointed hour, the network representatives came to our room to pick up sealed envelopes containing a note from us setting the minimum bid for the opening round. They returned to their hotel rooms, and came back an hour later with their bids safely sealed in envelopes.

We set the opening-round minimum at $165 million, but ABC chose to bid $208 million, presumably to show it was serious. NBC and CBS bid $165 million. We hiked the minimum for the next round to $225 million so that ABC might wonder if it had been outbid by one of the others. As the bidding pro-

BILL NEMETH · DENNIS CRESSMAN · CAROL SCHMALTZ · RON KNELLER · WANDA SMITH · DONNA MELNYCHYN · HELEN CAMPBELL · KIMBERLEY PODRASKY · SHANNON JOHNSON · ERIKA SCHULTZ · RHODELLE ROBERTSON · RONALD OLSON · WILLIAM VICKERS · KATE ROBERTSON · BRUCE NEWMARCH · CYNTHIA O'REGAN · SHANNON WILSON · GRACE MCMILLEN · SANDY SKOREYKO · JAMES WRIGHT · ROBIN MACDONALD · ROBERT BALFOUR · RICK LEVITT · CATHY PITTS · SHANNON DEE STEPHENS · CELINA BONDARCZUK · ALAN STEPHENSON · BEN PETERSON · MARIANNE YEOH · REGINA LICHTENFELD · KATY GRASS · PHIL ANDERSON · DEBRA RICKMAN · DWAYNE

ceeded, we varied the pattern of increases to keep everyone guessing. In each of the first two rounds, there were requests for one-hour extensions to allow the networks time to think over what they were going to do next.

When the third-round minimum reached $265 million, CBS dropped out. We didn't immediately tell the other two that CBS was no longer in the bidding, and for this we were later criticized. One round after CBS had stopped bidding, ABC and NBC noticed they alone were picking up our sealed envelopes, and asked whether CBS was still in. Pound said no. They were upset we had not volunteered the information, but we had felt no obligation to release it because, at the beginning, when we set down the rules, we had not provided for that eventuality.

We sat in our conference room most of the day. The bidding kept us busy only 15 minutes per hour, so the rest of the time we were free. Bill Warren, Dick Pound, Danny Russell and I played bridge. Madame Berlioux worked on a huge IOC correspondence file. Bill Wardle, who was responsible for the bid more than anyone else, spent his time reading a novel appropriately called *Poor No More*. Starting at noon, Wardle sat with his feet up and read. He finished the whole 832-page novel in the 11 hours we were there that day.

I remember looking at the book jacket thinking how appropriate the title was. Later I got a chuckle when I glanced at a couple of passages in the book that seemed to echo our own situation in an ironic way. The hero of this potboiler is a despicable lout, but his enthusiasm for playing to win was a cartoon reflection of our own:

> Craig took a pull at his julep and lit two cigarettes. He handed one to Sue. "[. . .] I guess I thrive on strife. The challenge thing. To put together a deal, to make two and two come out nine, to know that everybody's hand's against you and still whip the bastards to their knees. . . . Yeah." His voice hardened. "I like it. I wouldn't be without it. Take me away from the messes and the troubles and I'd wrinkle up and die like an old tomato." [Robert Ruark, *Poor No More* (New York: Fawcett, 1959), p. 725.]

As the day wore on, we experienced a strange combination of excitement and boredom—but it was already clear we were indeed poor no more.

The bidding lasted through six rounds, with ABC leading the whole way. NBC typically bid either the minimum or a little more. But as the hours passed, the numbers kept mounting. To avoid any possibility of tip-offs we agreed none of us would leave the room unaccompanied. If someone wanted to make a trip to the bathroom, someone went with him or her to make sure there was no attempt at bribery. Network representatives were not allowed into our conference room.

During one of the extensions, I went shopping for running shoes with Danny Russell.

Our own estimate was that $265 million was the real value of the TV rights contract. When the bidding went beyond $265 million, it occurred to us for the first time that we might get far more than we had ever dreamed. We had thought of almost all the options except the one that involved the networks paying too much. We were euphoric, of course, but as the numbers continued to soar we also became concerned. If we were paid too much could it create resentment and difficulties later? We might not be able to provide value equal to the exorbitant sums now being offered.

We couldn't stop the bidding, but we did begin reducing the increments between rounds. Then, with the bid level in round four set at $280 million, ABC jumped its bid all the way to $300 million. It was a clear sign ABC had had enough.

We had also had enough, and decided to give that signal by leaving the minimum bid for round five at $300 million. For the first time ABC would know it was the highest bidder. NBC, seeing this enormous jump, would likely call it quits. We felt sure that the next round would be the final one and ABC would win the TV rights with a $300 million bid.

ABC must have breathed a sigh of relief. Sure enough, ABC's bid again was $300 million. The network clearly believed it had won. But NBC was not prepared to roll over and play dead—it matched the ante with an equal bid of $300 million. Both networks had matched our minimum.

"What do we do now?" Dick Pound exclaimed. We actually thought of awarding the bid to ABC based on the fact that they had reached $300 million first, but having established the rules of play, we couldn't arbitrarily change them in the middle of the game. So we offered a modest variation to make it easier for both ABC and NBC. "We intend to reduce the bid time from one hour to 15 minutes," we said, "and if you agree we will make the minimum raise one million dollars. Each of you will know exactly what the other network has bid. Do you agree to these new rules?"

"Yes," they said wearily. "Let's get on with it."

We decided to toss a coin to see who would win the right to go first. NBC's Arthur Watson was asked to call. The coin went up, but Watson was suddenly seized with indecision. As it flew in the air he could only say, "Ah, Ah . . ." It was not until the coin lay on the table that he blurted out "Heads!"

"Arthur," we said, "you have to call before the coin hits the table. Therefore ABC wins the toss, and has the right to choose who goes first." ABC chose to follow NBC's bid.

In 15 minutes, representatives of both networks came back in and NBC said, "NBC bids $304 million." Not $301 million, which was the minimum, but $304 million. We all got the clear message that anyone who thought NBC was finished had better think again.

ABC's Arledge and company curtly walked out. At this point there wasn't a lot of joking or friendly conversation. In 15 minutes ABC came back, but it was not Roone Arledge this time. His first lieutenant, Jim Spence, marched into the room and announced, "ABC bids $309 million."

The competitive psychology was intense. ABC had raised the ante by $5 million! Not $1 million, which was the minimum, not $4 million, as NBC had done, but instead: "I'll see your four and raise you five more." Corporate egos were taking over; it was no longer just a matter of price. ABC's anger was apparent. So was its clear determination to broadcast the Calgary Winter Games to Americans.

Another 15 minutes went by. The phone rang in our room. It was Watson from NBC. "Would you please ask Roone Arledge to come down?"

"We'll ask him, but it's up to him," we replied. "He doesn't have to come if he doesn't want to." We phoned ABC's room and asked, "Is Roone Arledge there?"

"No, he's not," ABC answered.

"NBC is prepared to make its next bid and it has requested that Roone be down here."

"We'll be down right away."

The rest of the ABC team came down, but there was no sign of Roone Arledge. When everyone was assembled NBC's Watson spoke: "NBC would like to congratulate Calgary for conducting the finest television bid in the history of the Olympic Games. We regret very much that NBC will not be present to televise to all the people of America the best Winter Games in history."

The entire ABC team turned without saying a word and walked out. We shook the hands of NBC's executives and they politely accepted our invitation for some refreshments in the lobby bar.

Before joining NBC and our team in the lobby, I went to a phone booth in the Lausanne Palace. I've used this phone booth a number of times since, and every time I get the willies thinking about what it was like to describe the events of that day to an anxious group back in Calgary. It was approaching midnight in Lausanne, so it was about 4 p.m. in Calgary. I called the OCO'88 offices where a full contingent of the local media had gathered, awaiting the result of a two-year effort that meant so much to our Games.

When I announced the astonishing number of $309 million U.S. ($386 million Canadian) there was a moment of silence and then a loud cheer on the other end of the phone. I was pelted with questions, but they were not typical media questions probing for fault or weakness, but simple questions about what had happened. The reporters all understood the significance of our coup. It was the richest television rights contract ever.

That decision to refuse NBC's offer for unilateral negotiations had probably meant at least $50 million in extra revenue for us, and $50 million eventually turned out to be about the size of the

Games surplus. The quality and style of the Games would not have been the same if we had sold the farm for the first good offer.

I had planned to go jogging in my new shoes the next morning with Donna DeVerona from ABC. I was curious to see if she would show up. Sure enough she did, and while we jogged along the lakeside (I was wearing my new runners) I asked her what had taken place in the ABC hotel room the night before.

"Roone was just livid," she said. "The money got to be too much, but he had made a commitment that he was going to get these Games, and he had to carry through. It was a tough night for ABC."

We were worried our record-high contract might result in a difficult relationship with ABC, but our concerns were unjustified. Roone Arledge later moved up the executive ladder. He was replaced as the head of ABC sports by a tough ex-marine, Dennis Swanson, who was brought in by Capital Cities, a large publishing and broadcasting company that purchased ABC in 1985. We continued to have a superb relationship with ABC, and never once did they attempt to break the agreement. They had bought and paid for the best ever. Now we had the obligation to deliver—an obligation that was also an opportunity.

When we got home we told our lawyers, "Read the ABC agreement every morning before you come to work to make sure we never violate one single word." We didn't want to provide a reason for ABC to wriggle out of it.

ABC was ultimately happy with Calgary because we delivered more than we had originally promised. When ABC wanted something, even if it didn't seem entirely reasonable to us, we tried to satisfy the network. We bent over backwards to make up for the fact that ABC had paid too much. ABC later confirmed it would lose at least $40 million on the deal, although I'm sure that was more than made up by affiliate revenues and future returns on network ratings.

After the Games, Dennis Swanson called to say how much he appreciated the fact that Calgary had done everything reasonable to accommodate ABC—even beyond the strict terms of

our thick contract. It is a compliment to ABC, as well as to Bill
Wardle and to Dean Walker, who was in charge of Broadcast
Relations at OCO'88, that never once was the contract used to
settle a difference of opinion between us.

Dividing the Pie

Long before Calgary's ABC rights contract was written, we
had completed a crucial negotiation with Samaranch and
Berlioux on the sharing of television revenues. Samaranch had
come to Calgary for the first time in February 1982. We showed
him around and he expressed pleasure with our early plans.
On the way to the airport in the limousine, I asked him if we
could reopen discussion of the television rights in the contract
we had signed in Baden-Baden. He agreed to listen. I was
pleased with his fairness because during the bid phase, when
would-be organizers are scrambling for votes, they are not in a
good bargaining position. Madame Berlioux wrote the contract
and all bidders were forced to sign in advance of the bid, a tactic
similar to the one we used for our TV contract bids.

In our Baden-Baden contract we had agreed the IOC would
take one-third of the television revenues, and from our two-
thirds share we would pay the costs of the host broadcaster. I
told Samaranch that my experience in the Olympics was limited, but in the Calgary oilpatch it was quite common to form
joint ventures between two or more companies with common
objectives and different resources. United we stand, divided we
fall. In a joint venture, the profits are divided only after all the
costs have been paid.

"What concerns me about the Baden-Baden contract that
we were forced to sign is that it doesn't have the best interests
of the Olympic movement at heart," I explained to Samaranch.

"Why is that?" he asked, his curiosity piqued.

"The contract we signed says that the IOC will take one-
third of the revenues and we will take two-thirds, but we have
to pay one hundred per cent of the expenses for producing the
TV signals. This lopsided arrangement gives us an incentive to
cut corners on host broadcaster expenses. If we cut corners, the
presentation of the Games will be poorer and the TV rights will

be worth less than if we go all out for high quality. I propose that we change the contract to allow us to deduct a reasonable amount for the value of host broadcaster costs, and then we will split the remainder one-third, two-thirds—as you would in a joint venture."

"That sounds reasonable," he said thoughtfully. "I agree."

He got out of the limousine, shook hands and was gone. I had never seen such a pragmatic negotiation in my life, and I couldn't help but wonder if he would honor his agreement. But I shouldn't have wondered. Samaranch dispatched Madame Berlioux to Calgary and we eventually agreed the first 20 per cent of television revenues would be deducted to cover host-broadcaster costs payable by OCO'88. When we later got the unexpected ABC bonanza, the 20 per cent we had agreed upon provided us with more money than expected. With that money we were able to provide substantially better broadcaster services, including computerized results systems and improved physical facilities for broadcasters at the venues. Instead of getting two-thirds of the revenue, we ended up getting 72 per cent.

The IOC, for its part, got more than twice the money from Calgary TV rights than from all previous Winter Games put together. When you believe there will be plenty to share, it's easier to cut a win-win deal.

The ABC contract established funding for the Calgary 1988 Olympic Winter Games representing more than half our operating budget. It was a tremendous bonus for Calgarians.

Because of the focus on the television marketing of the Games in Calgary, some important changes have been made to the Olympic movement. The Winter Games have come closer to being an equal of their summer counterpart. The Winter Games were extended to 16 days. Television coverage increased almost 50 per cent—from 63 hours in Sarajevo to about a hundred hours in Calgary. Ultimately the IOC decided to hold Winter Games in the two-year intervals between Summer Games, rather than having both Games in the same year. And by 1990 the IOC had modified the TV revenue-sharing package, leaving only 33 per cent for the host city because of the huge revenues available from television coverage of the Games. Most importantly—more people are participating in these great global festivals of sport and peace as spectators. Only television can make that possible.

CHAPTER NINE

The Golden Rule

Those that have the gold make the rules.
ANONYMOUS

T HE ABC CONTRACT made it clear to the world that OCO'88 was no longer poor. That had some negative consequences. Although Gerry Regan was one of our biggest allies, he was also the first of many federal sports ministers to start squirming to get out of the $200-million federal commitment. As time went by and our revenue situation looked more and more healthy, it became clear that we didn't need the $200-million as much as we once had. Even Iona Campagnolo would not have agreed to pay $200 million if she had been able to foresee the success of our marketing program, and our ability to squirrel away our resources as a legacy for future athletes. In 1988, in fact, we ended up allocating about $150 million to sports endowment funds as a legacy of the Games. But we didn't like the notion that Calgary should be penalized for our success in producing revenues, and we weren't prepared to let the feds off the hook.

If you go down to the Calgary Petroleum Club for lunch and over dessert your lunch companion says, "Sure, I'll take 30 per cent of that deal," you shake on it and it's settled. You send the paperwork around to him when you get a chance. Not for a moment do you doubt the other guy's word; if he let you down his reputation would be shot and he'd be finished. To me this sort of straight shooting was just a normal part of how the game was played. It didn't take long to realize that the federal government was used to playing by different rules.

The Regan Legacy

Gerry Regan and I had once agreed at a meeting attended by Peter Lesaux, assistant deputy minister of sport, that the government would pay the $200 million indexed to 1981 dollars. Inflation was still running high, so indexing the amount was important. Peter Lesaux was always friendly and supportive, and he mouthed all the right words. But I soon became aware of his true game plan—he authored an internal government report stating that the indexing of Olympic funding had never even been discussed with OCO'88.

When I learned of the report I was furious. I picked up the phone and called Gerry Regan's office in Ottawa. Lesaux returned my call and when I confronted him with his convenient lapse of memory he said, "Frank, you're mistaken. There was never any agreement on indexing."

"Peter, I'm not mistaken," I said. "I know exactly what was agreed upon and the money was indexed to 1981 dollars." I demanded and got a meeting with Regan, and in Lesaux's presence said, "Gerry, I'm very disappointed your assistant deputy minister is trying to convince me we didn't agree on indexing. You know full well that was part of our deal."

To my great relief Regan answered, "You're absolutely right. Of course our money contribution was indexed to 1981 dollars." Peter Lesaux squirmed. To me he looked like a rat in search of a hole. "But," said Regan, abruptly ending my sense of relief, "I'm afraid I can no longer agree to that."

"We're counting on it," I said, "and it's already agreed to, it's done."

"No, it isn't done, because my colleagues won't let me do it," he replied. "It's too expensive, it's too much. You must consider some compromise."

"I'm not sure that we can," I said. "How can we make financial commitments if we keep compromising our position?"

"If you don't, it will jeopardize the whole deal," he said. "I can get you the $200 million, but I cannot get it indexed to 1981." Although he argued that it should not be indexed at all, we finally agreed to index it to 1982 dollars. That negotiation cost us about $20 million. It was not to be the last time the feds would try to chip away at our original deal.

Even with our compromise, no matter how many times the federal government restated its intent to pay the $200 million, it seemed we would never get the agreement signed. We continued negotiating with the bureaucracy, but somehow never got ahead. It's been said that when a bureaucrat winks, he opens one eye. We couldn't even get them to wink at us.

Gerry Regan had accompanied us to Brisbane, Australia, for the 1982 Commonwealth Games. At that time, Edmonton was bidding to host the Universiade Games, and Gerry Regan and I attended a party to help promote Edmonton's bid. Unfortunately, the Universiade bidders had been bungling their relationship with Regan and the federal government. The bidders had claimed to have federal support for things that the federal government had not yet been consulted about, and they had excluded Regan from decision-making where he felt he should have been included. After attempting to greet the guests at the party gracefully, Regan left the Universiade bid party muttering, "It will be over my dead body that these clowns get any federal funding." That day he withdrew his active support of the Edmonton bid, and although they ended up winning, they also got far less money from the federal government than they had expected.

As we left the Universiade reception, Gerry Regan told Jeanette and me he had received a telephone call from the prime minister saying he had been promoted to minister of international trade, and Senator Ray Perrault would be taking over from him as sports minister. Perrault would be the fourth minister we had worked with in four years.

The announcement saddened me. "Gerry," I said, "I'm really going to miss you. You and I have made an important deal and we were counting on working with you to make it happen. We would have been a good team." I was sure Regan would have signed the $200-million deal, but now I was worried we would have to begin again with a new minister.

"Frank," he said, "don't worry. You'll get your money. I have them sufficiently pregnant." This graphic expression was Regan's personal guarantee that the rest of his cabinet colleagues would support the funding, even if he were no longer minister. I would later have to call on him to get him to remind more than one of his successors in the sports minister's office of the commitment the government had made. On one such occasion I visited his Parliament Hill office. Regan was, as usual, rushing to another engagement, and was changing even as we spoke from his business suit into a tuxedo. Standing there in his boxer shorts, searching for his shirt and bow tie, he repeated his promise: "Don't worry, Frank, I told you that you would get the money and I'll make sure you do." Gerry Regan was a man of his word, and it is partly thanks to him that the Calgary Games were a success.

Senator Ray Perrault, Regan's successor, wasn't an elected member of Parliament, but was appointed minister of fitness and amateur sport. The Trudeau government had few elected representatives from the west and they needed a western minister in cabinet. Perrault had the best of intentions, but he was never able to accomplish much for us. It seemed to me that he relied too heavily on his advisers. We had to backtrack and help him reach the right decisions about the Games. We often seemed to be on the verge of losing the $200 million altogether. His major accomplishment was a new federal commitment of $25 million to a "Best Ever" athlete-development program pointing toward future Olympic gold. He also gave us our first $5-million advance to keep our current finances in shape.

Deals Versus Ideals

Perrault lasted only a few months, and was replaced by Céline Hervieux-Payette, a young Quebec member of Parliament. She was our fifth sports minister in less than five years, and won the award as the most difficult one to deal with. Her outwardly friendly manner belied the fact that the $200-million Olympic contribution was simply not on her agenda. She was bound and determined not to hand the money over.

We had agreed that wherever possible Olympic facilities would be constructed by governments on behalf of the public, who would own and use the facilities after the Games. This concept kept OCO'88 out of the complex field of project management, leaving the design and construction of all Olympic facilities up to the bodies ultimately responsible for them. OCO'88 simply negotiated funding agreements and established critical design specifications that would meet Olympic standards.

Political realities being what they are, we knew it would be best if federal dollars were used for tangible projects rather than to support something boring like the organizing committee's operating costs. Politicians must have something concrete to point to when they commit public funds. The Olympics in Calgary were a project with plenty of political sizzle, and the feds wanted to be able to maximize their political credit—even though the $200 million in federal funds were from non-tax sources. As the grand opening of the Olympic Saddledome approached I grew increasingly concerned that if the feds didn't get in on that project, it might become difficult to get them involved in any major way with the Games at all.

In October 1983 the opening of the Saddledome was rapidly approaching, but Hervieux-Payette was still dragging her feet. The key member of her staff responsible for the Calgary Olympics, Anita Slazak, was playing silly tactical games, and we were getting absolutely nowhere.

Toward the end of 1983, Hervieux-Payette announced with great fanfare that a deal had been struck to fund the Calgary Winter Games, including the Olympic Saddledome. But when Anita Slazak presented the final federal position to the OCO'88 board, it contained conditions that reduced the financial commitment of the government while expanding its control over board decisions. This made us bitter. We had just concluded an agreement with the provincial government for its $125-million share, but trying to work with the federal government was like being bitten to death by a duck.

Bill Warren and I were two of the few remaining people in Calgary to believe we were going to get the $200 million from the federal government. Peter Lougheed didn't believe it, Ralph Klein didn't believe it, and even some members of our board of directors didn't believe it. But Bill and I had invested too much time in laying this $200-million cornerstone. We were committed to hanging on to it. We had been fast-talked, cajoled, and cheated by successive ministers and bureaucrats trying to avoid paying the money. Even the best ones had played their own Olympic games.

Earlier, Hervieux-Payette had agreed the federal government would pay its one-third share of the Olympic Saddledome. Then Peter Lesaux got into the act and convinced her that since the Olympic Saddledome was going ahead anyway, and since it was really not being built for the Olympics but for professional hockey, the federal government should not get involved. We had presented evidence to show that the Olympics had been the main spark for the Olympic Saddledome, and the hockey team was only a secondary beneficiary. Lesaux, using his own brand of logic, had refuted our evidence, and once again talked his minister out of participating. Hervieux-Payette angrily accused me of misleading her.

"Lesaux is wrong," I said, "and I can prove it."

"You'd better," she replied, "because we are not going to pay anything for a professional hockey arena." We diligently prepared a detailed chronology of events, including letters from the premier of Alberta and the owners of the Calgary Flames, to confirm that we had been the first to approach the city to build the Olympic Saddledome to support our Olympic bid. We had systematically eliminated every objection she and her people had thrown at us. Even the name selected for the arena included the word "Olympic," helping to confirm its *raison d'être*.

Bill Warren and I were travelling back from Europe when we arrived in Ottawa for a meeting I had arranged with Hervieux-Payette. We spent time on the plane getting our strategy together and shook hands, agreeing never to give up.

We went directly to Hervieux-Payette's Parliament Hill office. She invited several others to the meeting, including

Senator Jack Austin, a federal hatchet-man, and Senator Bud Olson from Alberta. The same familiar crowd of bureaucrats sat ringing the inner circle, taking copious notes on everything that was said. Bill Warren and I may have looked like Custer's men at their last stand. But it soon became obvious the meeting was not being run by Hervieux-Payette, but by Austin. Austin's message was simple: the feds couldn't afford $200 million. They didn't have the means to pay it now that the Olympic lottery was gone, and if we wanted any funding at all, $120 million was the best offer.

"A deal is a deal," we insisted. "We expect the Government of Canada to honor the commitment made by Gerry Regan and Iona Campagnolo." We said we expected $200 million, indexed to 1982, of which $30 million would be paid within two weeks at the opening of the Olympic Saddledome.

Austin replied that it was $120 million or nothing. If we did not accept that, the government would withdraw entirely. We had prepared for the possibility of such a threat. "We believe you will honor your obligations and you won't embarrass us or the federal government by reneging on our deal," we replied. "There is no reason whatsoever for Calgary not to receive everything it is due." We reminded them all that Calgary had received virtually nothing in federal distribution of wealth in the last decade. Now it was time.

"If you leave this room without agreeing to $120 million, there will be no further negotiations," Austin threatened.

"We are sorry, Senator, that you are taking this strong position," we persisted. "We don't want the Government of Canada to withdraw from these Games, but we will not accept less than $200 million. If you doubt that an agreement for $200 million already exists you should check with Gerry Regan."

Then we stood up and left.

We sensed we had won, in spite of the government's ultimatum. To be on the safe side, however, we immediately got on the phone to Gerry Regan saying, "They're doing it to us again!"

"I'll talk to them," he said. We made calls to Calgary members of Parliament and others we knew in the government.

CHUCK JAMES • SUE MOFFATT • BRYAN BENNY • KRISTINA LINDSTEN • SEAN SOUTAR • COLLEEN DERBY • MAUREEN BENSON • DAN DOWNE • JUDITH SHEANE • MARY TAYLOR • WOLFGANG STAMPE • DON MAXWELL • LILLIAN RHODES • DAVE FILUK • GARY GARDINER • FIN JOHNSTON • BOB BUSCHGENS • JANICE FOSTER • BRENDA BECK-EDWARDS • SHIRLEY THOMAS • DAVID SALMON • SHARRON KASER • MICHELLE CURTIS • YVONNE WUOTILA • PAT ALLON • LINLEY BIBLOW • LOUIS KAMENKA • STAN KALUZNICK • MICHAEL WASYLENKO • MARILYN CARLSON • D.J. MOSER • GRANT LYDIATT • CLAYDON GORVEATT • GLEN WOO • MARCEL SZYSZKOWSKI • TRUDY CAMPBELL •

We pulled out all the stops. For 10 days we lobbied, each day bringing us closer to the opening of the Olympic Saddledome. "Calgary's going down the tubes," we said. "We're about to lose a major plank in our financing." It would be a terrible embarrassment if the feds bombed out, a national disgrace, well-covered in the international press.

I got a phone call from Hervieux-Payette. "We've reconsidered our position," she said. "Please plan for my attendance at the Olympic Saddledome grand opening. I'm not certain, but I believe we will be participating."

"I'm delighted to hear that," I said. "We will have time to prepare the bronze plaque to include your name." Everyone likes to be remembered in bronze.

The night of the Olympic Saddledome opening I met Hervieux-Payette at a party at the home of a local Liberal organizer, Darryl Raymaker. She took me into a corner and discussed the issue. "It's true," she said, "we have decided to pay you the money, but there may be certain conditions."

"What are the conditions?" I asked, remembering countless previous head fakes from the minister's bureaucrats.

"The federal government will require much greater participation in the affairs of the organizing committee."

My memory flashed to a larger-than-life image of Mayor Klein in Baden-Baden demanding precisely the same control over OCO'88. I listened dispiritedly as she continued. "There will be other conditions. We will talk about them later. But I have the funds approved and we will be participating in the Saddledome opening tonight."

As I drove to the Olympic Saddledome I felt sorry that this government leader, like so many others, could not stick to governing and nothing more. The Golden Rule was in effect: she had the gold so she wanted to make the rules.

At the opening of the Olympic Saddledome that night, Hervieux-Payette was loudly booed by the first audience ever to be in the building. Calgarians have a happy faculty for letting people know where they stand. Our problems with the feds had been well-covered in the news media. When the announcer said

Hervieux-Payette was handing me the envelope containing a cheque for $30 million for the Olympic Saddledome, however, the crowd responded with loud cheers.

Backstage, I met Bill Nield, our treasurer. "Now, I don't want to carry around a $30-million cheque," I said to him, "so we'd better get this sucker in the bank." I opened the envelope. It was empty. I swore. "I don't believe it," I said. "They did it to us again." It was like a taunt from the feds: Here—deposit *this!*

Two weeks later, we received the full $30-million payment from the Government of Canada in the mail.

CHAPTER TEN

The Gift of Good Examples

It's amazing what you can observe just by watching.

YOGI BERRA

IN THE BEGINNING most Olympic organizers don't fully understand what is expected of them or where to place priorities. The best Games are organized by those who learn from prior Games and have the courage and vision to use what they learn to improve the Games that follow.

By the fall of '83 the staff at OCO'88 had increased to nearly 50 people, from which we selected a 29-member team to go to Sarajevo. For some original CODA people it was their second Winter Games, but for most it was the first. Jeanette and I decided to take along our two sons, Dave and Steve, so they could for the first time share in the Olympic experience.

Dave was 17 years old; he had been an avid skier and was quickly developing into a competitive runner in middle distances. He had received a high-school award the previous season as the top male track athlete and was looking forward to an even better season in his senior year. A few weeks prior to the Sarajevo Games he experienced an injury from training that at the time we thought was a stress fracture. (The injury did not go away, and put an end to Dave's running. Only years later did we finally get a correct diagnosis. The problem turned out to be compartment syndrome—an inflammation of the calf muscle sheaths that causes severe pain during exercise. The problem is easily corrected by surgery.)

Steve was 14 years old when we went to Sarajevo and was also an active skier and track athlete, but his first love was basketball. The boys' older sisters, Diane and Linda, had been good basketball players, and Steve worked out regularly on the basketball court we have at home.

The trip to Sarajevo turned out to be an important family bonding experience. For the first time our two sons could feel for themselves the intense emotions that come with the Olympics.

The Games of Ice and Snow

The opening ceremonies at Sarajevo took place on a beautiful day, warm and calm. About 50,000 people were assembled for the show, which featured local people dressed in futuristic costumes reminiscent of the Michelin Man. I will not forget the sight of thousands of performers walking to the stadium, and later walking home, since apparently transportation was unavailable for them. I was astonished to find that during the whole opening ceremonies most of the people in the stadium were standing. We were among the privileged few with seats.

A brown smog covered the city, the streets were bare, and the only snow in evidence was barely visible through the thick haze on the nearby hills. That evening, as part of nature's plan, the skies opened up and snow began to fall. By morning nearly two feet of snow had fallen on the streets—and it kept falling. It was an amazing sight to see large groups of workers out shovelling the snow from the major streets by hand! The mechanized snow-clearing equipment amassed from all over Yugoslavia was still not adequate to cope. Similarly, the amount of electrical power required for the Olympic Winter

SHEILA BILTON • HOLLY MYERS • JUAN FLORES • PATEL KIRAN • SUE LOUNSBURY • MELBA DANIELSON • MARTA POROPAT • JIM GORSLINE • WAYNE LO • GORD CALDWELL • LESLEY MURRAY • JAMES DUSTAN • JACK WILLISON • AL BLACK • FRANK PORT • GALE DEAN • KEITH DOWNIE • JEFF STEPHENSON • NICK ZEKULIN • BOB VICKERS • FAY VANDERWAL • DANY DESLONGCHAMPS • MICKEY KUZIO • MICHAEL CASEY • RON DEANS • MARGARET PATTERSON • HELLY VISSER • CLARENCE SERVOLD • GORDON COOK • WENDY WATSON • ELLEN COUCH • ELEANOR LLOYD • RICHARD GREEN • BRENDA DE WITT • JULIEANN COWIE • MARTIN BLAKE • MARIE SIROIS • ADA LOGULLO • JACK BLACK • BILL

Games was so great that power brownouts were allowed to occur in other parts of Yugoslavia so that adequate power could be available in the Sarajevo area for the operation of the Games. To welcome the world, the people of Yugoslavia made sacrifices.

The snowstorm caused other difficulties. The airport at Sarajevo had a runway too short for big international flights. A DC-10 charter jet from Canada trying to land in the snowstorm skidded off the end of the runway. Like all its Winter Games predecessors, Sarajevo lacked an international airport. Calgary would be the first host city of the Olympic Winter Games to offer this important advantage.

The people of Yugoslavia should be proud of the facilities they built for the Sarajevo Games. The hockey arena, in a city that had no previous exposure to hockey, seated 8,000 people. One of the difficulties facing organizers is ensuring that new facilities will be used after the Games. For this reason, alpine villages cannot easily compete with modern cities near the mountains for the right to host Olympic Winter Games. Sarajevo, because of its size, was able to find successful solutions to questions of legacy and facility after-use. For instance, the hockey arena has become an indoor sports centre, used for skating, gymnastics, winter training, trade shows—and yes, a little hockey as well.

The combined bobsleigh and luge run was not considered great by the International Bobsleigh Federation. Some competitors complained, but it was more than adequate for fair competition. In contrast, the ski-jumping facility was marvelous. Dave and Steve went with us to the ski-jumping area, joining a crowd of at least 50,000 people. When the Yugoslav jumper was preparing to come down, the crowd began to yell, "Yugo! Yugo! Yugo!" In Sarajevo the Yugos flew further than they ever had before, thanks to the hometown crowd cheering them on.

The weather was snowy and foggy, but favorable on most days. The massive snowfall created havoc in the mountains— the downhill courses were covered with soft, wet snow and had to be prepared for racing all over again. The men's downhill was postponed on four occasions, until finally on the fifth try the event was completed. Too much snow can provide organizers with problems even more costly than the problems of too little snow. Yet winter city bidders often brag about the tremendous snowfall in their region. It's good to have plenty of snow in January to allow course workers to create a championship ski hill and keep it in top shape, but organizers should pray for no snow during the Games period in February.

At the men's downhill the crowd of a few thousand was much smaller than we had expected. After watching the top-seeded skiers compete, we took the chairlift to the top to see how the mountain had been extended by Yugoslav engineers to meet the minimum vertical requirements of the International Ski Federation. The men's downhill racers started in a chute located on the third floor of a new restaurant perched on top of the tallest hill. The skiers launched themselves down the chute, right through the building, and out onto the hill.

Clearing the Air

At Sarajevo I realized Bill Pratt had become uneasy with my constant presence. Perhaps it was as a result of several social functions to which both Bill and I were being invited. On most occasions, President Samaranch, as a matter of protocol, would invite Jeanette and me to sit at the head table beside him and his wife. Bill and Millie Pratt were usually invited to sit at a table with Madame Berlioux and other Olympic officials. I had thought our roles were clear. Bill, as president, was chief operating officer; I, as chairman, was chief executive officer. The leadership role was comfortable for me, after five years working with our old friends in the international sports scene. In early 1984 Bill Pratt was still the new boy on the block. As Dick Pound said once, "The IOC tend to eat their young." Bill still had to earn his stripes.

One day, standing in the lobby of the IOC hotel in Sarajevo, I mentioned to Bill some OCO'88 problems that needed his attention. Unexpectedly Bill blew his cork. He wheeled to face me and said, "Frank, for God's sake, either get in or get out!"

I glared back at Bill and said, "Bill, you should have no doubt . . . I'm in!" I turned and walked away. I was more disappointed than surprised by his outburst. I realized I had some work to do making Bill feel more comfortable with his role in OCO'88. He obviously felt capable of doing a bigger job than he had been given.

We had arranged to meet at Sarajevo's International Broadcast Centre about an hour later for a tour of ABC's facilities. Bill was already in the room with several of our key executives when I entered. I looked at him, my face clearly expressing the fact that I was bothered by his earlier offensive. Once again Bill was full of surprises. He walked across the room, gave me a great big bearhug and said, "Frank, I'm sorry." It was the only time in all the years I've known Bill Pratt that he apologized for anything. It was not the only time, though, that I received a bearhug from this man, who often shows strong emotion.

VIP Transportation

Like many other special guests of the Sarajevo Organizing Committee, we were assigned a car and driver. I found Ralph Klein anxiously pacing in the hotel lobby one morning, waiting for his driver to arrive. As he stood fretting about being late for an event he wanted to see, a casually dressed man walked directly toward him. Ralph, feeling relieved, strode forward saying, "You must be my driver."

"Not quite, sir," answered the man. "I am Crown Prince Harald of Norway but I would be pleased to drive you wherever you need to go." Our chagrined mayor laughed heartily and became an instant friend of the Crown Prince, who is now the king of Norway.

Quick on His Feet

The story of Canada's top speed skater at Sarajevo, Gaetan Boucher, will not soon be forgotten. Gaetan had won a single silver medal in Lake Placid, skating in the shadow cast by the great U.S. skater Eric Heiden. Gaetan had been a strong medal contender for 1984 until a year earlier, when he broke his ankle during a skating mishap. He had worked himself back into competitive form and had been rewarded by being selected to carry the flag at the head of the Canadian team as it marched in the opening ceremonies.

In his first race, the 500-metre sprint, Gaetan finished third, just $\frac{9}{100}$ of a second behind the silver medalist, Yoshihiro Kitazawa. It was a surprisingly strong finish, and Gaetan's favorite 1,000- and 1,500-metre races still lay ahead. A day later, in front of the whole Canadian hockey team and many members of Team'88, Gaetan won his first gold medal. He predicted he could repeat his performance, and the next day he did not disappoint his small but enthusiastic Canadian cheering section.

We all watched as Gaetan Boucher won the 1,500-metre event to become the fastest skater in the world and Canada's greatest medal winner in Winter Games history. Canada's venerable IOC member, Jim Worrall, presented the medals that evening in the central square of Sarajevo. All of us stood transfixed as Gaetan mounted the stand, took the number-one spot, and bowed his head to receive the gold medal around his neck. We felt tingles as the Canadian flag was raised and *O Canada* was played. Our sons noticed the tears rolling down their mother's cheeks. Steve said to me, "Look Pop, she's at it again!"

Jockeying with Jacques

Just before the Sarajevo Games, Céline Hervieux-Payette was replaced as minister of fitness and amateur sport by Jacques Olivier. Olivier made the trip to Sarajevo as part of the Canadian delegation. We made arrangements through the office of Anita Slazak, still the federal government's top bureaucrat in charge of the Calgary Olympics, to have Olivier speak on behalf of the federal government during our report to the IOC session. Peter Lougheed would speak for the provincial government, Mayor Klein would make a statement on behalf of the city, and Bill Pratt and I would make the business presentation on behalf of OCO'88. The politicians were there to show the strength of our partners and to take some credit for their contributions.

We still hadn't signed our $200-million funding deal with the federal government, and our board was growing increas-

• DON SMITH • KATHY PAPAVACILOPOULOS • GAYLE GRAHAM • SAVINDER DHILLON • SARAH LEETE • STEPHANIE CHIA • DIANE MCCLENNON • ROBERT TUFFNAIL • LINDA HUTCHISON • MEREDETH MARTIN • JOHN KRPAN • SAM HARBISON • DONNA RHODES • GLENN MACDONALD • CONSTANCE SMITH • DAVE ROWAN • DAVID WILLIAMS • BARRY ADAMSON • THERESE AMANN • SHERRY HRYHORIW • EUGENE SEEWALT • LINDA FRIZZLE • PAMELA HOLLO • JOHN MARTIN • TED GILES • CATHERINE LEE • BRIAN PELLAND • CYNTHIA BELL • FRANCOISE SIGUR-CLOUTIER • BARBARA CRABTREE • PHYLLIS LOEWEN • SHIRLEY SIMMERING • MARNIE KELLY • ROSALYNN HORNE • FROUKJE VAN DORSSEN

ingly impatient with the feds' seemingly endless delaying tactics. Using Olivier in our presentation was a tactical move to confirm the federal "pregnancy" started by Gerry Regan.

Jacques Olivier, the sixth sport minister in five years, summoned me to our first meeting the day before our Sarajevo report to the IOC. When I walked into his room Olivier greeted me by saying, "So, you're Frank King. I've heard a lot of things about you. I hear you're pretty tough and one-sided in your negotiations."

Olivier's aggressive, adversarial approach irked me. "I think you've heard wrong," I answered. "We have good relations with all our partners, but we do expect them to honor their commitments fully."

"That isn't what I've heard," he replied. "I've heard a lot of bad things about you and your OCO'88 people."

"I can't imagine who you might have heard these things from," I said, silently and sarcastically acknowledging what I suspected was the work of Anita Slazak and Peter Lesaux, "but I can assure you that you are dealing with an organization that can be trusted. We have never failed to keep our promises. Unfortunately, I can't say the same for some of your predecessors, and I hope this isn't going to be the case with you."

"I'm not saying it's true, I'm just telling you what I've heard about you," he said. I appreciated his candor but I was annoyed and concerned about the situation, which could undermine our progress and rob us of more valuable time for organizing the Games.

"I've got an idea," I said. "Why don't you call some of your trusted Liberal friends in Calgary who know us personally, and ask them whether we are straight shooters." I gave him the name of a few leading local Liberals whom I knew well. "Then talk to Gerry Regan. You'll find out what the government is committed to."

Since he had started on this aggressive note, I decided to air some of my concerns with his operation as well. Two things were of particular concern to me. First was the fact that we still did not have our contract for the $200 million, and second was the problem of Anita Slazak, whom I did not like. I thought that she was influencing the formation of policy in a way unbefitting her position as a second-tier bureaucrat. I was concerned because I felt that at every step she was doing what she could to undermine our efforts. Olivier listened carefully, saying nothing.

We discussed the speaking order for OCO'88's report the next day. The order had already been agreed to by the mayor and Peter Lougheed, but Olivier insisted he be allowed to speak last, in place of Lougheed. I argued that Lougheed, an old friend of many IOC members, had been positioned last in the presentation so he could talk effectively about government support. This was appropriate, because his provincial government had, at that time, been the only one to provide full support for our new Olympic facilities.

Olivier insisted we do it his way or he wouldn't speak at all. In exasperation I went to see Lougheed, who was clearly upset by the minister's power play. He was, however, quite used to federal political confrontations by now. Lougheed and our team met with the minister, and Peter coolly predicted to Olivier that, based on what he had learned from their first encounter, "not only will your government be defeated, but you will lose your seat." He was right on both counts.

After the meeting between Lougheed and Olivier, Peter said to me, "I don't wish to get into a public confrontation with the minister. Let him speak when he wants and I won't speak at all, I'll just appear with you and smile."

"I appreciate the offer," I replied, "but I don't want to lose the impact of your comments to the IOC. Yours is the only government seriously committed to the construction of Olympic facilities. I will organize two or three IOC members to ask questions, which I will then direct to you for response. You can make your presentation during the question period which will, in effect, give you the last word."

"Fine," he said. "You organize it any way you want."

The next day it was my job to introduce our delegation to the full IOC session.

After Mayor Klein had spoken I introduced Peter Lougheed. For Jacques Olivier's benefit I said, "It is a great pleasure for me to introduce the Honorable Peter Lougheed, premier of the Province of Alberta. Mr. Lougheed has been premier of Alberta since 1971, leading the province through its period of greatest economic growth.

"Mr. Lougheed is a former member of the Canadian Olympic Association and personally assisted with two bids from the City of Calgary to host the Olympic Winter Games. He was with the Calgary delegation for the successful bid in 1981 in Baden-Baden. He has been premier during the staging of two successful international sporting events in Alberta, the Commonwealth Games in 1978 and the Universiade Games in 1983. Mr. Lougheed's government executed a full agreement for support and co-operation with the Calgary organizing committee in December 1983. Mr. Lougheed has accepted the kind invitation of President Samaranch to attend the IOC session and the XIVth Olympic Winter Games in Sarajevo. And he has agreed to answer any questions you may have concerning the role of the Province of Alberta."

And then I said, "It is my pleasure now to introduce Canada's new Minister of State for Fitness and Amateur Sport, the Honorable Jacques Olivier." Olivier spoke briefly without substance, and then questions from IOC members were handled eloquently by Peter Lougheed.

Crosbie Cotton, the Olympic reporter for the *Calgary Herald*, had caught wind of the belligerent attitude of the federal government and it didn't take long before the headlines back home became damaging to Olivier. Olivier made several ill-conceived remarks at Sarajevo, including one about making Calgary's Olympic funding conditional on hiring bilingual coaches for bilingual teams. His comments were not well received at home, the papers eventually joking that Olivier was making a habit of opening his mouth only to change feet. Especially odd was Olivier's self-congratulatory declaration to the media that he had personally saved Calgary's credibility by appearing on our behalf in front of the IOC in Sarajevo. The Calgary press made short work of the minister.

In contrast, OCO'88 was in a position of improving strength. We had just negotiated the ABC contract, and the IOC had quickly approved our new 16-day Games schedule, along with our extra sporting events. We were on a roll.

In Sarajevo Olivier gradually began to see for himself that we were responsible people with the difficult task of controlling a complex project. Just by watching, Olivier learned quickly, and by the time he left Sarajevo he was in a much more receptive frame of mind. As we parted he promised to look into my concerns and get back to me soon.

A few days later Olivier called me in Sarajevo from Ottawa. "I've checked it all out," he said, "and you're quite right. I now agree with you, and I'm prepared to take action to help. I now understand that your group is doing a good job. Why don't you come to Ottawa on your way home, and we'll work this out together."

"That's not possible," I answered. "I'm travelling with my family and I have personal business appointments back in Calgary."

"That's fine," he said. "If you can't come to Ottawa, I'll come to Calgary and we'll finalize the deal."

I probably could have gone to Ottawa, but at this stage I preferred not to. It was partly a matter of convenience and partly one of gamesmanship. We wanted to play the game on home turf. We had found that whenever we went to Ottawa we were overwhelmed with bureaucratic arguments and empty promises. Besides, Calgary was really beginning to look like an Olympic city. Many of the facilities were now under construction and I wanted Olivier to see them, to foster in him a sense of involvement. I had been away from home for a full month. So I decided not to go to Ottawa and instead to invite Olivier to Calgary.

Olivier did come to Calgary, where he became an instant Olympic enthusiast. He even began negotiating our funding agreement fairly. Our elected representatives rely on advice from staff who have all the facts at their disposal, but may not have a proper perspective. The experience of the Games showed that most ministers were able to detect bad advice, discount it, and act on their own political judgment. Being accountable makes all the difference.

Another Ultimatum

A few months earlier, Anita Slazak called me at 7 a.m. at my home as I was preparing to leave for a meeting of the board of directors of OCO'88.

"Could you come down to the meeting early?" she asked. "I would like to discuss something with you."

"Sure," I said. "What would you like to discuss?"

"I can't tell you on the telephone, but I would like you to come down half an hour early if you can."

Since I was ready to go, I left early and met her in the boardroom before the others arrived.

"Frank," she said, "I am bringing to you a serious message from the federal cabinet. You are going to have to accept some terms if we are to have an agreement. If you do not accept these terms, the federal government will withdraw from the Games."

She continued as I listened in shock. Here we go again, I thought. "First of all, we won't be giving you $200 million. We will not be contributing all the money you have requested." She went on to list a number of other terms regarding the role of the federal government and ended by saying, "You must agree before we sign."

"Well, Anita," I said, "I think you already know this is totally unacceptable. The deal you propose has already been discussed and rejected and frankly, I don't believe the federal government will take that position." Mixing my metaphors, I told her she was way out in left field and playing with fire. I told her I had lost confidence in her and would deal directly with the minister on issues of importance from now on.

She answered defensively, "I didn't think you would believe me, but I assure you this is the official position of the government. I have been asked to give you the message, and I intend to deliver it to the board even if you try to stop me."

"I won't try to stop you," I said. "On the contrary, I insist you tell the board. If you don't I will, so please tell them in your own words."

Anita was about to cook her own goose. I knew the board well, and this kind of arrogant, unilateral proposal would really make the other partners' blood boil. The provincial government would feel badly used, because it was using Heritage Fund dollars while the feds were planning to use Olympic funding gained from lotteries and coin and stamp sales. The city would also be upset, because Anita's approach would expose municipal taxpayers to increased risks. And I knew how Maurice Allan, Roger Jackson, John Lecky, Bob Niven, Dick Pound, Bill Warren, and Jim Worrall would react. They were all experienced businessmen who would bridle at games of bureaucratic brinksmanship.

I thought Anita would come on less strong with the board than she had with me. Amazingly, she escalated her performance. She repeated the ultimatum in aggressive and dictatorial terms, saying that if we did not accept the terms at this board meeting, the Government of Canada would be withdrawing funding from the 1988 Olympic Winter Games immediately. There would be no negotiations.

One by one the other members of the board rejected the ultimatum outright. Bill Warren spoke calmly and deliberately about the disgraceful record of unfaithful conduct of the federal government. Maurice Allan (a representative of the COA) spoke of underhanded blackmail tactics. George de Rappard, from the provincial government, said he wasn't surprised the feds were about to screw the West one more time. Bob Niven asked, "How can the feds introduce a sports pool to raise funding for the Olympics and then announce they will refuse to fund the Olympics?" I spoke only after everyone else. I said this was a turning point in the life of the organizing committee and if we agreed to accept this type of treatment we could not continue to run the Games as they should be run—by citizens.

The board of directors of OCO'88, with the lone exception of Anita Slazak, passed a resolution to reject the proposal presented by the federal government.

Later, when we had gained the confidence of Jacques Olivier, I told him of the confrontation. I had to know whether our problem was with the minister or the messenger. He agreed that perhaps Anita should not have represented the government's position in a "take-it-or-leave-it" manner.

"I hardly need to suggest what you should do now," I said.

"You're right," he answered.

After Anita Slazak's departure from the federal scene, Olivier began to resolve the long-standing issue of the federal government's participation. He researched the facts honestly, fairly, and quickly. He also recognized the work that had been done by OCO'88 and the reasonableness of our outlook. Having $200 million in non-tax funding coming from the federal government was, at last, being viewed as an investment in a once-in-a-lifetime opportunity for all Canadians.

The federal Olympic funding agreement, signed by Olivier in Calgary on March 30th, 1984, committed the government to $200 million, indexed to 1982 dollars, as well as providing other essential government services such as police, immigration, customs, and external affairs. The signing was a particularly welcome moment for Bill Warren, because he had worked tirelessly to ensure the Government of Canada did not renege on its commitments. Now OCO'88, the Government of Canada, the Province of Alberta, and the City of Calgary were all solid partners. It is remarkable that the three levels of government were able to work together on a major ten-year project, share the credit, and actually enjoy the experience.

Despite his inauspicious debut, then, Jacques Olivier ended up doing two great pieces of work: signing the Olympic funding agreement and removing Anita Slazak. We all promised to stop referring to him by his early nickname, Jacques Strap.

Los Angeles

In the summer of 1984 we took our OCO'88 team to Los Angeles to witness the private-enterprise style of Peter Ueberroth, Harry Usher, and company. Our mission in Los Angeles

LEMON • LAUREN PISESKY • BOB SWAINGER • GWEN SCAMAN • RICK BLACK • HELGA CATTONI • LINDA ANDERSON • CARA SNIDER • BOB CAIRNS • GERRY CEBALLOS • ED LEE • INGE OLSON • KENNETH TAYLOR • ANNE FREY • EVELYN KEELER • HAZEL WALKUT • ANNE STEWART • SHAWN MCCREA • ADAM HEDINGER • JOYCE BRAYTON • STUART HUTTON • GERHARD SCHUBERT • AL MCCUE • MARIANNA TUDDA • FRED STOREY • GRAHAM UNDERWOOD • EDWIN UNVERRICHT • ANN MURPHY • CAROL MAKI • DONALD MCMECHAN • SHARON BENDER • DORIS TAYLOR • CHOE CHING • IAN FITZGERALD • YOLANDE HALL • SHELLEY STOKES • DREW GNAM • LINDA BLOWER • AIDAN WALSH • BEV

provided another lesson in crisis management. We had already learned in Sarajevo that keeping the Olympic show operating involved a litany of pressure-cooker decisions. The L.A. organizing committee allowed us to work behind the scenes in their operations and technology departments, observing the venue-management system in action.

The Los Angeles Games, like at least five Olympic Games before them, were a subject of controversy. The absence of countries friendly to the Soviet Union hurt the Games to a degree, but other members of the Olympic movement responded to the opportunity by sending larger teams. The younger athletes who received a surprise chance to compete with the best must have had a wonderful experience, but that experience could not make up for the disappointment of the many athletes who were denied, by yet another boycott, the chance to be Olympians.

The Calgary mission spent most of its time working inside the LAOOC management structure, learning how to manage crises. We watched the organizers handle volunteer deployment problems, a helicopter crash on the freeway, a runaway automobile near the Olympic Village, ticket delivery problems, and more. They did well.

The Calgary group decided to hold a reception in Los Angeles for visiting members of the Olympic family from around the world. Our people prepared a huge welcome sign, which was prominently displayed over the doorway through which our guests arrived. Ralph Klein, Bill Pratt, and I stood at the door to greet visitors, and the rest of our team chatted with them inside the large reception area. I was glad to see Chick Igaya in the lineup at the front door. Years earlier I had become a friend of Chick's, a popular Olympic silver-medal slalom skier from Japan and now an IOC member. When Chick and his wife, Akiko, arrived at our reception, he quietly pulled me aside to comment on our huge sign which (we thought) read WELCOME in six languages, including Japanese. Chick pointed out that the Japanese sign should say KANGEI, which means welcome. I looked at the bold characters, which meant nothing to me, and asked "What does our sign say?"

DORSCHEID • NORMAN JORDISON • JOHN PICKETT • CHARLES HAYES • IAN CATTERALL • KATHY MASSEY • RITCHARD NOONAN • CINDY MCFEETERS • STEPHEN EDGAR • MIKE BENSON • KENNETH COOK • NICK MOORE • BILL LYNCH • JOHN HELTON • HENRY PATRAM • ROBIN ARTHURS • CHRISTINE DYER • PEGGY AMATT • JOY KOSTEN • JAY BYER • PATRICIA CATTANEO • RAY EVANS • RT HALL • JERRY GAINER • CAROLLE WOOLGAR • MAXINE GRASLEY • LAWERENCE SCHWEITZ • JAN CZEPURYK • CLARENCE GLESSING • WILLARD SOLTYS • LILY KOREN • MARTHA TIMM • GINA SEIBERT • THOMAS ELBEL • DONNA MCWILLIAMS • LORI BARKLEY • MELANIE REILLY • GABRIELLA KUTFEJ •

Chick smiled and replied, "It says DO O ITA SHI MA SHI TE, which means "you're welcome" or "think nothing of it." It was not the message we had intended to convey.

LAOOC, the organizing committee for the XXIIIrd Olympic Games, had protected itself against failure by flooding the project with volunteer workers in the last few months before the Games. Prudent early fiscal management had allowed Ueberroth to be in a position to fix any last-minute problems with unlimited buying power. Our OCO'88 team was impressed with the crisp management style, which was needed to overcome some weak planning in the two years leading up to the games. We decided on the spot to adopt a system of delegating authority at each sports venue to a qualified business "venue chairman" rather than allowing the venues to be managed by the "sports chairmen." The choice of the venue-management system, also used at the Edmonton Universiade Games, would create some controversy for OCO'88 in years ahead.

We borrowed several ideas from L.A.'s accreditation and ticketing but were not impressed with the VIP transportation system. The system of assigning one car and one driver to each IOC member seemed an inefficient way of using the fleet. It was hard on the volunteer drivers, some of whom rarely left the parking garage, and it was complex enough that it didn't work well for the VIPs either. We vowed to change the IOC transportation system in Calgary—a decision that led to confrontation with President Samaranch.

We were inspired by parts of the Los Angeles arts festival and ceremonies, and determined to go for maximum goose bumps in Calgary. I was impressed with the song performed by people from dozens of countries at the L.A. opening ceremonies:

> Reach out and touch somebody's hand
> Make this world a better place if you can.

People in the Olympic Stadium joined hands and swayed back and forth in time to the music. It was a perfect evocation of the Olympic spirit. Los Angeles and Sarajevo had been superb Olympic hosts, and both had given Calgary the gift of good examples.

CHAPTER ELEVEN

More Fun and Games

Trust in Allah, but always tie your camel.
ANONYMOUS

JEAN LAPIERRE WAS APPOINTED by Prime Minister John Turner in mid-1984 to succeed Jacques Olivier as sports minister. I met Jean for the first time at the home of Jim Nutt, the Canadian Consul General in Los Angeles. Lapierre invited me for a stroll around the block, during which he described how he had been briefed about the Olympics. As he spoke, my spirits sank. It sounded like the same old broken record of attitudes we'd heard from previous new ministers.

Gerald Berger had replaced Anita Slazak, and even though we had been building up a certain amount of trust in him, Lapierre's comments now led me to fear that we might really have slipped backwards. It seemed all the ground we had gained with Jacques Olivier might have been lost.

My fears were soon dispelled, however, when Lapierre concluded by saying, "What I've been told is clearly a bunch of bureaucratic bullshit, and I'm going to put a stop to it. We intend to deliver the goods. I don't believe you should have to use your valuable time dealing this way with the federal government. We will honor the contract we signed. From now on you can work directly with me and bypass the bureaucracy altogether."

When John Turner's Liberal government was defeated only two months later, I was sorry to see Lapierre go. He had been a straight shooter who had done what he could for us. He had been working hard to save the sports pool, a project that by then had proven poorly conceived and unworkable. By the time the project was cancelled, the federal government had lost more than $30 million. In his last weeks in office, as the sports pool's demise became imminent, Lapierre had already been grappling with the question of how the government would fund the Olympics without resorting to tax revenue.

I visited Lapierre after the defeat of the government and asked him what he would have done with the sports pool. He said his administration had already written legislation taxing all lottery revenues at the rate of three per cent, which would have raised approximately $60 million per year. If the feds couldn't control the lottery system, they did have the power to tax it.

With the September 1984 election of a Conservative government came an increase in influence from strongly Conservative Western Canada. Soon after the Tory election, I called up Peter Bawden about the appointment of a new sports minister. Bawden was a former MP who was the senior Conservative party adviser on appointments in Alberta for the federal government. "Peter," I said, "I have lots of experience in dealing with sports ministers and I know the qualities that will be important to Calgary as we approach the Olympics. I'd like to see Otto Jelinek get the job."

Otto Mobile

I had met Otto Jelinek, the MP from Oakville and a former world-champion figure skater, several times. I got to know him best at Sarajevo, where he was part of the CTV color commentary crew for figure skating. A native of Czechoslovakia, he and his sister Maria had won the world pairs figure-skating championship as Canadians in 1968. I appreciated his strong commitment to free enterprise and found his forthright personality refreshing. I don't know whether my representations made a difference, but within a week Otto Jelinek was our new sports minister—the eighth we had dealt with in seven years!

Otto greeted me as an old friend, so we got off to a good start. Gerry Berger briefed Otto quickly and accurately and was helpful in bringing him up to speed. Otto knew about our previous problems with the sports bureaucracy, and for the first half-dozen times we met he was careful to ask my opinion of Gerry Berger. He wanted to make sure history wasn't repeated. We said we had no reason to distrust Berger.

Overall, Otto Jelinek was a superb sports minister. He visited Calgary frequently and used his enthusiasm and personality to promote the Olympic Games. There were, however, two incidents that caused me concern. The first took place while I was out of the country on business for 10 days in February 1985. After about a week I called the office to see how things were. Val Wheeler, my executive secretary, told me Berger was polling the board of OCO'88 to acquire support for a request from the minister for a change in the federal funding formula.

"Val," I said, alarmed and annoyed, "someone's playing games with us. Gerry Berger doesn't have authority to poll the board."

I called Bill Warren to find that Berger was trying to change our agreement so a federal payment of $30 million now due OCO'88 could be deferred until the year of the Games, three years away. Since it was clear our revenue situation was now robust, the federal government felt it could get away with deferring payment until after the Games. The funding schedules were so complicated that when Berger polled the board members some agreed, probably not understanding the full financial impact of Jelinek's proposal. If we agreed to the changes it would cost OCO'88 about $9 million in lost interest.

I called Gerry Berger, saying, "What are you trying to do? This is ridiculous!"

"I've received instructions from the minister," he said. "I've been told that's the way we're going to handle the funding."

"What then does our written agreement mean?" I asked. "We are entitled to receive our federal money now."

Otto Jelinek had been motivated to attempt this manœuvre by the funding needs of the federal government's Best-Ever Program. Ray Perrault had been the one to introduce the idea for this program, which was aimed at preparing Canadian athletes for the Games. Perrault had committed the government to paying $25 million to help produce the best-ever Canadian Olympic team to go along with our goal of the best-ever Olympics. Unfortunately, Perrault had never identified how he was going to fund the program, and now, to help do so, Otto apparently hoped to plunder $9 million from OCO'88.

Bill Warren and I met Otto Jelinek in a hotel room in Ottawa to resolve the issue. Jelinek said, "Look, Frank, you are absolutely right. We owe you the money and we may have to pay you the money, but for God's sake, help us. I don't have any other way of funding this program. We need this money for the Best-Ever Program."

I looked at Bill Warren for a sign of support. It was barely visible. "Okay," I said, "we'll do it as a gesture of good faith." It was our second such gesture. We had already ceded $20 million to Gerry Regan when we agreed the money would be indexed to 1982, and this was another $9 million to Otto Jelinek. It was a curious reversal of roles. OCO'88 was increasingly being called upon to give funding to its partners. I recalled how we had contributed to the Olympic Saddledome overrun and how we had agreed to pay for the media village originally promised by the City of Calgary. It was, in fact, an ominous sign for the future.

Everyone Out of the Pool

One of the first acts of Otto Jelinek was to cancel the sports pool created by Gerry Regan. Jelinek then had the difficult task of raising money from provincial lotteries to replace the original Lotto Canada funds and the failed sports pool. I told him about Lapierre's idea for a three-per-cent lottery tax, but

Otto rejected the plan, preferring to convince the provinces, through negotiation, to allow him to raise one-time funding for the Olympics.

Otto Jelinek was a convincing sports promoter who needed $100 million in provincial lottery aid. Somehow he pulled it off and got all the provinces to help fund the Calgary Games. He raised an additional $40 million through the sale of Olympic coins and stamps, and some more through the sale of a new Maple Leaf gold coin with a face value of $100 and a retail price of twice that. Altogether, Otto was able to come up with enough money from non-tax sources to cover our full $200 million.

We continued to have a good relationship with Otto. On one of his frequent trips to Calgary he decided to attempt the terrifying slide down the Olympic luge track. When asked to describe the experience, he said it was "the ultimate laxative."

He and his wife, Leata, came to our home for dinner one night in 1986. After dinner Jeanette cornered Otto, and with characteristic enthusiasm presented to him the fabulous education curriculum program she had been responsible for organizing as head of OCO'88's education committee. OCO'88 made kits available to every school in Alberta. Otto loved the program, and was later instrumental in making it possible for the kits to be distributed throughout the country so that all Canadian children would have the benefit of understanding the Olympics better.

At the same dinner we also had a long discussion about our relations with the media and the problems we had been having with their penchant for creating negative stories. We were surprised, though, when Otto erupted the next day. At the unveiling of a new sculpture for the university speed-skating oval, Otto tore strips off the media for misrepresenting the facts.

"You guys," he said, "why don't you tell the truth? These are the greatest Games that are ever going to be held. These are great people here and you keep writing all this garbage about them. Why don't you shape up and get on side?"

It was an astounding tirade, but Otto was on a roll. "There are only normal business problems here in Calgary," he continued. "Nothing that you should be reporting the way you are. You are doing yourselves and the country a great disservice." Gerry Berger was in the audience and I could see him shift into panic mode. His face went absolutely white and I could see that he was wishing his minister would not say another word. Berger later accused me of putting Otto up to it, and added, only half-jokingly, that he would advise the minister not to come to my house for dinner ever again.

The Torch Legacy

As part of the contract for Petro-Canada's sponsorship of the Olympic Torch Relay, OCO'88 encouraged the sale of mementos, with proceeds being used for a sports-related project. Petro-Canada had estimated it could raise $2.5 million for amateur sport through the sale of Olympic glasses at its gas stations. The creation of this fund resulted in our second confrontation with Otto Jelinek. Several months later Jelinek came to me and said, "Frank, I view our association with Petro-Canada as four pillars. There's the federal government, the Canadian Olympic Association, Petro-Canada, and OCO'88. We already have $2.5 million and if we had another $2.5 million, we could do something really special. I am asking you to match the $2.5 million we have on hand to create a $5-million fund."

"Rather than four pillars, I see it a little differently," I said. "I see it like a milking stool that has three legs. There is the Canadian Olympic Association, there is Petro-Canada, and there is OCO'88. The federal government is not part of this deal. This money is not federal money, it is Torch Relay trust money created for OCO'88 by Petro-Canada. What you are asking us to do is match our own money. Our board of directors would find the idea unacceptable."

"Frank, I can't imagine you being so stingy. With all the money you have, it would be no problem for you to match this fund," he replied.

"Otto," I said, "OCO'88 made the deal with Petro-Canada to create this fund for amateur sport. We will not match our own funds. And I don't think the feds should use tax dollars, either. That's precisely why we worked so hard to create legacy funds. The COA and Petro-Canada should work out a deal to provide sport scholarships. Let private enterprise do it."

The creation of a $5-million Olympic Torch Relay Legacy Fund was announced by Otto Jelinek in Ottawa in December 1987. The funds were generated entirely by the people of Canada, who bought Olympic-legacy glassware from Petro-Canada stations. Today the Canadian Olympic Association continues to administer the money, and distributes it to promising young athletes who need financial help to keep training and competing.

After the Games, at least $4 million more was dedicated by OCO'88 to another endowment fund, to underwrite the hiring of coaches in winter sports. That was done in consultation with our ninth sport minister, Jean Charest.

Favored-Nations Agreement

Meanwhile, Bill Wardle and Dick Pound kept chipping away at increasing our international television rights revenues for the Games. We soon learned about the enormous gap between American commercial television and European television, which had far less commercial content in the mid-1980s than it does today.

President Samaranch and Marc Hodler took a personal interest in explaining to the Calgary organizers that, for a number of reasons, we could not expect substantial cash payments for European TV rights. The major broadcasters in Western Europe operated independently but worked together under a monopolistic umbrella arrangement called the European Broadcasting Union (EBU). Olympic organizers have traditionally bargained with the EBU rather than with individual TV networks in each country. European TV broadcasting is more state-owned and operates more as a public service than does Canadian or American TV. The huge TV rights payments from ABC and other U.S. networks are only possible because of the mature commercial markets they serve.

Nevertheless, we had counted on at least $10 million U.S. from EBU for the Calgary TV rights. We were shocked when

EBU offered only $5.9 million U.S.—even though Samaranch and Hodler had personally intervened to encourage EBU to pay a fair price. The apparent inequity in payments received from ABC ($309 million U.S.) and EBU ($5.9 million U.S.) left us disappointed. Worse, we were concerned that an attempt to correct the unfair situation by American legislators might jeopardize our solid financial foundation and future revenues for Olympic sport. The imposition a year later of a 10-per-cent telecommunications withholding tax by the United States government justified our concerns, although our agreement with ABC was grandfathered out of reach of the new tax.

Samaranch was openly disappointed with my reluctance to accept the price and terms of the EBU agreement that he and Marc Hodler had personally negotiated. He made sure he had the support of Mayor Klein before he flew to Calgary on a mission to get me to back off my position. Dick Pound had warned me that "the boss usually gets what he wants" and that I risked having my private parts bronzed and made into bookends if I protested too much. We found an acceptable compromise when I agreed to accept the price if Samaranch would allow OCO'88 to renegotiate the terms of the EBU deal. It was the best we could have hoped for under the circumstances.

In future, now that commercial television has arrived in Western Europe, this group of favored nations will have to carry a bigger part of the cost of major media sporting events such as the Olympics.

Chapter Twelve

A Solid Foundation

When prosperity comes, do not use all of it.
Confucius

THE YEARS 1985 AND 1986 were spent building up the OCO'88 organization, setting up thousands of milestones in detailed plans, and marketing the Games to sponsors, suppliers, and licensees. The final success of the Games was to a large extent the result of work done during those years.

We were always amazed by the public opinion surveys showing massive support for the Olympic project—even though local politicians constantly railed against OCO'88 and the media played follow-the-leader with rumors that leaked regularly from City Hall. The Olympic Games are an unrivaled international celebration of human achievement. To Olympic organizers, however, the Games represent a swarm of parochial problems. The trick in organizing the Games, as elsewhere in life, is learning to reach beyond the day-to-day minutiæ toward the promise of the Olympics themselves. Now that the Games are over and the fear of failure is no longer there, it is easier to put the facts in perspective.

VAN VLIET • SYLVIE HISLER • MARK PERRIN • ALLAN BELZBERG • PAUL HATFIELD • JIM COMFORT • GILLIAN BRISCOE • MATTHEW MOREAU • DON NELSON • JANE SIU • BARB ZACH • JIM SUCHLA • DEBORAH BOLAM • AL STORDY • HYNEK STUPKA • GEORGE PETROPOULOS • KARL KUHNLEIN • IRIS ANSELL • DENNIS PASCHKE • VICKI BOAN • DAWN RYAN • CATHIE MAIN-OSTER • PAMELA KURYLUK • BRYAN MURRAY • CRIS KNEBEL • LOIS GLUCK • DENNIS CARTER • FRED GUY • CATHY SAWCHENKO • SHIRLEE GOULD • SUSAN OSLER • JILL PEDERSEN • BILL MCTAGGART • PADDY CAMPBELL • GRANT KITZUL • BRENT ALLARDYCE • ELAINE ZAMERUK • WENDY NUMRICH • ROBERT SINGLE • JERRY

Indecent Exposure

When Ralph Klein, Dick Pound, and I signed the Olympic contract in Baden-Baden in 1981, the City of Calgary (and, in effect, its taxpayers) became liable, at least theoretically, for paying the total cost of the Games. It is a requirement of the Olympic Charter that the host city assume all liability. From the beginning, however, we set our sights on reducing that liability. We succeeded: when all was said and done, city taxpayers shouldered a scant six per cent of the cost of the Games.

In order to achieve the low exposure to financial risk that OCO'88 sought for Calgarians, it was necessary to convince the federal and provincial governments on the one hand and private enterprise on the other to share in the cost of the project. It was precisely this that had caused me to reject Klein's demands that the city be given voting control of the organizing committee. If the city were running the project, then it would be hard to convince private enterprise or the other levels of government to get involved in a big way.

In order to protect itself against financial failure, OCO'88 established strong controls against spending money we didn't have, a practice unfamiliar to most governments. While the City of Calgary was running up a huge deficit for its own capital projects, we were limiting spending to match money we could raise. As our marketing program began to produce record-breaking revenues, we gradually loosened our visegrip on spending, but we always protected our position with large cash reserves and prudent contract management. In short, we hedged our bets. We focused our attention, above all, on the enormous ABC television rights contract. The board of directors approved a proposal from our volunteer insurance committee to spend $4 million to insure about $120 million of our ABC contract—if ABC revenues had failed to materialize it would have exposed our Achilles heel. We also earned nearly $15 million by anticipating trends in the rate of exchange between U.S. and Canadian currency.

We didn't want taxpayers to have to guarantee our financial performance and we didn't want politicians to be accountable for our actions. So we developed a contract with the City of Calgary that specifically excluded the city from having to make good on any debts or obligations of the organizing committee.

If city councillors ever understood the massive safeguards built into our Olympic funding formula, they certainly didn't bother to share their understanding with the people of Calgary. Right up until the day the Games started, the greatest concern of the people remained the prospect of the city losing its shirt in an Olympic financial orgy. The ghost of Montreal was real for many Calgarians, but city council chose to stay a safe distance from the action until it became evident the complex steps we were taking to safeguard our finances were going to succeed.

The Old Boys' Club

Ralph Klein delighted in calling OCO'88—and on one occasion the IOC—"the old boys' club." It seemed like a bad joke, coming from our own mayor, because by this time we had become a highly motivated group of thousands of volunteers from all parts of Calgary. We had met all promises and exceeded all major goals, so when the mayor occasionally portrayed OCO'88 as an élite private club it was never taken too seriously. But Ralph continued to press for more city council representation and for open board meetings, even though only half the events were now to be held in Calgary itself and the risk of financial exposure had been reduced to very low levels. He was amply supported by the editorial stance of the *Calgary Herald*.

"Ralph," I said, "If you try to take more control over the Games, the other governments will never stand for it, private-enterprise sponsors may back off, and we'll be left with a financial mess. I'm not sure many of the best people will volunteer to work for government-run Games."

Contrary to their public positions, both Ralph Klein and the ombudsman of the *Calgary Herald* admitted to me privately that they were not concerned about our rejection of the notion of open board meetings. Their public protestations to the contrary were, in my opinion, little more than posturing.

Klein and the media believed that OCO'88 needed an official opposition. That idea was okay in principle, but in practice it created friction between City Hall and OCO'88 in the early years and sapped public support for our organization. Maintaining public confidence ended up costing us more management time and much more money than we had foreseen.

A Leak of Faith

As a matter of policy, OCO'88 did not publicly discuss personnel matters, or financial contracts that had not yet been awarded. To do otherwise would have been to breach the privacy of our people and jeopardize impending deals. To safeguard confidentiality, we asked our board members not to discuss such matters with reporters, nor to distribute board-meeting documents to them. In spite of this, reporters somehow usually got hold of the most newsworthy information. They would then be in a position to speculate on what the board of directors would do, prior to our meetings.

This put us in a dilemma in media interviews: we were not prepared to lie, and we could not breach confidentiality. Instead, we learned to mumble. We answered the tough questions with long, complicated sentences that were generally unusable in print or on TV.

At the same time, we tried to track down the source of the leaks. Within our organization it was widely believed that the mayor's office was responsible. In an effort to unmask the culprit, we marked each board member's documents with a personal copy number, which could be used to identify the pages with the board member who had received them.

If we were confronted by reporters on any confidential issue, we would usually ask them to demonstrate that they had real information and were not just talking through their hats. Occasionally reporters would let us glance at copies of documents to verify their own credibility. Once in a while, copies of OCO'88 documents even appeared on TV newscasts. But the copies that showed up in reporters' hands didn't have copy numbers on them.

After the Games, Mayor Klein often bragged publicly about the fruitless efforts of OCO'88 to mark the documents in order to nab the party responsible for leaks. He confirmed that his office had simply whited out the copy number on pages given to the media, so that the document could not be traced back to him. What he didn't know was that we had been one step ahead in this little game. Anticipating that the mayor's office would white out the copy numbers, we included special hairline coded marks on his copies of the most sensitive documents. The marks looked like little glitches in the photocopying—we called them Xerox marks—but they allowed us to identify the source of leaked documents.

Thus, when a reporter showed me a copy of a confidential document, even when the copy number had been blanked out, I could still tell at a glance if it had come from the mayor's office.

The game of leak detection worked, but we were a bit like a dog chasing a bus—what were we going to do about it once we caught it? Nevertheless the exercise was good for a few chuckles.

In order to temper the mayor's opposition to our Olympic management process, we made it a practice to brief him about upcoming decisions. On one such occasion OCO'88 had decided to hire a vice-president of communications to help our sagging public image, and had advertised for the new position. We had a rich response, including an indication of interest from a recently appointed member of our board, Jerry Joynt. On the spur of the moment, I pulled a prank on Klein—one that bore interesting fruit.

It hinged on the name John Francis, which had cropped up sometime before in connection with a controversy surrounding Bill Pratt. In the early years of his presidency Pratt had been criticized for awarding a small contract to the public relations firm of Francis, Williams & Johnson. The problem was that Bill had previously owned almost one per cent of FWJ and had briefly served as a director. Although Pratt had held no interest in FWJ for several years, the media linked them together and headlines about Pratt and his "old friend" John Francis proliferated.

A factor that likely contributed to the extra media scrutiny of FWJ contracts was that John Francis had supported Ross Alger and designed Alger's unsuccessful mayoralty campaign against Ralph Klein. Francis was *persona non grata* with Mayor Klein, and Klein had the media's ear.

On the day I called on Klein we had just completed our evaluation of all candidates for the new post of vice-president of communications. Our first choice was Jerry Joynt, who had served as a volunteer in a similar role with the Western Canada Games in Calgary, but we had one other candidate on the short list. I decided to discuss the nominees with Ralph Klein a few days before our board meeting.

On my way down to the mayor's office, a diabolical idea popped into my head. Suppose I added the name of John Francis to the list of candidates— even though he had neither applied for nor ever been considered for the job! In the mayor's office I got the expected reaction: "You can't be serious!"

"Why not?" I asked innocently. "John Francis is superbly qualified."

"I don't mind either of the other two candidates," countered the mayor, "but I won't be able to support the nomination of John Francis."

That same night, CFCN-TV carried a headline news story saying it had learned Calgary public relations specialist John Francis was to be appointed OCO'88's new vice-president of communications at Friday's board meeting.

We received dozens of calls from the media requesting confirmation of the John Francis appointment. Of course, we denied that his name was being presented to the board and asked them to check their sources of information more carefully in the future.

The board approved the appointment of Jerry Joynt from a list of two. Despite occasional time out to have fun and to play games, we were beginning to build a solid foundation capable of sustaining us in the difficult times ahead.

Management Style

While Bill Warren and I were busy building partnership deals with the three levels of government, Bill Pratt was busy picking people who could perform for us.

Some local politicians and representatives of the media were making a big noise even though we were changing weak people for strong people in senior positions. I regularly chatted with Bill Pratt about the old bromide: It's not the people you fire who will hurt you, it's the ones you don't fire. "In the final analysis," I said, "people will blame only OCO'88 if the Games are not perfect. The politicians will be nowhere to be seen if there are problems. Do what has to be done to get the best people because the Games are like mumps, we only get them once." We found it strange that we had to spend so much time explaining to the media that not every employee we hired was suitable for the responsibilities we assigned.

Montreal and Lake Placid had strongly government-controlled Games where the management style was oriented toward political patronage and vote-getting—they were a lesson in how to influence friends and win people. Los Angeles and Calgary had Games controlled by business people using a survival-of-the-fittest management style. In our case, that style was adopted during the early bid years. Olympic organizers must resist pressure to take populist actions that might have immediate popular appeal but would lack long-term effectiveness. The best Games organizers will always be more concerned about the next generation than they are about the next election.

We were aware that in difficult times we might need to seek the support of a strong board of directors to preserve our goals, so we held a campaign to attract new board members. Over 300 applications were received in response to our Canada-wide advertisement. The selection process was designed to find people with a love for sport, dedicated to the volunteer concept, and committed to running the Games like a business. We wanted people who shared our dream for staging the best-ever Games while creating the maximum legacy for the community. We rejected political opportunists and members of pressure groups.

It was evident to our 12-man board there was a deficiency of women in sports administration. This is not because women do not participate in sports, but because they do not often continue on to become sports administrators. Several outstanding women had submitted their names, however, and we were delighted to accept them as members. We also chose representatives from Montreal and Edmonton, whose Games had inspired us in the beginning. We also placed among our board members businessmen, former athletes, and people who represented the Chamber of Commerce, the Calgary Exhibition and Stampede, the University of Calgary, and the Town of Canmore. The City of Calgary had four representatives, including the mayor, and there were three representatives each from the Province of Alberta and the Government of Canada.

The board of directors of OCO'88 took its mandate as a steward of resources seriously. The board was generous in its support of projects that would clearly benefit sport or the community, and it had the courage to say no whenever a superfluous proposal was received.

Members of the board, working as liaison officers within all the major committees, helped the organization keep a focus, watch over deadlines, and maintain the attitude that we should be the best ever in everything we did.

After the ABC and government contracts were signed, it would have been easy to rest on our laurels. But with the encouragement of the board, we kept management running hard to achieve even greater results.

In 1985 and 1986 good news arrived regularly at OCO'88, and we found little to be concerned about. Coca-Cola signed a record sponsorship agreement with us, contracts with governments were signed and sealed, the sports venues were all approved and put under construction. Sporadic Chicken Little media reports to the contrary, the sky was not falling and we knew it wasn't. Our biggest regret was that the public was not yet able to enjoy the same quiet sense of confidence in how things were going that we behind the scenes were beginning to experience.

CHAPTER THIRTEEN

Jiminy Tickets

When one part suffers every part suffers with it.
1 CORINTHIANS 12:26

I FIRST MET JIM MCGREGOR in the hallway of the Olympic office in 1986. He approached me with a beaming smile and a firm handshake. I had heard about Jim's record as the ticket manager for both the Commonwealth Games and the Universiade Games in Edmonton. He enjoyed a reputation as the most experienced Games ticketing man in Canada.

Bill Wardle hired McGregor as the manager of ticketing to develop the plan, priorities, and objectives for our ticketing system. We began calling him Jiminy Tickets. Among McGregor's early recommendations were low ticket prices, widespread public distribution, and first-come first-served sales. The board had no difficulty accepting these objectives. We expected to be able to match the high interest in the Winter Games with the largest spectator seating capacities in their history. We wanted the people of Calgary and all Canadians, as well as visitors from dozens of other countries, to have easy access to the record number of tickets that would be available.

The lower-than-usual Olympic ticket-pricing policy would make the Games more accessible to average-income families and help us reach our optimistic sales forecasts of about 1.6 million tickets for sporting events and another 150,000 for arts festival events. Nearly two million tickets would be available in total.

McGregor's plan was simple: application forms would be made available the day before tickets went on sale, and tickets would be issued on the basis of the date and time of the postmark on the envelope in which the applications were received. The applications with the earliest postmarks would be filled first.

On the morning of September 30th, 1986, newspapers across the country contained an application form. People could also pick up forms in branches of the Royal Bank across Canada. Special mailboxes in Calgary were established in front of City Hall and in other key places. Everything seemed ready.

Cross-Threaded

The first problem with McGregor's plan was discovered just a few days before the launch when it was brought to our attention by the *Calgary Herald* that Canada Post does not stamp mail with a time, only a date. McGregor had failed to check that, as well as other important details.

Another problem surfaced in the days before September 30th. I appeared as a regular guest on a CHQR radio talk show with host Dave Rutherford, and on one occasion I brought Jim McGregor with me to help answer questions about the forthcoming ticket launch. I thought it would be a good chance to promote ticket sales and to explain how our ticketing system worked.

During the course of the show, a caller asked Jim what percentage of tickets would be reserved for the Olympic family, sponsors, and television rights holders. McGregor's quick response was, "We're not really sure, but somewhere around 10 per cent should be enough."

I was surprised at his answer. I knew OCO'88 had substantial contractual obligations to our sponsors and the media, obligations that could far exceed the 10 per cent McGregor had quoted. On a talk show 10 days earlier on CBC I had been asked the same question, but I had given a different answer. I had said it would be about 10 per cent for the Olympic family and another 10 per cent for media and sponsors, making a total of 20 per cent. At that time we were unsure about what sort of ticket reserves were needed to meet our contractual obligations because we had not yet received responses from foreign countries or from our sponsors.

When McGregor answered 10 per cent I quickly added, "Of course, that's only for the Olympic family, and in addition to that we will need about another 10 per cent for sponsors and the media." As McGregor and I walked back to the office, I asked what the right number would be and why he had used such a low estimate. He indicated that perhaps my number would be closer to the final figure, but since he wasn't sure he hadn't wanted to raise concerns by using a number as high as 20 per cent. I cautioned him that frankness with the public was essential, and asked him to check the figures more precisely and let me know at the earliest moment.

I soon learned that while I had been using the 20 per cent estimate McGregor had been using the 10 per cent figure extensively in public without my knowledge. Getting cross-threaded on some issues normally doesn't matter much, but this was an issue that affected most of our public and it damp-ened years of effort to build support and confidence. It also planted the seeds of concern about McGregor in my mind. He had known all along that 10 per cent was too low a figure. His willingness to use a number publicly that he knew was wrong showed a casual attitude toward the truth.

The Gold Rush

On the first night of ticket sales I left work about 7:30 p.m. to meet my family at the Olympic Saddledome for a hockey game. As I drove up the driveway from the underground park-ing garage at City Hall I found a traffic jam. My first thought was, "This is incredible, so many people trying to get to the hockey game!" A second later I realized these people were not going to the game; they were driving around the block so friends or spouses could jump out of the car to deposit ticket applications at the special Olympic ticket mail box in front of City Hall.

I knew at that moment we had a problem. We had a gold rush on our hands.

Jim McGregor had confidently predicted that on the first day we should expect about 17,000 applications representing as many as 200,000 ticket requests, out of the total of 1.8 million sports tickets. In other words, 10 to 15 per cent of tickets would be sold through first-day orders. It seemed strange to me, though, that people would be driving their cars four-deep around City Hall in order to deposit application forms if a total of only 17,000 orders were to come in Canada-wide.

Public interest in Olympic tickets had been grossly underestimated. On that first day alone the OCO'88 ticketing department received a staggering 53,000 applications, most of which were for prime events such as hockey finals, figure skating, and the opening and closing ceremonies.

The distribution of tickets for Olympic events is made complex by virtue of the fact that organizers have to operate within strict rules established by the Olympic Charter. Access to the Games must be provided to everyone who by the provisions of the charter has a right or a need to be there. That includes not only the IOC, athletes, coaches, and officials, but also National Olympic Committees, International Sports Federations, and certain citizens of participating countries. Tickets must also be provided for other participants, including three levels of government, all sponsors, television rights holders, and about 4,500 members of the media, who carry the Games to the rest of the world. Added together, this amounts to a substantial list of people.

As far as I know, Calgary's Games were the first where citizens were so enthusiastic that virtually all high-profile events could have been sold out locally many times over. It is easy to agree that international visitors must have their place in the Games, but for local people who do not receive any tickets to priority events, it was hard to understand how the system was fair.

Many of our premium events had 10 ticket applications for every seat available, so 90 per cent of applicants were left unsatisfied.

Media and the public began to complain that too many tickets were going to the Olympic family and not enough to them. It was frustrating that when accusing OCO'88 of misleading the public the media clung to McGregor's 10 per cent number, rather than my estimate of 20 per cent, which was accurate. Although I was the chairman and chief spokesman for OCO'88, my number was seldom quoted.

The media did much to keep negative pressure on OCO'88, rather than trying to clear up a messy situation by telling the story fairly. Senior Olympic reporters understood our predicament and were in a position to tell the truth. The media had found a weakness in our plan and, true to form, they decided to shake the trees to see how many big apples would fall out. At one point the *Calgary Herald* even accused members of City Council of receiving free Olympic tickets. The aldermen (who were wrongly accused) complained to the Alberta Press Council, which censured the *Herald* for its story. But with stoic editorials the *Herald* stood fast, refusing to admit it was in the wrong.

It is not the job of the media to promote the Games or sell tickets, but citizens have a right to expect balanced coverage of major controversies involving public opinion and the reputation of the community. On this occasion the public didn't get what it deserved.

Black Friday

McGregor had not finished doing damage. On Friday, October 3rd, 1986 at 5:30 p.m., Bill Pratt walked into my office with a stone-cold expression on his face. "Frank," he said as he closed the door tightly behind him, "we've got a problem. Our security people tell me there are some irregularities in the ticketing department." My heart sank.

"From what we understand," Bill said, "Jim McGregor has established a private mailbox to receive ticket application forms from the United States. In addition to that, the names of our U.S. customers have disappeared from the computer list. There are other problems too."

Never mind the other problems for a second, I thought. First things first. "What action has been taken so far?" I asked.

Bill said he had called in Harley Johnson, OCO'88's manager of security and a high-ranking officer with the Calgary Police Service. Johnson had frozen all files and records and was taking control of Jim McGregor's private mailbox. He was also in the process of giving McGregor a polygraph test so we could quickly determine what to do next.

"Have you called the police?" I asked.

"Not yet. I'm leaving it in Harley's hands for now."

"I don't think that's enough," I said. "I think we should call in our auditors to be sure we have control of the situation internally. If McGregor is involved, there may be others. We don't know to what extent a conspiracy might exist in our ticketing department."

Bill agreed, so I got on the phone and called Fred Abbott, the leading partner from Coopers and Lybrand, our auditors. I found Fred at home preparing to go to a football game. "Fred," I said, "I don't want to discuss this on the phone. I can only tell you I need to talk to you urgently. Can you get down here right away?"

"Done," he said, and hung up. By the time Abbott arrived I had been further briefed. We asked Fred to bring in a team of special auditors to review and take control of all files and records in the ticketing department, and to be sure not a single dollar or ticket was misappropriated. So far none had been. We also asked Fred to provide a report on the state of our controls and procedures in the department.

When I was sure I had done what I could for the moment, I left the office, leaving instructions that I was to be contacted as soon as the results of the polygraph test were in. Throughout the evening I fidgeted, but further word didn't come until the next morning, when Harley Johnson called me at home. He reported that during the night the polygraph test had been run on three occasions, and each time the results had been inconclusive.

"Harley, don't give me the gears," I said. "What does 'inconclusive' mean?"

"McGregor's mental and physical state were such that we could not get reliable polygraph results from him," Harley replied. "His heartbeat, respiration, and perspiration were so irregular that the test results are ambiguous."

"Does that happen often, or is it in itself a sign that we should be concerned?" I asked.

"At this point we should not assume Jim McGregor has done anything legally wrong, but he is extremely distraught at the damage he has done both to OCO'88 and to himself."

"Have you been in touch with the police?"

Harley answered that the police had contacted him because they had received a phone call from a lawyer in Portland, Oregon, who complained about having to send her ticket application to a numbered Calgary postal box rather than to the organizing committee. The U.S. applicants had been directed to pay the Canadian dollar price in U.S. dollars. The inquiry had resulted in the police looking into a private company called World Tickets Inc., to which cheques from some 8,000 U.S. applicants had been directed. World Tickets Inc., said Harley, was owned by none other than Jim McGregor.

I asked Harley whether the police were likely to do their own investigation, and he said they almost certainly would. Harley agreed to continue his investigation and to share any information we had with the Calgary Police Service.

At 4 p.m. on Monday, October 6th, Calgary Police Chief Ernie Reimer asked to see Bill Pratt and me. When he walked in his expression warned us the news was serious. He advised us the police were on their way to Jim McGregor's house to arrest him on four charges, including fraud.

For the first time we had a real public-relations disaster on our hands. I hadn't thought it possible for more fear and anger to be focused on the Olympics than it had been with the Saddledome story, but I was wrong. This was far worse. The McGregor episode added enormous fuel to the public frustration already created by the high demand for tickets and the poor system for their distribution.

We had lost a lot of credibility and were breathing our own exhaust. Our ticketing and communications departments fought back with a barrage of information. We had made sure full details of the ticket distribution plan were released in late October of 1986 and again in early November. The *Calgary Herald* published a full explanation of the distribution of tickets. Astoundingly, two months later the *Herald* ran several stories stating OCO'88 had never released those ticket facts.

We implemented a series of measures to correct the inequities of our original ticket lottery system. We appealed to sponsors and government partners to reduce their ticket allotments. They co-operated generously. We developed plans to expand the number of seats available for several of the premium events—2,400 extra seats were installed in the Olympic Saddledome for hockey and figure skating, and 10,000 temporary seats were added to McMahon Stadium for opening and closing ceremonies.

The precious extra tickets made available by this recovery program were carefully allocated to a broad group of people who had been on our waiting lists for at least a few premium events. Months later, returns of tickets from foreign countries provided some further relief for Calgarians anxious to attend at least one of their favorite events.

In the end, the Calgary Games had about three times as many tickets sold as any previous Olympic Winter Games. But even with those numbers, we had missed a chance to make many people happy.

Postscript

In May 1991 I saw a familiar headline in an unexpected place—the front page of the *European,* an English-language daily newspaper published and distributed throughout Europe. In big bold letters it read OLYMPIC TICKET FIASCO. The article said:

> An international row is building up over Barcelona's plans for next year's Olympic Games in Spain. Critics claim that tickets for the games will be limited to a privileged few and that accommodation will be exorbitantly expensive. European nations are incensed that

only 6,000 seats out of 60,000 will be available for foreign fans to witness the main Olympic festival—the athletics.

The crux of the problem is the limited seating in Barcelona's main stadium, the Montjuic. Sixty thousand seats are far too few for Olympic competition. Half the stadium seats will be allocated to what is known as Olympic family—International Olympic Committee members, sponsors, and athletes.

We can expect some variation on this theme to show up in newspaper headlines every four years or so.

CHAPTER FOURTEEN

Only Who We Are

What do we have to offer? Only who we are.
1981 CALGARY OLYMPIC BID FILM

W E STARTED THE OLYMPIC PROJECT with no money, no facilities, and no experience in organizing major sporting events. So we offered what we had: ourselves—the people of the Calgary region. Who we were turned out to be our greatest asset. The Calgary Olympic Winter Games will be mainly remembered not for their surplus or their legacy of fine sports facilities, but for their friendly, competent people. Ninety-seven per cent of our workers were volunteers who received no money for their efforts.

Although the whole Olympic movement finds its best people through volunteer service, top IOC members were amazed by the smoothly co-ordinated performance of our volunteers. They were even more surprised to find doctors, lawyers, mothers, and teachers taking time off to drive IOC officials to their venues. "Volunteers" in some parts of the world are simply those who agree to do a job rather than being told to do it. For example, think of the distinction in the army between a

HENRY VAN AKEN • LIGAYA ALLMER • CATHY CHAN • PHYLLIS BATCHELOR • RAY YOUNG • ORREE DEMCO • RENE EDWARDS • JIM LAUTNER • DEAN KIT-TLESON • JONI MALLABONE • TERRY DEGERNESS • DAVID PAULSON • GARRY KOLODYCHUK • LYNN MOEN • ALISON DOUGLAS • ANNA WALKER • RICHARD REITBAUER • BARBARA TARDIFF • KAREN BODARD • DIANA MCKELLAR • BOB MCKENDRICK • ROSE NIELSEN • RAYMOND GORAL • RICK POLO • AL SCHABER • BRUCE LAWRENCE • CAROLINE RODMAN • MAUREEN DEFOE • PATRICIA WARREN • MICHELLE EMMOTT • CATHERINE HEDLIN • BOB KEIGHAN • MAX PELT • ALAINE MCGUNIGLE • MALCOLM FAILLE • JOHN CONTI • DAVE SHIMA • SUSAN TABOR • KIM KENDAL-KNITTER • RANDY

volunteer and a draftee. Such "volunteers" get paid the same as everybody else. The concept of working entirely without financial reward is not common in major sporting organizations around the world except at the executive level.

Years from now the example of our Olympic organization will still provide a model for others to emulate. But it was not created without pain.

It would surprise no one to learn that not everyone starting out on the Olympic journey would make it to the finale. As the organization grew from a small, closely knit core group to more than 20,000 workers, responsibilities were assigned and subsequently divided and shared. During its entire life, the OCO'88 organization was in a state of change. Some people fear change and oppose it. But change also creates opportunity for progress.

OCO'88 relied on an excellent core of paid staff working together with the best volunteers from the sport and business community. The idea was simple, but the implementation was tough. All our volunteers were asked to attend extensive training sessions for at least a year before the Games. They were schooled in the history of the Olympic movement, in protocol, and in procedures specific to their particular duties. Every driver and hostess visited each venue several times to familiarize himself or herself with the facilities. Prospective performers were required to have perfect attendance at practices. The expectations upon our volunteers were considerable.

Murphy's Law

In September and October 1986 all was not quiet on the western front. Brian Murphy, the last surviving member of a rebel group of middle managers in the sport and operations area, decided to resign. He left his letter of resignation in an envelope addressed to me marked PERSONAL AND CONFIDENTIAL, and walked out the door.

Murphy had wanted to pay his senior volunteers in the sports department $50,000 a year, a breach of policy Pratt had resisted. Murphy also strongly disagreed with the decision to use a venue-management system like the one that had been used in Los Angeles.

I notified Bill Pratt that I had received Murphy's resignation. The letter was sharply critical of Pratt's personal management style. Bill, immediately recognizing the political implications given that Ralph Klein had so often been critical of his handling of personnel situations, went down to the mayor's office to explain the circumstances surrounding the resignation.

This proved a costly mistake for Pratt. The mayor's office promptly leaked the confidential letter to reporters, who had another heyday, claiming that Murphy had been squeezed out. Stories stated that most of OCO'88's good people had now been lost as a result of conflicts in management style with the bull-headed president, Bill Pratt.

Murphy's resignation was, for OCO'88, a more significant turning point than just the loss of a middle manager would imply. Once again the mayor came charging in on his white horse, swinging his sword in the direction of Bill Pratt's head. Klein had never been a big fan of Pratt's and this was, to him, more evidence of Pratt's unacceptably iron-fisted management style. Klein portrayed Murphy as a hero who had dared to stand up to Pratt and had been forced to resign as a result. Murphy's resignation followed closely upon McGregor's suspension, and, although the two were unrelated, it must have looked like the beginning of a trend. If two dominoes had fallen, perhaps more would follow. OCO'88's public image was in trouble. Maybe, I reflected glumly, that's why they call it Murphy's Law.

On this occasion I was firmly on Pratt's side. But Ralph had buckled on a bigger sword than usual. He didn't restrict his comments to name-calling as he had in the past; this time he demanded a public inquiry into OCO'88's administration and management. This got the media excited. Reporters love a good scrap, and Ralph, as was often the case, was happy to give them one. Public reaction to the mayor's suggestion was quick and enthusiastic. Soon vigilantes would be saddling up and going after Pratt themselves.

I could not allow this public lynching to take place. Where would the mayor find members for a panel of public inquiry? The few people with enough experience to understand the complexities of the Olympic organization were almost all already part of OCO'88. OCO'88's management had achieved more than previous Olympic organizers, but in a public inquiry, that might be lost among the calls for Pratt's blood.

In the past we had learned that when we faced a problem it was often possible to find a solution by reformulating our predicament in positive rather than negative terms. I visited Ralph Klein with a suggestion. I proposed that we select three distinguished members of our board to carry out an internal study of our management capability. In this way we would be sure that knowledgeable people familiar with the Olympic Games would contribute to constructive solutions rather than destructive ones The mayor agreed to my plan. The three members selected were Ian Douglas, a senior partner in an accounting firm; Bob Brawn, a well-known businessman and former president of the Calgary Chamber of Commerce; and Don Sprague, an Edmonton businessman and former member of the board for both the Commonwealth and Universiade games.

The terms of reference of this three-man committee, under the chairmanship of Ian Douglas, were developed and approved by the OCO'88 board of directors, and the Douglas Review Committee, as it came to be known, began interviews with senior managers and board members. Members of the staff were also invited to approach the committee on a confidential basis.

The Douglas committee did a fine job. The members had background knowledge of the Olympic organizing committee and understood the constraints under which the management of OCO'88 had to operate. (The principal constraints were three. First, OCO'88 was accountable to the IOC; second, OCO'88 was under various contractual obligations through the Olympic charter; and third, OCO'88 had imposed upon itself a commitment to finance the Games from non-tax sources.) The committee worked quietly and professionally behind the scenes. After one month Douglas presented his preliminary findings to the board, and requested an additional month to prepare his final report.

An Amazing Feet

Meanwhile Jeanette and I travelled to Mexico for a meeting of the Young Presidents' Organization, where we and about 400 others experienced a rare demonstration of the power of the mind. Anthony Robbins was hired by YPO to teach interested members how to fire walk. The graduating exercise of the seminar was a stroll across 14 feet of red-hot coals in bare feet.

Robbins took our group through an evening of mental preparation involving a discussion of the delicate balance between the mind and body. He expertly provided us with the courage to use our minds to overcome fear and to do something that had been unthinkable two hours earlier.

We watched the workmen take fresh coals from a huge bonfire burning in the hotel courtyard. Then, using the mental preparations he had taught us, Tony Robbins walked across the coals in his bare feet. We had all asked ourselves whether we would do it too—I had decided that it was a chance I could not miss. If others could do it so could I. It was an acid test for my theories about the power of positive thinking.

We had three hours of mental preparation—then the time came to walk on hot coals. Tony Robbins's wife clutched my arm before I stepped into the glowing red-hot bed and yelled, "Are you sure you want to go?"

"Yes," I said. She repeated her enquiry with even greater force and I said, "Yes, I'm sure!"

"Go!" she screamed in my ear.

I stepped confidently onto the coals with head erect, looking forward, not down, saying as we had been taught, "Cool moss! Cool moss! Cool moss!"

Beneath me my bare feet felt only the texture of the searing coals but amazingly there was no pain nor even a feeling of heat. When I reached the other side in five deliberate strides I raised my arms and let out a Calgary "Yahoo!" John Ferguson, a fellow member from Edmonton, had just completed his red-hot journey on another pit next to mine and greeted me with a giant hug. "Frank, we did it!" John and I left that exercise with a profound appreciation for the limitations that fear can place on our performance. Perhaps most of our challenges are mental, not physical.

Employee Number 372

One of the recommendations of the final report of the Douglas Committee was that I become the full-time leader of OCO'88, with particular emphasis on developing volunteers, public relations, communications, and other aspects of the organizing structure. The report made the options clear. I would become the full-time chief executive officer, or we would lose Bill Pratt to the wolves.

At first I was disappointed to think my efforts as volunteer chairman had not been sufficient to maintain the cohesiveness that OCO'88 was now said to require. But I knew pressure from the mayor's office would likely continue against Pratt, to the point that he would be unable to do his job unless I was there to intervene. Mayor Klein and Alderman Hartman had warned me a couple of years earlier that they would do their best to oust Pratt. I had made it clear to Klein that I was determined to keep Pratt. Now, however, the conflict had escalated, and we had neither the time nor the energy to fight City Hall as well as prepare for the Games, just 16 months away.

I recalled how, when we had hired Bill Pratt, we had considered appointing him as general manager of OCO'88 rather than president. The latter title had been meant mainly to establish his international prestige, because de facto he was general manager. Pratt's capabilities as a manager are indeed substantial. While all the board members of OCO'88 were well aware of Bill Pratt's weaknesses, they were also ready to recognize his tremendous strengths as a fully committed disciplinarian for the Olympic organizing committee—and as a man with practical experience in solving problems. I did not want to lose him. He was doing the job we had hired him to do.

I was loathe to give up my volunteer status with OCO'88. I had been enjoying leading our volunteer organization through example. Besides, the timing of the recommendation could hardly have been worse for me because I was in the midst of a major restructuring of one of my businesses. The price of oil had dropped from about $30 to $10 per barrel, and a small high-tech oil recovery company in which I had a 55-per-cent interest was hit hard. Our partner in the company was the Ontario government. The government wouldn't put more money up and wouldn't let anyone else buy in either. Finding a way to get the government out without destroying the business was taking up a big part of my time.

At no time, however, did I give serious consideration to anything that would mean the loss of Bill Pratt from our team. The only thing for me to do was accept the committee's recommendation.

I gave the board a positive response, which included the terms I needed to operate successfully as a full-time employee. I took advantage of the opportunity to consult with senior members of OCO'88. Based on their input, I drew up a plan of action that included a number of radical changes to the organizing committee. First and foremost was the expansion of the executive management team from Bill Pratt and four vice-presidents to a total of 10 people, including three new vice-presidents, a press secretary, and myself.

After dozens of interviews with employees and volunteers, I responded to many of the other constructive criticisms of the Douglas inquiry. Soon I was refreshed and energized by the prospect of changing the management style of OCO'88. It had become tiresome for the public, the politicians, the partners, and myself to have OCO'88's image eroded and defaced so often.

On December 1st, 1986, I became a paid employee of OCO'88 for the first time. I received my identification badge as employee number 372 and wrote the following piece for the Team'88 newspaper, *Spirit of '88*:

> During the past few days as I discussed the recommendations of the Douglas Review Committee with many of you, I was reminded of an expression I have often relied on: The most successful people you will ever meet are those who respond positively to challenges. I was very encouraged, but not surprised, at the strength and the character of the people who make OCO'88 what it is: a strong but flexible organization. We have been able to constructively accept recent public criticism, learn from our mistakes, and make moves to improve

ourselves. Our strength has always been based on [our ability for] positive action. We have a fighting faith in what we are doing. We care about our image.

The board of directors has offered me a full-time position as chairman and chief executive officer of OCO'88.

After discussions with my family and my business partners, members of senior management, many volunteers at all levels, and members of the general public, I have decided to accept the position as your chief executive officer. I have been encouraged to do so by your kind and supportive comments. I am deeply honored to have received your help. I am strongly motivated by our achievements so far and by the promise of an even greater future ahead.

In addition to the appointment of a full-time CEO, we expect to receive the approval of the board of directors to expand the executive management team and to implement a number of the very positive changes recommended by the Douglas Review Committee. We will ask for your help in preparing an action plan for consideration by the board on December 19th, 1986. Considering the Preview'88 events and the Christmas season which is now upon us this is a considerable challenge. I am confident we can also review our people and our job assignments together and evaluate our needs quickly so that every one of us can focus on the road ahead rather than on the hood ornament.

The benefits of change are clear. We are approaching the last and most important year of organizing the Games. We have developed a superb set of facilities and a good financial base. Now we must work to achieve the strong support of the public we serve, a public who will provide the final essential ingredients of human energy and enthusiasm for the XVth Olympic Winter Games.

The greatest Olympic Winter Games have yet to be organized. We have that opportunity. We have that obligation. By responding positively to the challenges ahead we can succeed. The future depends on you.

One of the first things I did was to investigate the Olympic ticket distribution system. In December we were still under considerable attack, although some of the media noise had died down. Word came to me, however, that some employees of OCO'88 might have received special preference from the ticketing department. Bill Pratt and the human resources department had authorized a box to be placed in the OCO'88 office for the convenience of employees who wanted to buy Olympic tickets. That idea in itself was acceptable, but what happened to those applications was not. All of the people who had put their applications in the special box had received their complete orders from the ticketing department. When 90 per cent of applications were being refused overall, this had to be more than coincidence.

I moved quickly to unwind this new ticketing mess. The tickets were taken back and redistributed to the employees on the basis of a fair draw, offering the same odds of success as the original public draw. The original policy by which public tickets had been allocated had to apply to employees as well.

Some members of the staff resented my action, and I heard about it both directly and indirectly. In retrospect most realize, I hope, that the only way OCO'88 could maintain its dignity and the respect of the public was by dealing openly, fairly, and honestly according to the rules we ourselves had established. Nevertheless, stripping tickets away from OCO'88 employees was not the auspicious debut I might have hoped for in my expanded role as volunteer-turned-employee.

This first action served, however, as a signal that the chairman and CEO was not going to confine himself to being a member of the diplomatic corps, but a hands-on, working member of the executive management team.

CHAPTER FIFTEEN

Rocketships Don't Have Rearview Mirrors

If you work hard and smart you only have to work
half of each day. It doesn't matter whether it's the
first 12 hours or the second 12 hours.

HARVEY McKAY
BUSINESSMAN

I N MY FIRST DAYS as full-time executive officer I focused on
strengthening our executive team and improving public
and media relations. Morale was at an all-time low within
Team'88 and on the streets of Calgary. People were wondering
if our dream had become a nightmare.

Our executive management team had labored too long as a
group of five. The EMT spent a full 20 per cent of its time discussing and approving hundreds of detailed items. I decided
to streamline the management process and to bring some of
our bench strength into play. John Russell became vice-president of technology and Bill France was made our new
vice-president of sports. Gary Arthur became press secretary,
reporting directly to me.

DON • JOAN GOODMAN • KARE ASAK • FAY GATHERCOLE • JOHN MILES • KAREN NORTHCOTT • GREGORY MACCULLOCH • PATRICK HENRY • DANA HERGOTT • VIVIENNE RABB • SANDRA FOREST • WAYNE PAGE • JEFF MACLEOD • BRIAN FEA • PAUL KUELKER • BARBARA SCHMALZ • ENID O'NEIL • BARB KARWANDY • DIANE BINDA • LORNE DANIELSON • LANCE GRANT • JEANNE KEITH-FERRIS • RUARI MACKENZIE • HERMAN VAN VLIET • DAVID YIP • BILL VICKERS • GABRIELLE ENNS • MERLE LISKE • KEVIN DALTON • ARDEN BRUMMELL • BONNIE COMSTOCK • CHARLES CLARK • RUDOLF SUDRICH • SANDRA TRUEMAN • GARTH SWEENEY • JOHN LANDEEN • BONNIE BOGHEAN • BRIAN GRONBERG • SANDRA MILES • MARK KELLER • JOHN LANDRY •

Planning can be overdone on any project, but in a complex operation like the Olympics, without it you're dead. Bill Pratt preferred to manage by gut reaction and instinct. I decided to force a new focus on priorities and planning. I was disquieted to find that top management did not regularly review the financial reports of the operation, and financial forecasting was nonexistent. We quickly worked out a system of forecasting, which we used at each weekly meeting of the executive management team to help assess where we stood.

We were beginning to move fast at OCO'88 and we needed management systems that told us where we were going rather than where we had been. Rocketships don't have rearview mirrors.

Even though I wanted more attention paid to priorities, planning, and financial forecasting, I also wanted management meetings to be shorter. We began starting the meetings at 8 a.m. instead of 9 a.m. and finishing at noon instead of 4 p.m.

At the same time we began to strengthen the role of the volunteer board of directors, especially in the finance and budget area, where John Lecky was able to provide leadership in screening out requests for expenditures that had not been carefully worked out. The combination of a stronger executive management team and the strong participatory board of directors provided, at last, the "comfortable shoe" that OCO'88 needed.

As I walked the hallways of OCO'88 watching our team work, I was grateful we had managed to maintain our autonomy. The volunteer system works only when people are challenged to do something worthwhile for themselves and for their community. People need to be needed before they begin to perform at their best.

People have asked me how we motivated so many people to work so hard and sacrifice so much. The answer is that they were self-propelled. Their motivation came from within themselves, not from the leaders. It was magical to watch our people reach for new heights because they wanted to be the best. You can't finish first with a fifth-place attitude.

Because of the rather negative attitude that the media and the public had developed toward Bill Pratt, we agreed that for the moment he would be kept in the closet as far as public relations were concerned. I asked him not to do press interviews and instructed him not to contact members of the government, particularly the mayor or aldermen. All of this would henceforth be left to the professional communications department we were putting together. Not talking to reporters was no skin off Bill's nose; he didn't like them much anyway.

It was part of my job, as we approached the Games, to make sure the mayor stayed on side. During the IOC session in Istanbul in 1987 I met privately with Juan Antonio Samaranch to talk about the negative news stories that continued to appear in Calgary media coverage. Samaranch reiterated that it continued to amaze him that the media in Calgary reported so many negative or trivial matters regarding the progress of the organizing committee. Samaranch felt we were doing a good job, the facilities were fantastic, and the people of Calgary were generally happy.

Samaranch is a former politician, having been the equivalent of a premier in the Spanish province in which Barcelona is the largest city. He has also served as Spanish ambassador to the Soviet Union. He therefore has insight into the role of politicians in the Olympics. We concurred that if Mayor Klein was able to take more credit for Olympic happenings in the city—without taking control away from Olympic organizers—his guns would be silenced.

We agreed Samaranch would speak to Klein privately. In the meantime, Samaranch would also raise the issue of the Calgary media at the executive board meeting of the IOC the next day. Klein would be in attendance there, as well as Peter Lougheed, who, although he was no longer premier of Alberta, was a trusted friend of Samaranch's and now OCO'88's honorary chairman. I let our delegation know beforehand what Samaranch intended to say.

The next day, as expected, Samaranch expressed his surprise that the Calgary media were so negative, in light of generally good job that OCO'88 was doing of organizing the

Games. He said he expected the Games to be the best he had ever seen.

I responded, "Mr. President, this has been a source of frustration for us as well, but since we have an expert in public communication here, I will refer the question to Mayor Ralph Klein."

Ralph is never at a loss for words, but we were all surprised when his answer was, "I believe the problem with OCO'88 is that they are too open. They discuss their business in public far too much. The media has too much knowledge of what is going on inside the organizing committee and OCO'88 has lost control of its own stories."

I was both shocked and amused. I dared not raise my eyes to look at either Bill Pratt or Peter Lougheed sitting beside me, because I felt if our eyes met I would surely lose my composure and smile. I suppose it's possible that Ralph was pulling our legs, but I'm pretty sure he was serious.

After Ralph finished, I invited Peter Lougheed to add his comments. Lougheed pointed out that in Canada, and in Calgary in particular, an adversarial attitude was a traditional method of operation for the media. Supposedly the only stories that sell newspapers are negative ones, and indeed the media consider themselves to be "the official opposition" to whatever is going on, no matter how noble the cause. He said, "In my experience with two previous Games, when the event itself takes place and is successful, the media will become positive and will assume the role of having been part of the success story. Until then we can expect the news coverage to be largely negative."

A few days later in a private meeting, as promised, Samaranch asked Ralph Klein to help in the communication and public relations program for OCO'88. In an effort to be helpful, Samaranch told Ralph he thought the mayor should take over OCO'88's public relations program and run it himself. This, of course, had not been my intention when I asked Samaranch to speak to Klein and would have been an impossible scenario for our other government partners.

The story made headlines in Calgary. Reporters greeted my arrival at the airport with questions about this crazy idea. I called Samaranch to explain that I would ask the mayor to forget about such a notion, as it was totally impractical and would create serious morale problems for the employees of OCO'88, starting with myself. "Of course. You are entitled to organize the Games as you see fit," he said. "I thought this would be of some use but if you think not, do whatever you think is best. I trust you."

I said, "Thank you very much. That's what I hoped you'd say."

I also talked to Dick Pound, a member of the IOC's powerful 12-person executive board, who was horrified at the possibility of the mayor becoming involved with the actual organization of the Games.

Ralph Klein returned to Calgary a day later. Even before I had a chance to talk to him, he was saying he had no intention of serving in such a senior position with the organizing committee. "Indeed," he said, "my job as mayor would not allow me to do so." Ralph was right, and I heaved a sigh of relief.

We came up with a different solution. We created a mayor's public relations committee, a joint committee of OCO'88 and the mayor's office that would meet every two weeks. The members of the committee were Bill Payne, our general manager of media; Gary Arthur, our press secretary; myself, for OCO'88; Bob Holmes, the city's Olympic liaison officer; Rod Love, the mayor's executive assistant; and Mayor Klein. The committee turned out to be a godsend. From that time forward co-operation from the mayor's office was vastly better, and there were few occasions when the mayor and OCO'88 were caught taking different points of view.

The Fire of the Sun

Access to the Olympic flame is carefully guarded by the Greek Olympic authorities as a Greek national treasure, to the chagrin of some IOC members, who would like to see it under international control. While the Greeks may be overly possessive, they have managed to preserve some of the magic of 3,000 years of legend surrounding the ceremony at Olympia.

Our lawyer, John Richels, Bill Pratt, and I travelled to Greece in May 1987 to make arrangements for the traditional flame-lighting ceremony with the Hellenic Olympic Committee. The Greek National Committee provided us with a small bus for the day-long journey from Athens through Corinth to Olympia in southwestern Greece.

Our team stayed at the Olympic Academy, located just a few hundred metres down the narrow highway from the ancient site of the first Olympic Games. The low, austere buildings look something like a middle-class California motel, with a row of palm trees decorating the semicircular driveway out front. Lush vegetation covers the hillside behind the Olympic Academy, and a pleasant two-minute walk takes you down to "de Coubertin's Grove," where giant cypress trees surround the marble memorial stone that actually holds the heart of the founder of the modern Olympic movement.

The morning after our arrival at Olympia, we toured the academy with the proud director, Otto Szymiczek, and then proceeded to the site of ancient Olympia to learn something about our Olympic heritage.

The beginnings of the Olympic Games in ancient Greece are lost in antiquity. Some people believe the Games started with the mythical champion Hercules back around 1100 B.C., when he vanquished Augeus, the local ruler. To celebrate his victory, Hercules staged a sports competition among other champions from the surrounding region. The first recorded Games were held in Olympia in 776 B.C. The Games survived for more than 1,000 years, but hit a low point when the Roman Emperor Nero fixed a chariot race so he himself would win. Nero may have been the first political leader to assume he could use the Games as a political instrument. Such abuses may have continued until finally, in 393 A.D., the Emperor Theodosius ordered the Games discontinued and Olympia destroyed.

Today Olympia is the site of renewed public interest, since the ruins were discovered under 20 feet of accumulated sediment, the residue of centuries of inattention. The site clearly shows the former location of a huge resort hotel, the sports stadium, the Temple of Zeus, and the Temple of Hera, queen of the gods.

John Richels, Bill Pratt, and I, accompanied by our wives, and Gary Bobrovitz and cameraman Tony Carter from CFAC-TV in Calgary, toured the ruins together for several hours, hearing fascinating tales of Greek history and prehistory. John, Gary, and I ran the traditional Olympic course, from one end of the ancient stadium to the other and back again, using the original ribbed rock slabs as our starting blocks. The place is like a shrine to the traditions of two millennia. We Canadians lack for little, but we have no places that I know of that exude such a sense of antiquity.

The Greek officials at Olympia walked our group through the whole ceremony of the lighting of the Olympic flame. It starts at the edge of the ruins of the Temple of Hera, where a parabolic mirror is used to focus the rays of the sun on a piece of tinder. These days, they use 35mm movie film, which ignites almost instantly. The Olympic torch is lit from the burning film, and used in turn to light a flame in a small ceramic urn easily held in two hands. Then a young lady portraying a goddess takes the urn and carries the sacred flame to the stadium. In our mock ceremony, Jeanette, enthusiastically playing the role of goddess, carried an imaginary Olympic urn 50 metres through a short tunnel and into the ancient Olympic stadium. Her unlikely entourage of lesser "goddesses" included John and Charlotte Richels, Bill and Millie Pratt, Gary Bobrovitz, and me. In the stadium, the flame carried in the Olympic urn is used to reignite the Olympic torch, an exercise that we also acted out. We had fun—perhaps a little too much fun to suit our grave and formal Hellenic host.

The Olympic torch is then transferred by young Greek runners a kilometre or so down the road to de Coubertin's Grove for ceremonial speeches. From there the torch is carried by runners and vehicles all the way to Athens and its Olympic Stadium, which is not far from the Parthenon.

The Firefighters

We travelled back to Athens for a day with friends from the Hellenic Olympic Committee. We signed an agreement with them to secure the sacred fire of the sun from amidst the ruins of the first Olympic site.

Before we signed the agreement we agreed to do an interview with Gary Bobrovitz at the Athens Olympic Stadium, a magnificent 60,000-seat white-marble masterpiece built in 1896 in the Classical style—long and narrow, with tight corners, like the stadium in Olympia.

The Athens stadium was the scene of intense activity when we arrived at mid-morning on a beautiful sunny day. About 50 runners would run two-and-a-half times around the ancient running surface, a total distance of 1,000 metres. A new race was run about every 15 minutes. The runners ranged in size and shape from the sublime to the ridiculous. Some wore Adidas athletic garb; others wore jeans, white undershirts, and even street shoes. We learned this was a competition among Greeks applying for employment with the Athens fire department. It seems everyone requires a modest level of physical fitness in order to fight fires.

Not to be denied our own chance to run in the Olympic Stadium as we had in Olympia, John Richels, Gary Bobrovitz, and I changed into our running duds and innocently lined up at the back of the pack of future firefighters contending for a job. The gun sounded and we found ourselves picking our way through the first wave of Greek couch potatoes.

With one-and-a-half laps behind us and 400 metres left I said to John, "Let's go for it or we won't have enough ground to catch those rabbits up front." We turned on the jets and closed on the serious runners, who had pulled away from the pack. I could not resist the chance to see if I still had some of the stuff that had carried me past Joe Womersly eight years earlier. In a last-minute sprint I passed all but one fellow who matched me in the last few strides to the tape. We crossed the finish line together.

As we slowed down, a Greek official corralled the first few runners into a special corner of the stadium. I had been selected to be a member of the Athens fire department! I laughingly bowed out, explaining I already had a few fires to fight back in Calgary.

PLATE 31 The Canadian Forces' Snowbirds perform a colorful Olympic flyby over the ceremonial teepee and the 2,200 Olympic athletes at Calgary's opening ceremonies.

PLATE 32 Cheered on by the Olympic athletes, 12-year-old Robyn Perry bounds up the stairs with the Olympic torch to light the Olympic cauldron. ▶

PLATE 33 Torchbearer Cathy Priestner (left) and the Perry family congratulate Robyn Perry after the opening ceremonies. ▼

PLATE 34 The mass Olympic choir, in an Olympic-ring formation, singing the Olympic theme "Come Together in Calgary " at the opening ceremonies.

PLATE 35 At the opening ceremonies, ethnic dancers and the Calgary Stampede Band perform while an array of balloons in the Olympic colors are released.

PLATE 36 Performers at the awards ceremonies held nightly at the Calgary Olympic Plaza.

PLATE 37 Traditionally dressed Native children get a chance to "share the flame."

PLATE 38 An Olympic volunteer monitors the bobsleigh track during competitions.

◀

PLATE 39 A volunteer worker makes final preparations at the 90-metre ski jump at Canada Olympic Park as a crowd of 50,000 looks on.

▼

PLATE 40 Taking a break from Olympic duties, this volunteer parks in a no-parking zone for a bite to eat.

▶

PLATE 41 President Samaranch greets the volunteer Olympic drivers stationed at the IOC headquarters in the Palliser Hotel.

▼

PLATE 42 This man had a close shave with an Olympic barber.

PLATE 43 Olympic skating fans at the Olympic Plaza display their pride and affection for Canadian Olympic hero Brian Orser.

PLATES 44 AND 45 A new Olympic culture, pin trading, flourished during the Calgary Olympic games.

PLATE 46 The mayor squared. Paula Andrews was both mayor of Canmore and mayor of the Canmore Olympic Village.

PLATE 47 From right to left: Jeanette King, Juan Antonio Samaranch, and his daughter Maria Theresa, at Nakiska during the Games.

PLATE 48 An Alberta field mouse watches as a volunteer prepares to inflate a balloon during the Olympic Balloon Festival.

Plate 49 An Olympic volunteer passes out candles at the Olympic Plaza. ▲

Plate 50 Kids light their Olympic candles from the torch held by the Man in Motion, Rick Hansen. ▼

PLATE 51 Raymond Gafner, IOC member from Switzerland, presents a bronze medal to Karen Percy at the Olympic Plaza.

PLATE 52 The two Brians. Orser (left, with white Stetson) and Boitano (right) share the podium and the admiration of the crowd at the Olympic Plaza.

PLATE 53 There's only room for one at the top. Elizabeth Manley squares off with Katarina Witt during the women's figure-skating competition.

▶

PLATE 54 The biggest Olympic torch in the world. Fireworks and the flame on the Calgary tower light up the Calgary skyline. In the foreground, the Olympic Saddledome.

▼

PLATE 55 My sense of duty compels me to put this photo in. This is the OCO'88 board of directors (and three guests) at Games time. Back row, left to right: Terry Roberts, Bob Brawn, Barry Mitchelson, Don Sprague, Bob Laidlaw, Jane Edwards, George Cornish, Norman Wagner, Paula Andrews, Walter Sieber, Bob Kasting, Diane Hunter, Roger Jackson. Front row, left to right: Wendy Bryden, Bob Holmes, Dick Pound, Gerry Berger, John Lecky, Jim Worrall, Marc Hodler, Juan Antonio Samaranch, Bill Pratt, me, Peter Lougheed, Bob Niven, Maurice Allan, Bill Warren. Missing and presumed absent are Ralph Klein, Lyle Makosky, Ian Douglas, George de Rappard, and Lee Richardson.

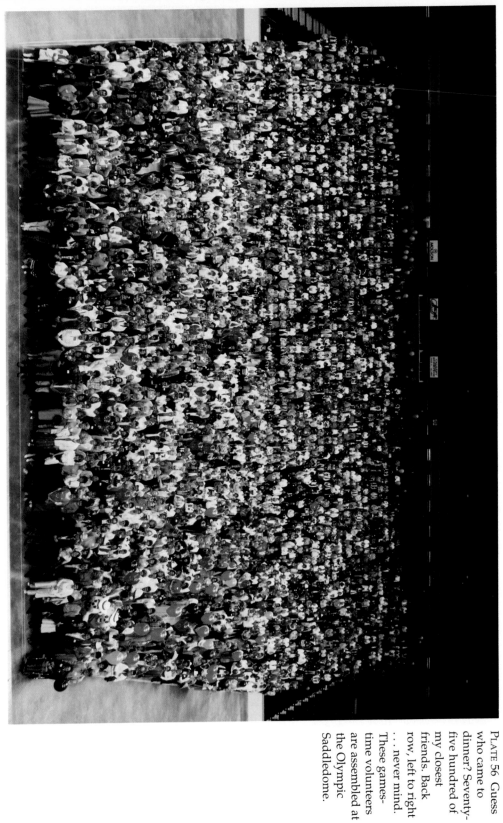

PLATE 56 Guess who came to dinner? Seventy-five hundred of my closest friends. Back row, left to right . . . never mind. These games-time volunteers are assembled at the Olympic Saddledome.

PLATE 57 Thank you Calgary—we did it! Fireworks mark the climactic finish of the best-ever Olympic Winter Games.

Chapter Sixteen

Setting the Stage

In art the best is good enough.
JOHANN WOLFGANG VON GOETHE

THE OLYMPIC GAMES are widely accepted as the most important sports festival in the world. But de Coubertin and his followers had more than that in mind. The writings and speeches of de Coubertin are filled with a philosophy, Olympism, that inextricably links physical performance to spiritual development. He saw the Olympic Games as a means to the development of a complete human being—body and mind tuned to perfection. It was an idea borrowed from the ancient Greeks.

The modern expression of this philosophy has been the presentation of cultural, architectural, and educational programs in conjunction with the Olympic Games. The larger, summertime version of the Games almost always succeeds in putting together an excellent cultural program to complement the sporting events. But the smaller Winter Games often run out of money, enthusiasm, or both before an equivalent cultural event is included. If Calgary was to be the best host it could be, then we would need a first-rate Canadian festival of arts. The board of directors of OCO'88 accordingly authorized $12.6 million for Calgary to put on the biggest, longest, and best cultural festival ever included in the Olympic Winter Games.

About 200,000 tickets were sold to 258 cultural events held over a five-week period from January 23rd to February 28th, 1988. Millions more enjoyed free performances, exhibitions, and coverage of festival events by the media. More than 2,200 artists and performers displayed their work to an international audience. Most of the talent was Canadian, but international artists were brought in as well.

The performing arts component included a dozen dance troupes, the finest Canadian musical ensembles, operas, philharmonic orchestras, half a dozen choirs, chamber music, variety entertainment, jazz, and more than a dozen stage productions. The visual arts program was equally impressive. *The Spirit Sings: Artistic Traditions of Canada's First Peoples* was put on by Calgary's Glenbow Museum. The exhibition billed itself as the most ambitious and complex museum project ever undertaken in Canada. It included artifacts from Native and non-Native collections from 16 different countries. Many of the items had been given as gifts to early European visitors to the Canadian territories centuries ago, and had not been back to Canada since.

In addition to *The Spirit Sings,* the chiefs of Treaty Seven tribes organized powwows, cultural performances, youth conferences, and Native fashion shows. The western theme was extended to include rodeo. We received rave reviews from Europeans, who had only seen rodeo events on TV and were thrilled to get a chance to see the real thing.

The Spirit Sings became the target of an Olympic boycott by the Lubicon Indians from Alberta's Peace River country. By appealing directly to potential lenders of Native artifacts, Chief Bernard Ominayak was able to gain worldwide attention for his small band's claims for a land settlement. Ten out of a hundred museums contacted for contributions to *The Spirit Sings* project declined to make donations as a result of the Lubicon appeal.

Like most Olympic arts festivals, ours included art posters, but Calgary outdid many other festivals by putting giant posters of Canadian paintings on billboards nationwide. Three distinctive arches were also built in Calgary, and one of them, which formed the dramatic entrance to the Olympic Village at the university, was recreated in miniature and presented to Juan Antonio Samaranch as a gift for IOC headquarters.

A photographic display of hockey masks, a philatelic display, contemporary art, a crafts exhibition, commemorative medals, and previous Olympic posters were displayed as well. The organizers showed no lack of creativity or initiative.

In the field of literary arts, a writers' festival and book fair was held, as well as a poetry sweatshop, a film festival, and literary awards programs. Attendance was excellent.

Wintershow '88 involved roving bands of performers entertaining delighted visitors on the streets of Calgary and in malls and shopping centres. An international snow-sculpting competition was held at Prince's Island, and an ice-sculpting competition at Canmore.

At the gala opening of the Olympic Arts Festival, which took place in the Saddledome, David Foster performed the themesong "Can't You Feel It," and Oscar Peterson debuted his *Olympic Suite*. The high point of the evening for many, however, came when Sports Minister Otto Jelinek and OCO'88 President Bill Pratt skated a vibrant duet together. Otto, a former world skating champion, had to show the lead to Bill, who hadn't skated in 20 years and had to borrow skates from Steve Bozek, then of the Calgary Flames. The crowd loved it.

Canada is a country with as many different cultures in its makeup as the Olympic movement itself. The arts festival captured that diversity and richness and put it in a showcase for the world to see.

The Strength of Sampson

Way back in the middle of 1984 we had decided to get started organizing our ceremonies. Bill Pratt had suggested inviting Eddie Roberts, administrator of the legal firm Bennett Jones in Calgary, to head our volunteer ceremonies committee.

I liked the idea because Eddie had performed similar duties for the Calgary Stampede's Grandstand shows.

The key person behind the ceremonies would be the executive producer. Roberts and his team looked all over Canada for the right person. They did not look farther afield, because we wanted the ceremonies to be organized by a Canadian. They chose Paddy Sampson, a former employee of CBC and the creator of numerous world-class productions in Toronto and Ottawa.

The first time I met Sampson I was impressed by his panache. Paddy is probably five feet five inches tall and 106 pounds soaking wet. He always wears a flat cap and horn-rimmed glasses. He has been a Canadian for most of his life but his Irish brogue links him to his past. He is quiet and caustic and the best executive producer in Canada. I told Paddy we could not control the quality of sporting events and we could not control the weather, but we could control the quality of our opening and closing shows. It was our chance to express our unique Canadian personality. The opening had to get the Games off to a great start with plenty of goosebumps. The closing had to be an emotional farewell that would make people remember our Games forever.

Paddy's response was characteristic. "Do you want the 1,000-goosebump model or the 2,000-goosebump model?" He understood the assignment all right.

One of the most difficult tasks I had over the next four years was leaving Paddy Sampson alone to do his job. In all the years of struggle to put together a dream that would meet the expectations of so many people, I felt the burden of responsibility for the ceremonies more than any other one thing. I almost had to nail a foot to the floor to keep myself off the ceremonies team. I often warned Paddy that I could barely manage to restrain myself. He helped by keeping me well-informed and by sharing snippets of information about his progress.

Most of the music used in the opening ceremonies was written and recorded in Calgary, and I received an invitation from Paddy one day to go down to a local recording studio to hear the recording of Olympic themes for the parade of athletes. I had expressed the desire that this be very stirring music. It was being prepared and recorded under the direction of an old friend, Tommy Banks, a western Canadian musician and TV personality. Tommy and I had grown up together in Calgary, where we put on magic shows as youngsters for which we charged two cents admission. The magic show was the same, but the admission price had inflated some in 40 years.

Members of the Calgary Philharmonic Orchestra were hard at work recording their music when Jeanette, Paddy, and I arrived. We sat and listened to a recording of a few bars of one of the marching themes to be used for the opening ceremonies. Ten members of the string section were recording their particular element of this piece.

Each time they played the bars in question I thought it sounded wonderful. Each time, though, the director behind me would say something like, "No, somebody is slightly flat. Play it again." They would. It would still sound fine to me but there would be another complaint. Finally, after nearly half an hour, the few bars of music were recorded perfectly. I remember commenting to Jeanette that these "musical athletes" were preparing for the Olympic Games in much the same way as sports athletes: by doing it over and over and over until they got it right.

Sampson wanted to have authentic western dancing for the opening ceremonies. He wasn't sure where to find authentic modern western-style dancers so he asked where the action was. He soon found himself in country-and-western bars on Calgary's south side.

Night after night Paddy mingled and watched young people enjoy themselves Calgary-style. When he saw people he wanted he asked them if they would dance in the ceremonies of the Olympic Winter Games. They laughed at first, not believing he was the executive producer for the opening ceremonies and he wanted them in his show. Eventually, though, he got nearly 400 of them to turn out to practice. This time it wasn't in a bar or a club but a dusty vacant warehouse. Paddy had created the Caloco Dancers.

• RON CARRELL • JOHN MACBEATH • BONNIE MAKSYMOWICH • ART TEPPLER • DAVE SMITH • KAY RAYMENT • GREIG MILLER • LINDA SAMPSON • WILLIAM RUTHERFORD • SANDRA DOERKSEN • ANNETTE DEL GUERCIO • KRISTINE BLIGH • EDWARD BATTLE • GREG JONES • ALAN KING • EVA BERMAN WONG • KEN JONASON • JIM CLARK • KELLY MACDONALD • AMY MARTIN • BARB GERBER • GUNILLA KAY • LENARD HOFFARTH • ED HEMMES • SUZETTE SMITH • NORMAN HOWDEN • MARIA FERNANDES • DONNA SANDERSON • MARK CHRISTENSEN • BARBARA COOKE • ROSALBA GIANNATELLI • TERRY CARLSON • RAY SRIGLEY • LYNDA LEONARD • BARRY WRIGHT • SUSAN SCHAN • KAREN PARTRIDGE • JEFFREY MELLOR • MIKE KEARNS •

By October 1987 there was still a lot of work to do and some of the Caloco Dancers were tired of giving up their Sundays to practice for the opening ceremonies. With morale waning, Paddy called me and asked, "Could you possibly come down and give them a little pep talk?"

I went to a Sunday-morning practice and spoke to them. "Most of you might be asked to do something world-class once in your life if you're lucky. This could be that one time. You may not realize it, but when you are dancing in the opening ceremonies on February 13th, 1988, one-and-a-half billion people will be watching on television." A rousing cheer interrupted my words. "All of you are going to your own world championships. All of you are part of a team working at the world-class level.

"This has often been described as a once-in-a-lifetime opportunity. But it's more than that; it's a lifetime opportunity. It's a chance to do something you will never forget. It's what I call rocking-chair stuff, because one day you will be able to reminisce that you were there, on February 13th, and you were part of it. It's a matter of choice between being the best you can be—and perhaps being recognized as the best in the world—or doing nothing. The choice is yours."

Immediately after that, the dance director took the microphone from me and said, "All right. We've had difficulties with some people not wanting to come to these practices. I'm going to make it easy for you. I'm going to ask all those who do not want to come to practices to stand where you are. All those who are prepared to come to practices and, as Mr. King has said, to be part of the best dance team in the world, move now to the side of the hall."

People started to move to the side of the hall. I saw several who hesitated for a moment, their eyes shifting from side to side to see what their colleagues were doing. Then they too moved to the side. And so one hundred per cent of the Caloco Dancers decided to stay with it. When I checked back with Paddy in later months he confirmed the problem was gone. "These guys are on a roll straight toward their own piece of history," he said.

At the opening ceremonies the Caloco Dancers, the men dressed in blue greatcoats and the women in bright pink dresses trimmed with white fur, became a human kaleidoscope, whirling and recombining to form wonderful patterns. They were Olympic champions, and the world watched them dance.

Victory in the Bored Room

Eddie Roberts put together a team of solid professionals and over 10,000 volunteers ranging in age from four to 70 who did everything expected and more to set the stage for the Games. Letters that came in after the Games referred more often to how wonderful the opening and closing ceremonies were than to anything else. The ceremonies really did give organizers their best opportunity to express the personality of the Calgary community.

Olympic tradition had established a pattern for opening ceremonies. An initial welcome segment was to be followed by the entrance of the athletes, the official opening speeches, the raising of the Olympic flag, the lighting of the cauldron, the release of doves, and a closing entertainment section. Paddy Sampson wanted to rearrange our ceremonies for maximum emotional impact. I asked Paddy to give me a written description of his new scenario. I was concerned about our ability to get it approved by the IOC executive board because we knew that changing Olympic tradition was not easily done. In the past, the athletes had always paraded into the ceremonies partway through, stood for a time, and then paraded out before the ceremonies ended. We wanted the athletes to enter early and, for the first time in Summer or Winter Games, be seated to enjoy the entire show. This seemed logical, because the show was intended above all else to honor and welcome them. But it had never been done that way before.

We had forwarded a written ceremonies scenario to the IOC, but in addition I was asked by President Samaranch to describe the ceremonies plan to the executive board. Once again I chose the mumble strategy. I decided to read the scenario script in full detail in the most boring monotone I could muster, hoping nobody would notice any deviation from tradition. It worked. The executive board was not anxious to hear such trivial details and the members tuned out. They trusted Calgary anyway to do the same good job on the ceremonies that we were doing on almost everything else.

Making a Scene

Hugh Dunne, Paddy's assistant, approached me quietly one day six months before the Games to see if I liked the idea of everyone in the stadium wearing colored ponchos to create a living scene in the stadium. I loved the idea. He said he wasn't sure Paddy liked it and he needed some help to convince him. Paddy was cautious but flexible so we decided to go ahead with the idea.

We talked Coca-Cola into helping pay for the ponchos because Paddy's budget was by now committed to other things. When the ponchos arrived a few weeks before the opening ceremonies we found Coke logos had been printed on the outside. Olympic rules forbid any commercial advertising at official events. Quick-thinking John Richels, who had taken over as boss of the ceremonies area when Frances Jackson-Dover quit, took the ponchos to nearby Spy Hill jail and made arrangements for the inmates to turn 62,000 capes inside out and remove the labels.

Some of the inmates decided to take the opportunity to participate personally in the grand opening of the Olympics. We found several capes with obscenities and other personal embellishments, including one cape that read, "Help me, I'm being held captive" in bold black ink. We had to sort through them all as they were placed in order on the seats and remove the offending ones. During the ceremonies our hostesses had spare ponchos in all colors on hand in case we had missed one or two personal messages from the hoosegow.

CHAPTER SEVENTEEN

Sharing the Flame

We . . . have been reminded that this is a country
of small towns and big dreams.
PRIME MINISTER BRIAN MULRONEY
SPEAKING OF THE OLYMPIC TORCH RELAY

C ALGARY'S OLYMPIC TORCH RELAY turned out to be the
longest and most successful in Olympic history. As it
travelled across the country, the Olympic flame captured the hearts of Canadians.

Los Angeles showed us the light with its successful relay.
The Los Angeles organizers had struck on the idea of finding a
corporate sponsor to cover costs of the torch caravan and then
the idea of charging all comers $3,000 per mile for the privilege
of running the torch. Runners got to keep their torch-relay T-
shirt as well as their own torch. America fell in love with the
Olympic Torch Relay, and more than $10 million was raised
and donated to local amateur sports clubs.

A problem with the L.A. torch relay was the resentment it
created with the Greeks, who felt that selecting runners on the
basis of who paid for the privilege was not appropriate. It
could be argued that only the wealthy could run, although

· ELIZABETH MAAG · PAT LANG · PAUL FOSTER · DUNCAN CARSWELL · MORYN SHAH · KELLY BROOKER · MIKI SIARKOWSKA · STEVE MOREY
· KATHY FEDORI · ESTHER WONG · LORNE BUNYAN · POLDI OLAFSON · CHRISTINE COLBERT · LYNN PARKIN · JENNY YUEN · LAURA
WESTGATE · LISA RYCKMAN · CORDELIA MCINTOSH · DAVID MELLOR · DAVID REJMINIAK · BILL PRATT · WILLIAM LIPSEY · MICHAEL
BULLARD · KIM TOMLIN · JIM HOBART · LINDSAY WATSON · MARGARET HERTER · LISA BUCK · WAYNE HARDOWA · JOHN WILSON · WALLY
BINDA · KATHLENE MERCER · KEN LAIDLAW · DONALD MILLER · LIESE MCDONALD · MARGARET STEEL · RACHEL ADAMS · PAT SCHROEDER ·

Peter Ueberroth contended that local communities often chipped in to be sure that underprivileged children or a local hero had a chance for glory too.

The idea of raising money as a legacy for community sport through the Olympics had a strong appeal to both Bill Pratt and me. Bill wanted to use the Los Angeles pay-as-you-go scheme. He once said to me, "I would give anything to be able to buy a kilometre for each of my grandchildren—there must be thousands more like me." I preferred the idea of opening up the Olympic Torch Relay to people everywhere.

To make it work, though, and still leave sports funding as a legacy, we needed a sponsor. Over the course of many months I met with Ed Lakusta, president of Petro-Canada, to talk about the relay. Ed and I talked philosophy, we talked cost, and we talked about the Olympic Torch Relay from every angle until the idea made sense to both of us. I wanted to be sure that a fund for the benefit of sport would be created through the relay. The project needed at least $5 million and yet we couldn't allow the commercialization of the Olympic flame. Lakusta had the vision to see how effective the torch relay could be in uniting the country behind the Olympic project and at the same time creating a legacy of funds for the development of future athletes.

Once Ed was convinced the relay would be a success he took the idea and ran with it. He agreed to sponsor the relay and to raise additional money by selling special glasses and other Olympic souvenirs as promotional items at Petro-Canada service stations. To put the project together OCO'88 also had help from Jungle Jim Hunter, the original Crazy Canuck skier.

Petro-Canada agreed to pay the projected $5.5-million cost of the torch relay. More important, the company provided the people power from its national network of dealers and employees. It also diverted millions of dollars' worth of corporate advertising into the Olympic Torch Relay program. The decision to do all this was a gutsy move by Ed Lakusta, but he was supported by Petro-Canada's chairman, Bill Hopper, the man who put the company together.

The creation of Petro-Canada, a government-owned company with its headquarters in Calgary, at the heart of the land of free enterprise, had left many western Canadians bitter. The Olympic Torch Relay was a public-relations dream for Petro-Canada. The big winners, though, were the 26 million Canadians who, as a result of the deal, got a chance to share the flame.

With the exception of the first and last legs of the 18,000-kilometre relay, running spots were assigned by a draw. Petro-Canada stations across the country distributed entry forms. All you had to do was choose what day you wanted to run; then you could fill in as many applications as you liked.

I remember meeting a young man as I was travelling on a plane to Ottawa during the relay. I was working on some Olympic papers as we flew and the young man next to me could not help but notice my work. He enquired if I was Frank King. I confirmed this fact and enquired about his interest in sport.

He said, "I've never been interested in sport or the Olympics before the torch relay came along, but I'm really proud about what's happening to our people with the torch."

He concluded with a remark that left an impression on me. "I've never filled in 22 applications for anything in my life before—but I did for the Olympic Torch Relay." We received more responses (6.5 million) than the numbers of votes cast in any federal election. Of course in a federal election you can't vote 22 times.

Bonnie and Clyde

One of the most delightful jobs that Bill Pratt and I retained as our own was the selection of the first and final Olympic torch runners. We wanted our choices to symbolize the great Olympic traditions of the past and the hope for an even greater future. We quickly agreed the first runners should reflect the past and the last runner the future. For the first runners, we wanted to recognize the contribution of all those athletes who had competed over the years. We wanted a woman and a man, and we wanted people with a story of past

· WILLIAM KALMANOVITCH · JASON GUREVITCH · BETY DILLMANN · LILY LOWE · KARI GUNDERSEN · DALE PAYNE · DEBBIE BALOG · BRAD MCMANUS · DONALD GOVER · MARC THIBAUDEAU · KIM GRATTIDGE · BRENDA DUNCAN · PATRICK BRENNAN · TOVE BAKKER · SHERRY BUCKLE · DAVID OPKO · TERRI MOELLER · KARIN ROSE · BRENDA SAUVERWALD · ELIO BRANDELLI · NELSON MERCER · TRISH SAVILL · JOHN G SMITH · SUSANNE KNIGHT · SUSAN CRAWFORD · MARGARET LAW · KEITH HANNA · LYDIA LASAK · PATRICIA MCCAMBLY · MAUREEN BELL-LANE · SHIRLEY MURRAY · PAUL CONLIN · IAN RAWES · BRENDA ROGERS · LINDA PYATT · GREG COULOMBE · GARY CORBEIL · JOAN

glories to tell. The choice of Barbara Ann Scott King and Ferd Hayward as our first torch runners, who would begin the relay in Signal Hill, Newfoundland, was easy.

On Saturday morning, November 7th, 1987, I picked up the telephone at my home and dialed Ferd Hayward's number in St. John's, Newfoundland. I had met Ferd for the first time a year earlier when I did a press blitz of Atlantic Canada. He had been the first native son of Newfoundland to have become an Olympian. At age 42 he had been the best racewalker in Canada, and he had represented Canada at the 1952 Helsinki Games.

The phone rang. "Hello," a quiet voice answered.

"Ferd, this is Frank King, chairman of the Calgary Olympic Winter Games."

"Oh yes, hello Frank, nice of you to call."

"Ferd, I'm calling to see if you'd be willing to help us out."

"Gosh, I'll sure try."

"As you know, in 10 days the torch relay begins in your home town and I'd appreciate it very much if you would accept the honor of being the first of two runners to carry the Olympic torch off Signal Hill."

There was a long pause. "Frank, I'm sorry, would you repeat that please?"

I repeated my question.

"I guess I did hear you all right the first time, but I was so shocked I couldn't believe it." Ferd said he would be greatly honored to run the flame, but he did not feel worthy. He asked if I was sure I wanted him. I told him I was quite sure.

Next I dialled the number of Barbara Ann and Tom King (no relation) of Chicago. Barbara Ann Scott was still the sweetheart champion of figure skating in the minds of most Canadians. She had won the gold medal in 1948 and returned to charm the proud people of her homeland. I told her that she was our choice to run the first kilometre of the Canadian Olympic Torch Relay with Ferd Hayward.

"Oh, I can't believe it!" she cried. "Let me get Tom on the line!"

I told Barbara Ann and Ferd that only our press secretary, Gary Arthur, should be trusted with any further discussion of arrangements. We wanted the public to be surprised.

On Monday I let Gary Arthur in on the secret. He was delighted with the choices and the fact that he would be solely responsible for getting our secret runners to Signal Hill undetected. He went to work immediately.

We had deliberately left little time, in order to lessen the chances of press leaks. Barbara Ann is a striking and famous lady, easily recognized. Gary had to find a way of getting her into St. John's without her being spotted. He suggested a disguise. "I'll come through the airport wearing an old shabby black coat and an ugly black wig," she agreed. "I've always wanted to be called Bonnie, and Tom often calls me Grace because I remind him of Gracie Fields. Why not call me Bonnie Grace?"

"Then Bonnie Grace you will be."

Gary promptly called Ferd to advise him to go into hiding at his son's country cottage to dodge the press. "Since Barbara Ann is to be known as Bonnie," Gary told Ferd, "from now on your name will be Clyde." The covert operation was on, and for several days, Gary's characteristic smile was a little more in evidence than usual.

Ferd called Gary almost daily for assurances that everything was okay. The media had been tipped off that Ferd would be an excellent choice. They hounded him with calls. Gary had told him that God wouldn't care if he told a white lie or two to preserve the secret. But one of the media guys got clever. Knowing I would likely have a hand in choosing the first runner, he deduced that our press secretary Gary Arthur would likely handle the details. Identifying himself as Gary Arthur, the reporter called Ferd to talk about the torch relay.

Ferd was bewildered when the real Gary Arthur called just half an hour later to discuss the same thing. "Gary, I just talked to you a few minutes ago," he said. "Why are you calling again?"

Gary decided he needed his own code name. "From now on you're Clyde Barrow, Barbara Ann is Bonnie Grace, and I'll be Gary Cooper." The code names were not sophisticated, but they did occasion a few chuckles among the participants.

Gary brought our RCMP torch relay security officer, Keith McMillan, into his confidence to help clear customs and arrange Bonnie's arrival in St. John's. Inspector McMillan's first assignment on the job was to meet the mysterious black-haired lady known as Bonnie at the airport. Standing unobtrusively in the airport lobby, he found no one answering the description he had been given. Becoming concerned, he surveyed every corner of the arrivals area. No one even slightly resembled the description of a lady wearing a shabby old black coat. He did, however, notice a well-dressed petite lady at the telephone as he walked over to make a call to Gary Cooper back in Calgary. While he was trying to get a line through, he was surprised to overhear her exclaim, "Gary, I've arrived in St. John's, but there's nobody here to meet me!"

Keith realized that what counts as a shabby old coat for some is quite different from what counts as one for others. Bonnie had arrived the only way she knew how—in style, in a gorgeous black fur coat.

I arrived in St. John's the next night, the evening before the beginning of the torch relay. Keith McMillan and Jim Hunter met me at the airport and we left immediately for a secret rendezvous with Bonnie and Clyde. We drove together through darkness out to the rural home of Ferd's son and daughter-in-law. We had been told by Ferd of this modest "country cottage" and had decided it was perfect for our hide-out. It turned out to be a huge Canadiana home. Ferd's son Hayward, I discovered, is a popular designer and interior decorator in Newfoundland.

After meeting Ferd's wife and grandchildren I spent a few moments touring the breathtaking "cottage" before we took a glass of wine and toasted the success of the "world's greatest Olympic Torch Relay."

As we toasted, I said, "Barbara Ann and Ferd—you are about to become a part of Canadian history for the second time. Carrying the first torch is more than an individual honor, because we are asking you to carry the torch on behalf of all the great Canadian men and women who have been Olympians through the years."

I looked at Barbara Ann. A small tear rolled down her cheek. "That's so beautiful," she said. "Thank you."

Then, using a fireplace sweeping iron as a mock Olympic torch, Jungle Jim Hunter walked Bonnie and Clyde through what their roles would be on stage the next day at Signal Hill.

Kilometre One

The Olympic Torch Relay made the effort of many years worthwhile for me. Canadians from coast to coast turned out by the millions to see the torch, to cheer, and to touch it. The prior efforts of Terry Fox, Steve Fonyo, and Rick Hansen helped inspire Canadians. Tina Turner sings, "We don't need another hero." In my opinion Canadians don't agree—we are still writing our best moments in history and we look forward to an even greater future based on the instinct of our people to achieve against any odds. The Olympic flame catalyzed that instinct. Canadians accepted the challenge to carry the flame 18,000 kilometres through the most difficult weather imaginable.

As the summer of 1987 had turned to fall, we had decided to assign Bill Pratt the responsibility for getting the Olympic flame from Greece to Canada. Bill had been "in the closet" for almost a year. The storm of controversy had subsided, and now it was time for Bill to get some well-deserved recognition for four years of hard work. He beamed when I told him I had decided not to go to Greece and that he and Dave Thompson would bring the flame to Canadian soil on November 17th, 1987.

John Richels was dispatched to Athens to make the final arrangements with the Hellenic Olympic Committee for the torch-lighting ceremony at Olympia. John made a deal with Bombardier to lend us a specially outfitted Challenger jet to carry the torch team to Greece and back to Newfoundland on November 17th. Ed Lakusta, Roger Jackson, and Bill Warren made up the rest of the mission, along with the chairman of our mascot committee, Lane Kranenberg. The torch team used

URQUHART · KELLY GARDNER · KAREN PERRY · JOAN BRUCH · MLADENKA FORSYTH · JULIA EDWARDS · MARILYN HUMMEL · LAURIE KREINER · VERA CUTHBERT · RON SCHWIEGER · GORDON MALCOLM · BORDEN MCLEOD · ROMEO ROJAS-WALSSON · WAYNE BULLARD · BJORGER PETTERSEN · LYNN PUNNETT · SUSIE ROBUTKA · MARG AUGUSTINI · CATHIE BELENKY · BARBARA METZ · RON CLARK · DEAN BEAUDOIN · ANNA MATOVINOVIC · LANCE MCGINN · EARL SORETTE · BARBARA DE BEER · LAURA PERRY · CAROLYN GINGERA · JUDY MAPPIN · DAVID FERRIER · JACQUIE MENSINK · SUSAN LEVITT · LYNNE DAVIES · BARBARA GOSLING · SHELDON GIBSON · JAMES BERTRAM

the flame at Olympia to light six miner's lamps, which they then brought back to Canada on the Challenger. The six lamps made it virtually impossible that the flame would go out on us somewhere over the mid-Atlantic.

The ceremony to welcome the flame to Canada was held in St. John's, Newfoundland. We didn't advertise the fact, but the Challenger carrying the flame had arrived in Gander the night before as a precaution against foul weather. Even knowing that, it was exciting to see the jet land in St. John's through the cold Newfoundland fog, precisely on time. Bill Pratt emerged with the sacred flame burning inside one of the brass miner's lamps. Otto Jelinek and Jim Hunter joined me in observing the flame's arrival at the airport.

Prime Minister Brian Mulroney, Premier Brian Peckford of Newfoundland, Mayor John Murphy of St. John's, Mayor Klein of Calgary, and CODA's "first four"—Niven, Warren, Jackson, and I—were all on stage when the flame arrived in the miner's lamp. Pratt and Jackson carried the lamp case; Niven carried the first torch to be used. The chairman of Petro-Canada, Bill Hopper, spoke briefly.

The wind was blowing so hard on Signal Hill that our torch relay team had become concerned about losing the flame when the window of the miner's lamp was opened. During countless trials the day before, they had not been able to get the wax-coated taper to stay lit while moving it from a miner's lamp to the Olympic cauldron on stage in the 50-kilometre-an-hour winds off the Atlantic Ocean. The solution was ingenious. Our crew obtained some wicks normally used to ignite underwater welding torches used on offshore drilling rigs. These wicks burn in wind, snow, and even underwater—you can't put them out.

The prime minister had been chosen to light the cauldron with the flame brought from Greece in the miner's lamp. I held my breath as he slipped a taper into the lamp. The ignition occurred with such enthusiasm the precious Olympic flame in the lamp was blown out! Fortunately, the prime minister had captured it with his taper and was able to light the cauldron with it.

There was cheering from the audience, but as the PM tried to acknowledge the crowd Jim Hunter, the master of ceremonies, noticed the lighted wick was still burning in Mulroney's hand. The prime minister's coat was being burned by little red-hot comets leaping from the exuberant wick. While continuing his job of emceeing the ceremony, Hunter relieved Mulroney of his Olympic sparkler and held it. Just before the flame reached his fingers, Jim nonchalantly dropped it and kicked the sputtering stub off the edge of the stage and into the snow. As the ceremony proceeded, the persistent device finally burned itself out.

I took the first torch—which had been lit three days earlier in Olympia—dipped it into the flaming cauldron, and held it above my head with my left hand.

"This flame belongs to all Canadians!" I shouted to the crowd as I held the first torch for all to see. My voice was hoarse from overuse; I'd had several tiring speaking engagements in the last 48 hours. As I announced that the first runners would be Ferd Hayward and Barbara Ann Scott King, the crowd of nearly 3,000 roared its approval.

As Jeanette and I left Signal Hill, we came upon Bonnie and Clyde just as they passed the torch to the next runner. Flocks of little children lined the road, and in the houses all the way to City Hall little hands framed faces with noses pressed against the windows. There the torch was to be given by Bob Niven to Mayor Murphy and Brian Peckford, premier of Newfoundland.

It was a cold, blustery day, but I felt warm and full of anticipation as I looked into the faces of the people of Canada.

Taking Up the Torch

It was the longest and coldest relay in history, and it brought out the best in millions of Canadians.

A family in rural Alberta received the happy news that their young son had been selected as an Olympic torch runner only to discover that he had mistakenly marked Day Nine on his application, rather than February 9th as he had thought. Day Nine meant he would be running in Prince Edward

Island, 4,000 kilometres from home. The mother had modest means to support her family and was not certain how she could finance such a trip, but she decided not to let that destroy her son's big opportunity.

The story of the local torch runner rapidly spread in the community. The people in the town held bake sales and rummage sales and some simply donated money. Everyone in the family shared the sacrifice of selling prized possessions to raise the fare. Included in the treasures sold were the boy's fishtank and all his pet fish. Somehow, together, the family and the community raised enough money for the whole family to go to P.E.I. to share the experience.

After the boy completed his run he was interviewed by the media, and the story of family sacrifice came out. "Was the whole thing worth it?" the reporter asked.

"I'm really going to miss my aquarium that Mom sold," he responded. "But I can always buy another aquarium when I'm older, and I'll never have a chance to feel this proud again."

I've got the feeling this young man is going to make out just fine when he's older. He learned to sacrifice in order to achieve something special. He taught me that success is often a matter of choice, not chance. He shared the experience with a caring family—I'm sure their bonds have been strengthened forever.

There were hundreds of wonderful stories along the relay route as well. One special moment came in northern Ontario at the end of Day 52.

The relay had been travelling all day long and had covered more than 350 kilometres on modified snowmobiles whose tracks had been removed and replaced with tiny wheels so they could travel on the highway. The relay organizers were at the point of exhaustion when they reached the final stopping place at 11 p.m. The temperature was −37°C. As the convoy drew to a stop at the top of a hill, the RCMP radio bristled with a message that there were at least 600 people waiting at the bottom to share the flame. They had been waiting for more than an hour in the frozen night, so the weary relay team decided to carry on one more stop.

It was an established tradition for the torch caravan to stop for impromptu celebrations wherever a group of significant size gathered by the roadside. In spite of the late hour and the bitter cold, this was another occasion for the torch to cast its spell.

Jim Hunter led the crowd through an explanation of the story of the flame, the aims of the Olympic movement, and the road ahead to Calgary. During a break when the song "Share the Flame" was playing, a man and his son standing near the podium caught Jim's attention. The man asked if his son could hold the torch, and pointed out that his son had lost his right hand in an accident.

Jim invited the young lad and his father onto the stage. The crowd seemed to recognize the boy immediately, and expressed appreciation for Jim's insight in recognizing how much this could mean. Jim announced the lad would now receive the torch that had carried the flame from Olympia, but as he handed the boy the torch the father intervened and took the torch into his own hands. For a moment Jim was annoyed, thinking the man was being selfish, horning in on something meant exclusively for his son. But the father had merely wanted to hand the torch to his son himself. Jim held the microphone to catch the boy's reaction.

The boy reached out with his nearest arm, which happened to be the one with a hook in place of a hand. The father deliberately bypassed the artificial hand, placing the torch instead where the other hand could accept it. The boy reached out his good hand reflexively and then withdrew it. Using his hook, he took the torch, saying, "No Dad, I'm not ashamed."

For a long heartbeat the audience was silenced by the boy's words. Then somewhere in the crowd a woman broke into *O Canada*. Others joined in as the boy raised the torch with his hook for all to see, and the whole crowd sang.

The torch travelled by air to the Northwest Territories and then by boat to the westernmost provincial capital, Victoria, before it was run eastward through the interior of B.C. to Alberta. Ed Lakusta and I had agreed to go out on several occasions to travel with the torch relay during its run through rural Canada. We chose a stretch near London, Ontario, for our first run and then we again joined the run near Trail, B.C., as it approached its Alberta destination.

I had enjoyed the first run so much that when I shared the stories back home with our sons, Jeanette came up with the idea that I should ask David and Stephen to join me for the second one. The boys jumped at the chance. Through the years they had benefited from our family's Olympic involvement, but they had also paid a price in terms of lost family time together. As Steve once said, "I'm used to eating alone—it's been 10 years with lots of frozen pizza."

The flight on Petro-Canada's executive jet to Trail, B.C. was an extra treat for Dave and Steve. I had invited Mark Tomlin, one of our many hard-working people behind the scenes at OCO'88, to join us on the trip. Mark's family lived near Trail, and he was thrilled to be coming home to run with the relay.

Our Challenger jet landed just before dusk. We relaxed for an hour in our motel room and then headed out to witness the torch arrival ceremony at Rossland, B.C. Nancy Greene-Raine, gold- and silver-medal skier from the 1968 Olympics, received the torch and was sent onto the course after Jim Hunter led us through a spirited version of *O Canada* and the now-familiar strains of the "Share the Flame" themesong. I'd seen the ceremony several times before, but I was still impressed with the magnetic attraction of the torch. The Olympic flame had a magical effect on people of all ages. All along the roadside people reached out seeking to touch the handle of the torch, as if to receive some form of spiritual nourishment. It was like a blessing.

As I stood in the cold night watching the uplifting effect the flame had on people, I thought back to several occasions when the supporters of the Lubicon Lake Indian land claims tried to bring public opinion to their side of the dispute by waving banners and signs at some of the flame celebrations. The so-called Lubicon "boycott" of our Games succeeded in drawing governments back to the bargaining table. Most Canadians would love to see this and hundreds of other Native land claims settled fairly. If this process is speeded up because the Olympics produced a platform for the Lubicon people, good. But the negative placards of Lubicon supporters along the torch relay route seemed out of place and ineffective. The public and the media moved unsympathetically around the protesters, and the message lost momentum. Under the glow from the ubiquitous Olympic-torch candles, people hugged and shook hands in friendship. There was no room for defiance or confrontation here, and the protesters' message was overwhelmed.

That night Ed Lakusta and I spoke to about 50 Petro-Canada workers who had arrived for a briefing before their week-long journey with the flame. Ed spoke about how proud and grateful he was that his company had accepted such an important project. He gave the credit for success to the un-precedented team effort mounted by Petro-Canada and OCO'88. He also mentioned the Government of Canada, which had chipped in with its "Celebration'88" awards for excellence to outstanding Canadians in communities across the country.

When I spoke, I suggested to the torch relay team that they had much in common with Olympic athletes who were also on the road to Calgary. What bound them together was a ren-dezvous with excellence. That night we could sense that these people loved being motivated by the challenge to do some-thing special. When the opportunity comes for most of us to do something extraordinary, we jump at it.

The next day, Ed, Mark, Dave, Steve, and I readied our-selves for a special day, running escort for the Olympic flame in the chilly mountain passes of southeastern British Columbia. The torch caravan was an impressive thing to be-hold. Thirty-eight vehicles ferried runners back and forth, carried the media, and kept supplies and security in hand. Each vehicle was numbered with Alberta license plates, from TORCH 1 up to TORCH 38.

Dave and Steve soon had the set-up cased and were anxious to get out on the road behind the runners. Dave looked forward to the run, as he had been a good middle-distance run-ner in high school until his leg injuries benched him. Steve

KOLSTAD · JUDITH CARVELL · DEL HALWA · NORMAN GRIER · JAMES STANLEY SUMMERS · DEBRA BORBELY · MICHAEL HUGHES · BRIAN VOLK · NANCY PALMER · EVAN CAPPON · MELVIN NIEMI · ROBERT HOWSON · PEGGY ECCLESTON · SHIRLEY HIGDON · INGO KALK · RUDY BOONSTRA · ROBERT GODFREY · AMUND JONASSEN · SHEAU-HARN YU · CHARLES ARSENAULT · SUZAN MALYSA · KEVIN WALDERN · GRACE ANDRADE · RON BERGMAN · MAGGIE WATSON · SUSAN PRIOR · ROSS MCSWEEN · DIXIE ANNALA · BIRDIE ARCHER · PETER BASSIN · VIC WIEBE, JR. · KERRY NOLAN · JIM BARBY · KEN BROWN · IRIS TRIGG · GEORGE MCDONALD · MIRKO ZATKA · MARY HILL · STEPHEN

wasn't so sure about the road running, but he had just completed three years as part of his high-school basketball provincial championship team and was still in good shape.

During the day our sons ran 15 kilometres with the Olympic flame caravan. As they ran they witnessed the hugs of friendship as the torch was passed from hand to hand. They saw first-hand the expressions of love—the hands held high waving Canadian flags, home-made torches, and Olympic flame-candles. They watched the caravan stop wherever unexpected crowds of children waited to share in the joy.

The whole caravan stopped to greet a lady waiting alone by the roadside. She wanted to touch the handle of the torch—and she burst into tears when handed the flame. She sat in her wheelchair and beamed as the torch caravan pulled away. It touched the boys deeply.

Half an hour later they were still running when a young woman took over the torch. She was running with a wineskin strapped around her neck and carried on her hip. I was riding in TORCH 4, the media truck, just in front of the young runner and the boys. I could see Dave chatting amicably with the woman. The loudspeaker operators in TORCH 3 behind the runner were joking with her as they often did with runners. Suddenly Dave peeled out of the escort pack and dropped back to the TORCH 3 mobile headquarters.

"TORCH 4, you should get the media folks over to talk to this lady—she has a story to tell," a voice said over the intercom speakers near my ears. When no one in our media vehicle responded, the voice from TORCH 3 made it quite clear. "TORCH 4, listen! This lady is running as a replacement for the relay runner who was selected to run this leg. He was killed in an accident a few weeks ago. The lady is his friend and, at the request of his family, she is distributing his ashes along his kilometre out of respect for his memory." We were dumbstruck with awe.

That night as we flew back to Calgary, Dave said, "Dad, thank you. I'll never forget this day." Steve said, "I loved running today. I've never loved running so much."

We heard many other fabulous stories. At least three women delivered babies shortly after completing their torch runs, one of them within an hour. Running the torch was a once-in-a-lifetime opportunity not to be missed for anything. The children born after the run will have their own Olympic tale to tell.

Kilometre 18,000

The final chapter in our Olympic Torch Relay story took place in Calgary at 2:13 p.m. on February 13th, when Calgary's Ken Read and Cathy Priestner ran the torch into McMahon Stadium. They represented all the men and women who had been recent Olympians, and they were now role models for our children.

The crowd roared as Ken and Cathy circled the stadium ringed with 88 torchbearers, one from each day of the record run. Native drummers struck up a beat as the torch moved around the perimeter of the stadium. Ken and Cathy stopped for a moment to share the flame with popular wheelchair Olympian Rick Hansen, and then moved onward to the stage at the north end of the stadium.

My heart jumped as I watched 12-year-old Robyn Perry bound from her sideline position onto the stage to receive the original Greek torch lit in Olympia nearly three months earlier.

She ascended the great white staircase bordered by the 1988 Olympic athletes from 57 countries who were, for the first time, seated and able to enjoy the opening ceremonies.

Robyn reached the cauldron landing. She paused, and acknowledged the athletes with three gentle bows. Then, skipping to the giant cauldron that had hydraulically risen from the floor, she stretched to her limit and lit the Olympic flame. In that moment, Robyn personified the hope—and promise—of the future.

CHAPTER EIGHTEEN

One for the Money, Two for the Show

If I have been able to see further than most, it is
because I have stood on the shoulders of giants.

SIR ISAAC NEWTON

I N SOME WAYS the story of Calgary's quest to host the
Olympic Winter Games is in the same western pioneer
spirit that drives oilmen to look for the "elephant" oilfield,
miners to look for the motherlode, or ranchers to build a new
Eden. No pioneer can ever tell in advance what he or she will
achieve, but the project is always exciting because he or she is,
in effect, inventing the future.

In 1982 our dreams had been questioned by many as the
usually sunny economic sky in Calgary turned temporarily
cloudy. OCO'88 was caught between our goal of the best-ever
Games and the worst economic period in Calgary since the
Depression. Our first priority was to find the money. Our second was to produce a top-quality show.

To reach our twin objectives would require a break-
through. We would have to change radically not only the way

CHRISTOPHER MILEJSZO • GREG STEWART • STUART VAUDRY • SUSAN RAWLYK • GORDON AUDLEY • STEVE BARCHAM • ROB MILLER •
KLAUS RICHTER • GEORGE PACHECO • TERRY GREEN • FRAN WILSON • CHARLOTTE FOORD • RICK DOELL • ROB DERKITT • SIMONETTE
KUHN • SUSAN MARSHALL • DOREEN BRANDLY • ESME' WILSON • ROBYN LEWIS • DAN FREE • JANET HARRIGAN • CORRI MORRIS • LARRY
STEIN • BLAINE MCGRATH • LORETTA MCKENNA • IRENE RECSKY • JOE NOLAN • JOHN MACKINNON • BRIAN TAYLOR • LIISI KOMULAINEN •
PAUL COLBORNE • DAVID SHAW • MARGARET CARMICHAEL • PETER PRIESTLEY-WRIGHT • PATTI LEMESURIER • THOMAS ZIMMERMANN •

the Games were managed, but also the Games themselves. The management of the Games must be carried out while keeping in place complex Olympic traditions, co-operation of three levels of government, contributions from private enterprise and support of the general public. The organization was responsible for operating at least a dozen different businesses, including engineering, construction, television broadcasting, media services, sports operations, publishing, entertainment, public relations, information systems, transportation, security, medical and food services, housing, and hosting.

Management by Participation

We had studied first-hand the management of the Olympic Winter Games in 1980 at Lake Placid and in 1984 at Sarajevo, as well as the 1984 Olympic Games at Los Angeles. We were struck by the fact that although the IOC owned the Games, there were few management tools that were passed on from one Games to the next. The IOC Charter provides some rules for organizers, and the IOC has Press, Medical, and Security commissions that link one Olympiad to the next. But the real meat and potatoes of the organizing was left to each new organizing group, largely without interference, or help, from the IOC. When it came to trying to figure out the right approach to take to manage the Games successfully, we were largely on our own.

Management guru Peter Drucker would probably characterize the typical Olympic organization as an example of "management by objectives" at work. With clear goals and strong rewards, the Olympic organizers of the past had almost always managed to achieve success.

But new management methods are sweeping businesses worldwide. Ordinary work is being turned into teamwork. Customers are working with suppliers to improve products and services. Middle managers are being asked to manage teams of people without top level supervision. Thus more people are given real responsibility for results. No one is left out. Leadership and recognition are shared. "Management by objectives" is being replaced by what I call "management by participation." The pyramidal management system belongs on the scrapheap of tired ideas. Management by participation developed out of our approach to solving a critical organizational problem.

It was evident that to succeed, we would need the help of thousands of people—the best people we could find. But many of the best people were already securely employed in their regular jobs and could not afford to leave them for a temporary term with Team'88. From the beginning it had been our plan to use a volunteer organization so we could attract top people. The problem was how to blend a small but strong full-time staff with a huge, highly skilled part-time volunteer corps without creating resentment.

We operated for several years with a centralized staff and committees of volunteers, each with its own chairman. During those early years I could often sense a lack of cohesion. For a while a sort of combat mentality proliferated, in which staff thought of themselves as "we" and the volunteers as "they," and vice versa. Bill Pratt and I actively discouraged this outlook. Russ Tynan, our general manager of volunteers at the time, even went so far as to have "US" T-shirts produced with a red bar through the words WE AND THEY. Pratt and I realized that the major weakness in our organization was a lack of good internal communication.

Our weak internal communications system in the early years of the organization created a field day for the Olympic reporters from the local media. With easy access to information from the mayor's office and some areas of discontent readily apparent, reporters could exploit the situation almost at will. Reporters were able to operate as information brokers, trading information from one source within OCO'88 for information from another. Thus at times they functioned as part of the Olympic internal communication system. But as time passed and a few of the more dissatisfied people left, the importance of the mission overcame the original weaknesses and good communication eventually allowed the team to jell.

Our internal communication was greatly strengthened when we joined the staff together with the volunteer chairmen in regular monthly meetings. It helped to know your buddy working beside you in the trenches. This was a turning point in the development of the character of our team. The shared leadership developed gradually. King and Pratt, seen by many as opposites, nevertheless served as examples of shared leadership and shared responsibility. The pyramidal management system was discarded. In its place, people were asked to take real responsibilities without several layers of supervision. This is what I call management by participation.

I can recall saying at one of our monthly Team'88 meetings that Team'88 was special. "We have our own uniforms, our own song, our own money, our own flag, and our own clear job to do," I said. "That's far more than many countries have to work with." The shared responsibility in everyone's hands was obvious. To succeed would require turning work into well-organized teamwork.

That was easy to say, but as the organization grew it had to evolve, and that inevitably generated some resentment. In each of the last three years before the Games, our organization doubled in size. Normally such a growth rate necessitates considerable reallocation of responsibilities. That wreaks a certain amount of misery among the personnel of the organization, and leads to conflicts, not all of which can be happily resolved.

I was always sorry to see anyone leave OCO'88, whatever the reasons. That was particularly true with Frances Jackson-Dover. She had approached me shortly after we had won the bid and we had immediately put her to work handling a variety of jobs, including media relations, communications, the arts festival, and ceremonies. Like almost everyone else, as the demands of her job grew, pieces of responsibility were carved off and assigned to others. Throughout, she remained one of our top managers, even though she and Bill Pratt had never been able to work within sight of each other.

Less than a year before the opening ceremonies, Frances and Bill came unglued over a reduction in the breadth of her responsibilities. Bill wanted Frances to focus on plaza ceremonies and opening and closing ceremonies. Frances wasn't happy with her proposed role, and in the verbal skirmish that resulted, neither party was prepared to compromise. I backed Bill in his decision, because he clearly had to be in a position to assign responsibilities to staff. Rather than give in, Frances decided to leave the team. Others picked up the slack, and we carried on.

Similar resentments over loss of authority arose as a result of the introduction of the venue management system. It was a serious factor in some of the resignations from OCO'88.

Venue Management

With numerous events taking place at each of six main venues the question of how to organize became critical for OCO'88. Operations at an Olympic venue require a multitude of services that have no direct relationship to any particular sport. Our sports chairmen and many others preferred to manage their events together with all related services themselves. That would mean, for instance, that if you had three different sports events in the course of a day at Canada Olympic Park, you would have three different people in charge of the park's operations. After careful study and some healthy debate, we decided to implement a venue-management system instead. Each venue was assigned a volunteer venue chairman responsible for its general operations. That left our sports chairmen free to focus on activities on the "field of play"—the crucial part of the venue.

The introduction of the venue-management system, however, did not sit well with our established sports chairmen, most of whom at that point had already been working with OCO'88 for three years. The sports organizations had been set up in the early years to help pick the best venues and to gain approval from the sports federations. Once the venues were approved and the critical sports work was done, the focus moved to preparing operational plans. When the venue chairmen, selected by Bill Pratt, were put in charge of venue operations, the sports chairmen felt they had been demoted and stripped of responsibilities. Although the decision was questioned at the time, it proved to be an essential ingredient of our success during the Games.

Preparing to Win

Just a month prior to the Games, we created a task force including Bill Pratt, Bruce Cleveley (Operations), Bill France (Sports), and myself. The purpose of the task force was to ensure that each team responsible for the operations of our venues understood its role. We invented a number of scenarios to test the theory that our teams knew how to play the game.

We asked one venue chairman: "What would you do if it was 10 minutes before an event was scheduled to start and only 10,000 people were in the venue while 40,000 were still lined up outside trying to pass through the ticket turnstiles?"

The chairman replied without hesitation, "I'd open up the gates and tell the people to come on in!"

"Great," we replied, "you're here to serve the people, not to make life miserable for them. For many people attending the Games will come only once in their lifetime."

We asked another: "What would you do if a truck backed into a fire hydrant at your venue and water was spraying everywhere?"

He said, "I'd call Bill Pratt and ask for help."

We said, "Why would you call Pratt—he's not a plumber! Call the public works department or a plumber yourself and get it fixed. Then call Pratt and tell him that everything is under control."

At the end of several days of focus on roles and responsibilities we had a team meeting to review what we had learned. The feedback proved that the exercise had been valuable. By direct and frequent contact we had reduced or eliminated doubt and fear that could have crippled our team in times of emergency. We had divided the project into manageable parts and assigned responsibility to capable people. And we had been able to identify where the gaps were in our detailed planning and training.

We were prepared for the XVth Olympic Winter Games. We now awaited the results of our efforts. When the Games came and the wind blew or accidents happened, our team responded professionally, applying their leadership skills with confidence.

There was no mental gridlock because the organization had competent leaders throughout. Everyone did his or her job and enjoyed doing it. We had built a team of giants. Since the Calgary Games the IOC has established several new commissions to help transfer the valuable business experience of past organizers to those on whom the future depends. The benefits have been substantial. The lessons learned from sport are often valid in business. In this case business has helped sport.

CHAPTER NINETEEN

Bright Ideas

The idea is there, locked inside. All you have to do
is remove the excess stone.

MICHELANGELO

THE CALGARY OLYMPIC WINTER GAMES provided many opportunities to Canada; one of them was a chance to bring
out the ingenuity of its people. Some ideas were borrowed from other host cities and improved upon, and some
of the ideas came from Calgarians themselves. Here are a few
of the best.

The Bear Facts

In February 1984 at the closing ceremonies of the Sarajevo
Games, Hidy and Howdy, the furry twin mascots of the
Calgary Olympics, made their first appearance. The lovable
larger-than-life polar bears began hugging their way into the
hearts of millions of people across Canada and around the
world. Hidy and Howdy were played by a troupe of about 140
Calgary students from Bishop Carroll High School. There were
six or seven sets of mascot suits, and public appearances were
carefully monitored to make sure the bears were never seen in

DWAYNE HAUCK • WILLIAM LAY • STEVEN CHAND'OISEAU • MARION MACKENZIE • SHIRLEY BELL • MATTHEW SNETSINGER • HARLEY
JOHNSON • KEITH OSBORNE • DAVID MARSURA • JUDITH TROWELL • CHERYL SIMONE-DOWNEY • JOHN MAHONEY • ROBIN DYMOND •
MICHAEL WALKER • TAMRA PURNELL • MARIE KNOX • KERRY ARCHBOLD • LINDA COURTMAN • BARRY CARBONETTO • DICK KELTIE • ANN
WILLIAMS • JIM NAY • KEITH MACELWAIN • IAN POOL • LEANNE HOWELL • KAREN BALCOMBE • KEITH TRAPTOW • CYNTHIA YOUNG • GARY
LADD • ELZBIETA MORRISON • KEITH BACON • SHAWNA ARON • BOB MERGNY • MICHAEL ADAMS • MARION KELLY • DENNIS MAYNARD •

public in two places at once. (We didn't want ugly rumors starting that they weren't real.) In all, the friendly duo made about 50,000 appearances at schools, community events, and sporting events of all kinds.

The selection of Hidy and Howdy as Olympic mascots and the program that resulted was one of the best ideas of the Games. The bears were cute and cuddly as well as big and friendly. Children loved their jaunty walk and howled with laughter when they attempted the winter sporting events. And because there were two of them, they could interact with each other. They danced and played and got their audience involved. Although the bears remained silent, they were able to delight audiences of all ages. We have dozens of pictures of Hidy and Howdy hugging people, and the people all have something in common—they're smiling.

During our visit to Lausanne in October 1986 our IOC liaison, Val Wheeler, was asked to play the role of Hidy and to greet President Samaranch as he emerged from the IOC session. Val had never been in the bear costume before. It is huge, warm, and awkward to manœuvre in. When Val saw Samaranch approaching she hustled toward him and bent over to give him a big hug but instead bonked him full on the forehead with Hidy's big bear nose. He was stunned by the assault but took it good-naturedly.

Hidy and Howdy, so far as I know, were the first twin mascots in Olympic history, and Hidy was the first female mascot for an Olympic Games. The bears were the brainwave of Calgary artist Sheila Scott, who won a public competition. The names were submitted by a 17-year-old Calgary student, Kim Johnston, who won a name-the-bears contest.

The World's Largest Olympic Torch

Our family was driving back to Calgary following a visit to Edmonton in the summer of 1983 and as we travelled Jeanette and I were discussing possible ideas for the creation of a permanent Olympic landmark in Calgary. Our older son, David, listened intently and as the Calgary skyline appeared over the horizon said, "You know Mom, if you really want to have an

Olympic monument, the Calgary Tower should become the world's largest Olympic torch." Another bright idea was born.

It took me several kicks at it to convince Bill Pratt and Jerry Joynt that I was serious when I said we were going to light up the tower. But once Jerry Joynt got Canadian Western Natural Gas involved, the idea really caught fire. Some of the best-ever pictures of Calgary were taken with the Calgary Tower flame burning for the world to see. The Olympic torches carried by 7,000 runners across Canada incorporated the tower's shape in their design.

The Calgary Tower must surely have been the biggest, highest and brightest Olympic flame in history. It created a special glow for Calgarians and visitors alike. The flame continues to be lit every now and then for special occasions.

The First Gold

During the opening ceremonies a thousand pigeons were released from their cages in McMahon Stadium. It marked the start of the first great Olympic Pigeon Race. Retired Calgary railway worker Sam Kolesuit was the owner of the first of 850 birds released to reach the designated finish line near the town of Bassano, more than 100 kilometres from Calgary. Sam's well-trained homing pigeon won the first Olympic gold of the Games for his proud owner. Pigeons, too, can live by the Olympic creed "swifter, higher, stronger."

Up, Up and Away

Kodak sponsored a hot-air balloon festival during the Games that featured 103 balloons from all over North America. High winds forced cancellation of flights on several days but on some of the calm, clear days it was an aerial fantasyland to see the brightly colored balloons—in the shape of propane bottles, gasoline pumps, a dinosaur, a cowboy hat, Mickey Mouse, and more—drifting across the Calgary skyline.

The Bishop's Rally

Bishop Paul O'Byrne put together a nondenominational religion committee that not only provided for the special needs of all athletes and visitors but also staged a religious rally at the Stampede Corral just prior to the Games. Bishop Paul and his helpers kept our focus on spiritual values and provided much-needed prayers for our success. We made a big mistake in not asking Paul's volunteer committee to handle the weather for the Games.

The Education Program

During our travels promoting Calgary's bid in early 1981, it was evident that in Europe, where the Olympics were traditionally held, young people had grown up with first-hand understanding of the Olympic Games and Olympic ideals. People in regions where the Games have been held learn more about sports, world records, names of record holders, and their country's top athletes. Olympics and World Cup competitions were always well-attended, with enthusiastic fans cheering for their countrymen. There was little of this in Western Canada.

We knew that educating young people was a leading goal of the Olympic movement. In late 1982 Jeanette, under the auspices of OCO'88's communications department, began collecting samples of educational material produced by other games: Edmonton's Commonwealth Games, the Brisbane Commonwealth Games, the Universiade, and the Lake Placid, Sarajevo, and Los Angeles Olympics. The idea continued to develop, until in 1984 staff were hired to put together teachers' manuals and organize educational activities.

Over 200 teachers of all grade levels and subject specialties worked on incorporating Olympic information into school curricula. By the fall of 1986, 1,700 Alberta schools had received resource kits consisting of a 500-page teachers' manual, posters, film strips, information pamphlets, and a video cassette.

The program was the first of its kind and the response to it was enthusiastic. The manuals showed how to incorporate Olympic information and examples into the teaching of practically every subject area. Students in phys ed could learn how to distinguish speed-skating skates from hockey skates. Students in math or physics could learn about velocity from examples using skiers. Students in chemistry could learn the secrets of snowmaking. Students in home economics could learn about high-tech fabrics for speed-skaters' suits.

Manuals were produced for Alberta elementary, junior high, and senior high schools. The Canadian government and the COA shared the cost of providing Olympic kits to elementary schools across Canada. The IOC headquarters in Lausanne requested copies, as did National Olympic Committees from 37 countries.

The Olympians

Kay Pringle tracked down all Canadian athletes from past Olympic Winter Games and invited them to participate in a series of public-speaking appearances at schools and at community events. It was important for young people to see former athletes becoming leaders in business and community affairs after their athletic years were over.

The Children's Gift

Hand-made greeting cards created by elementary school children were placed in the hotel room of each Olympic visitor. Many of our guests were so pleased they wrote personal thank-you notes to the child whose name appeared with the Winter Olympic scene on the card.

The Children's Ticket Fund

Although Bill Pratt was often credited with creating the Children's Ticket Fund, it was actually his predecessor, David Leighton, who originated the plan. As early as 1982 OCO'88 executives were being asked to speak at luncheons and banquets about the Olympic project. David's idea was to ask for a modest speaker's honorarium to be donated to a trust fund to finance the purchase of tickets to the Games on behalf of mentally or physically disabled children, and those too poor to afford it.

Over the years the Olympic Speakers' Bureau was developed and the money and donations trickled in, amounting to nearly $100,000 by 1987. Bill Pratt organized a final promotion by Coca-Cola and Safeway that pushed the fund over $300,000, allowing 12,400 children who would otherwise have been unable to do so to witness a once-in-a-lifetime event. The idea was magical. If the Olympic experience inspired even one young person to strive to do something he or she had never thought possible, then the Children's Ticket Fund was worthwhile.

Hi Mom!

What a perfect Olympic idea it was to invite the parents of Olympic athletes from all countries to stay in Calgary homes as guests. Rich Jones and Norma Leppert put together the plan. Labatt's sponsored the Canadian "Adopt-A-Parent" project by providing free plane fare and Olympic tickets to parents of people on Canada's Olympic teams.

Calgarians responded so well to the theme "Hold out your hand to make a friend" that more than 1,000 homes were offered when only about 300 could be used. About half those billeted were from Canada and the rest were from other countries. It was another Olympic first and an example of the warmth and generosity of the people of Calgary. Some of the friendships made and memories shared with parents of Olympians will last a lifetime.

Smoke Gets in Your Eyes

Dr. John Read, father of world-class skiers Ken and Jim Read, brought OCO'88 another bright idea. As a practising medical doctor actively involved with promoting athletic excellence, John Read asked OCO'88 to adopt a smoke-free policy for the Olympic Winter Games. We found the proposal attractive and consistent with the Olympic concept of developing a whole person through sport.

We found support for the idea from our chief medical officer and from our senior medical staff adviser. They worked out the details of removing ashtrays, posting No Smoking signs, and designating smoking areas to create the first Fresh-Air Olympics. The cardinal rule—maintained with vigor—was that no smoking was allowed at any place where athletes were present.

BURKE-GAFFNEY • LAURA DERBOWKA • GREG MACKENZIE • PATRICIA SUCHORAB • VAL WHEELER • RUBY MACLEOD • LORI WOYWITKA • HEIDI SCHMIDT • BRUCE FRASER • ROBIN CHARLEBOIS • BRIAN LEHMAN • PAT JENSEN • MARI-ANNE ALLAN • PAUL CONNOR • MARINA FLEMMING • RICKY SCHUH • WENDY MITCHELL • MARK BAECKER • KEN GALLINGER • CELINE DE SCHRYVER • JOAN MCCARTNEY • JOE PAWLAK • ERNIE MARCHIORI • SHELLEY STURROCK • ROSE WRIGHTSON • RAY KOKKONEN • DIANE GREGORY • IAN ROSS • JERRY HAASDYK • ARLO MOEN • JIM NORTHGRAVE • ERIC WILLIS • SHERRY DAHL • JERRY JOHNSTON • GORD LACHANCE • LOUIS GAAL • MARLENE NELSON •

OCO'88 received a World Health Organization award for its fresh-air achievement.

Team Petroleum'88

Bill Wardle's job was to find sponsors from among the biggest national companies. Only one sponsor would be chosen from each industry. But Wardle recognized the problem that would result in Calgary if we selected only one oil company as an exclusive sponsor, shutting out all others. The petroleum companies are major employers in Calgary. We needed their support in allowing employees to become volunteers.

To avoid the potential for problems, Wardle suggested that companies in the petroleum industry be invited to sponsor selected Olympic projects and to become a member of a joint industry sponsorship of the Games. The idea was brilliant and so the "Team Petroleum'88" concept was born. Wardle asked Doc Seaman, the soft-spoken and rock-solid chairman of Bow Valley Industries, who also headed Olympic fund-raising efforts in Alberta for the Olympic Trust, to lead Team Petroleum'88. (It was the same Doc Seaman who, together with his brother B.J. Seaman, Normie Kwong, Norman Green, Harley Hotchkiss and Ralph Scurfield, had brought the Calgary Flames NHL team to Calgary. When Kwong made speeches he would often joke, "When we bought the Flames at first it was just Kwong, Seaman, and Seaman. But we had to invite Green, Hotchkiss, and Scurfield to avoid being mistaken for a Chinese sperm bank.")

Wardle made offers of project sponsorship to the biggest players in the energy industry. Shell took an outstanding Indian artifacts exhibit called *The Spirit Sings,* Texaco took the arts festival hit *Porgy and Bess,* TransCanada PipeLines took the new *Naturbahn* luge run at Canada Olympic Park and the Athletes' Arch at the Olympic Village, and NOVA sponsored our computer services headquarters and Theatre Calgary. Most of the rest joined Team Petroleum'88 in funding both the Games and the Canadian Olympic team to the tune of more than $4 million.

Enterprise'88

Peter Lougheed, David Mitchell, and Norman Green came up with an idea to invite business leaders from around the world to the Calgary Winter Games. An ad-hoc committee known as "Enterprise'88" was created and a special business leaders' network established. The group of business people enjoyed Olympic events using tickets donated by companies and private citizens in Calgary who had bought the tickets already. The group met up in the mountains at Kananaskis Lodge to discuss business opportunities in Canada. Prime Minister Mulroney, Alberta Premier Don Getty, and Mayor Klein attended the main sessions even though their Olympic schedules were already crowded. Feedback after the Games showed that the goodwill generated by Enterprise'88 led to several new business opportunities and the creation of a network of friends.

The Albertville 1992 organizing committee expanded and improved the concept to create "Club de Coubertin." This group of sponsors was given an excellent package of ticket and other business benefits in exchange for financial support of the Games.

A Visitors' Centre

The Calgary Olympic Centre was a fresh idea. It was created in downtown Calgary at the base of the Calgary Tower as a means of communicating the Olympic story. The centre was filled with computerized slide and movie shows outlining the winter sports and Calgary's plans for the Games. Mechanized models of cartoon characters thrilled tiny children, and bigger children played computer quiz games to test their knowledge of sports. But the most popular shows were the ski-jump and bobsleigh simulators, which provided a thrill almost like the real thing. There was no charge for a visit to the Calgary Olympic Centre, thanks to the Canadian Pacific group of companies, who paid for the whole display, and several hundred hardworking friendly volunteers who managed the centre. Over more than two years, half a million people visited and enjoyed the Calgary Olympic Centre.

The Power of Excellence

A few months before the Calgary Winter Games I took the opportunity to visit the costume shop where the uniforms for the opening ceremonies were being prepared. Nearly 1,000 volunteers, mostly senior citizens and parents of dancers in the opening ceremonies, took their regular turn in a huge makeshift costume factory. There were rows on rows of sewing machines where costumes were already being prepared in a variety of brilliant colors. The unusual uniforms were to form part of the two-hour show for the world. The people working there received no tangible reward for their work, yet they were happy to be involved.

A visit to any one of the places where Olympic volunteers were at work always served to remind me of the tremendous untapped potential hidden in every one of us.

The Team'88 Clubhouse

The Olympic Volunteer Centre built by OCO'88 at McMahon Stadium was another great idea. It was the clubhouse for all Team'88 members. It had bright, functional workspace for volunteers as well as a large meeting hall on the second floor that was used as a volunteer training centre and for monthly public board meetings and frequent social club events.

During the Games it was converted to Club'88—a place where volunteers could relax, get refreshments, and have social contact with their buddies before they went home to crash. I asked Samaranch to visit Club'88 one night during the Games. He spoke briefly to the crowd of happy and tired workers. They cheered him wildly and he left touched by the energy and commitment of our people.

The camaraderie that made the Team'88 Clubhouse a special place had been fostered by events like the Team'88 Recognition Dinner held at the Stampede Round-Up Centre in May 1987. It was the largest sit-down dinner in Alberta history. The 8,000 people who attended consumed a total of 8,000 pounds of beef, 8,000 potatoes, 2,400 pounds of carrots, 12,000 dinner rolls, and 2,659 gallons of beer. It took under an hour to serve everyone.

LAURIE BAINES • DAVE SAUTER • GARRY WEETMAN • TREVOR CORNEIL • MARNEY ARMITAGE • ELIZABETH SCHOENING • PETER TAIT • ROSS HAYNES • HUGH DUNNE • MELANIE DUNPHY • DIANE BRUNETTE • MARC FOURNIER • DAVID ETMANSKI • BROOKE BAILLIE • ARCHIE EVANSON • BRIAN MEIER • GUDNY JOKULSDOTTIR • DORRIT REINHOLDT • ISABEL AITCHESON • RANDY TOPOLNITSKY • HELEN SAFARIS • DARREL JANZ • GARY CUMBERLAND • RICHARD NOBLE • GERDA GROOTHUIZEN • DON MACKENZIE • ROBERT SHARMAN • MIKE CHOW • PHIL CAREY • CARL WERBISKY • TUDOR BEATTIE • SHARON WINKCUP • KEVIN PACKER • DENNIS FLANAGAN • STAN HOWARTH • BOB SHAW • LINDA

The Olympic Plaza

In Sarajevo we watched the presentation of Canada's first gold medal to Gaetan Boucher in a downtown open area in the space between three buildings and a major street. People crowded in to catch a glimpse of the Olympic champions. They cheered and cried when the flags of the winners' nations were raised and the national anthems played.

In our travels together I had often remarked to Ralph Klein that every great city had taken care to create open places for people—broad avenues, parks, and plazas. The night Gaetan Boucher received his medal the tears of pride had barely dried before we had agreed that Calgary must have such a place. More than any other, Calgary's Olympic Plaza turned out to be the place where the Olympic spirit was kindled. It was a meeting place where athletes, visitors, and citizens could come together. The mix of joy and pride was perfect. So was the warm weather. Every night people mingled in the streets for hours dressed only in light winter clothing.

The brick sidewalks around the upper level of the plaza had been bought and paid for by citizens of Calgary who wanted to be part of Olympic history. For $19.88 you could buy a single brick with your name or the name of a loved one or friend on it.

OCO'88 bought a brick for each IOC member to say thank you to them for the honor of hosting the XVth Olympic Winter Games. Thousands of Calgarians and friends now have a permanent place at the official people place in downtown Calgary.

The Olympic Plaza medal ceremonies were a huge success. Crowds ranging from 30,000 to 60,000 packed the square every night to watch colorful entertainment by the Young Canadians of the Calgary Stampede and to cheer the Olympic champions. An enormous video matrix board was moved into place each night to provide a better view of the stage. Music filled the air.

Looking west from the Olympic Plaza you could see three large buildings framing the skyline. With the co-operation of Petro-Canada, the Royal Bank, and PanCanadian Petroleum, we were able to drape the buildings with 10-storey fabric screens. At night the giant screens were the site of shimmering green laser images of skiers, skaters, and tobogganers in action.

When our arts festival committee had suggested a laser light show, we had already been favorably disposed to the idea because of what we had seen in Los Angeles in 1984. The Los Angeles Olympics provided dramatic examples of what could be done with lasers, fireworks, giant skytracker searchlights, and music. During the Olympic Eve Gala at the Hollywood Bowl in 1984, Bob Niven and I had been introduced to the director of the projector light show. We had picked up a number of tips from him about how to use visual effects.

The finale each evening was the fireworks display, which featured huge starbursts exploding barely 50 metres above street level. Major streets had to be temporarily closed during the display, and special permits were required.

Just 50 metres away from the Olympic Plaza, Coca-Cola set up a large tent devoted to pin trading. pin trading at Olympic Games has flourished over the past decade. Today it serves as a popular part of the Olympic culture and to break the ice between strangers. The pin-trading centre was jammed all day long with barterers. Each night after the Festival of Lights show, part of the crowd would cram into the Coke Pin Trading Centre. We heard of prices as high as $250 for the rarest pins.

After the Games OCO'88 erected bronze plaques under the Olympic Plaza archways, listing the names of all the medal winners.

If It Won't Snow—Make It

Calgary winters in the years leading up to the Games seemed to be warmer and drier than usual. Team'88 didn't want anything to prevent the competitions from being perfect for the athletes. The construction of the covered Olympic Oval took speed skating out of reach of chaotic winter weather. The extensive and expensive refrigeration of the bob and luge track made that facility weather-resistant. Snowmaking facilities, using state-of-the-art designs, were installed at Canada Olympic Park, Canmore Nordic Centre, and Nakiska to provide more insurance that Calgary would have real winter conditions.

With warm dry weather in the forecast, we added one more safety feature. A chemical agent called Sno-Max was added to the snowmaking machines to increase their capacity by an amazing 30 per cent. By the time the warm snowless weather came, we had already covered all the venues with at least three metres of packed snow. We were glad we had the best modern snow- and ice-making systems to provide the essential elements of winter.

It is a common misconception that the warm weather was a problem during the Calgary Games. It was not. The winds were a problem, but warm weather was welcome, because we knew we had enough snow and could always come up with more. All in all, the conditions we ended up with were preferable to too much snow or extreme cold.

There were many more bright ideas that made the Calgary Winter Games special. Our community found new ways to express itself to the world. For those involved the memories will last forever and the benefits will long be felt.

The Calgary Olympic Winter Games will be remembered for the spirit of the people, a true reflection of Olympic spirit. There were many who participated, and there were no losers. That spirit is still alive and well and living in Calgary, looking for a chance to show itself again.

SLIMM · ROD COLBERT · DENIS DESJARDINS · CHERYL PHILLIPS · ANNA HEPNER · KAREN BUCK · STEPHEN TUPPER · MAUREEN ELLIOT · FRANK ARCHER · ERIC CLINE · JAMES DEJEWSKI · JOHN BRUCE · GLENN FAASS · HENRY PYLVAINEN · GARY ATHANS · ROY PINDER · HEATHER THOMPSON · VICKI BROWN · AHNE CRAWFORD-RIDLEY · LYNN MCKEOWN · BILL LOUIE · GORDON SCOTT · NICOLE SMITH · CAROLE RHYASEN · CHANDRA RUSSELL · HANCE MILNER · KATHERINE SALMON · DELIA CYR · KEN MORRICE · HEATHER MACCORMACK · BRENDA SILVER · DAVID HICKS · ELIZABETH MCGREGOR · ANDREW KRYZAN · EDUARD STARK · JOHN KLEMP · NORRIS BOWDEN · LIZZ DICK

CHAPTER TWENTY

Are We Having Fun Yet?

There is one thing stronger than all the armies in the
world and that is an idea whose time has come.

VICTOR HUGO

I GREETED JUAN ANTONIO SAMARANCH at the Calgary airport
at 9:50 p.m. on February 3rd, 1988. We met briefly with the
media and I suggested that weather could be our only
problem. Everything else for the XVth Olympic Winter Games
was ready.

We chatted amicably in the back seat of the limousine driving through the frigid night to the Palliser Hotel—IOC
headquarters. Our security officer seated in front found the right
moment to introduce himself and to politely explain the service
he and his RCMP colleagues would be providing. He concluded
by saying, "Mr. President, if you ever need this car, all you need
to do is call at least 24 hours in advance and we'll be at your
service." I blanched and uttered a silent oath. He had inadvertently stepped on a hornet's nest. For years Bill Pratt and I had
tried to convince Samaranch and the IOC executive board that
our own central radio-dispatch system of transport was superior to the old and inefficient dedicated car-and-driver system

used in previous Games. In recent weeks Bill Pratt had been unable to convince IOC Director Raymond Gafner of this, and had made matters worse by telling Gafner the IOC didn't have any idea how to organize Games and they should rely on organizers who know best what to do. Trying to sell that idea was like trying to sell a concrete lifejacket to a drowning man. Gafner had warned Samaranch of a Calgary plot to use an untried transport system, and Samaranch had called me seeking assurances the transportation system would be as always—a dedicated system with one car assigned to each IOC member.

The city looked cold and frosty as we drove down the hill into the Bow River valley, which cradles the tightly clustered office towers of downtown Calgary. Most foreign visitors are pleasantly surprised by the clean, sparkling view of this modern city, having expected a pioneer western town or a more typical winter alpine village. Samaranch had been here at least six times before. As we drove he carefully surveyed the pageantry in place on all the major streets, and, while he was pleased, he noted the IOC flag was not displayed as frequently as he had expected. Before we went to the hotel that would be his home for the next month I drove him to the Olympic Plaza. He was happy with the huge Olympic rings that dominated the plaza.

We met in Samaranch's room the next day. As expected after the conversation in the limousine the previous night, he reminded me of our commitment to provide each IOC member, NOC president, and sport federation president with individual cars. He spoke sternly about the extensive experience of the IOC in many previous Games and said there were some things they knew better than Calgary organizers did.

I acknowledged the value of the advice and experience the IOC had shared with us over six years. But I could not resist adding that we had carefully studied the IOC system of transport and had seen some problems we felt certain could be overcome with a radio dispatch system. I asked him if we could test our system during the first days before the Games so he could see the advantages.

"However, we have already agreed to use your system," I hastened to add. "If you insist, we will use the IOC system—

but we do not believe the system is efficient and we think it will result in serious delays in travel time for IOC members compared to our system." I could see Samaranch was irritated, perhaps because he perceived my remarks as impertinent. "I repeat, Chairman King—we have more experience than you and we have your word that each IOC member will have a dedicated car and driver." After all the years we had worked together Samaranch still called me Chairman King when business was being discussed.

It was a battle we had lost a year or so earlier. We had discussed the matter frequently at IOC headquarters but the IOC had stood firm behind tradition. I again confirmed our willingness to compromise. I should have quit sooner, because my aggressive stance had served only to entrench Samaranch's opposition. Bill Pratt had sat silently listening to our exchange. But he couldn't take it any more. He interrupted the IOC president, saying, "You have experience from many other Games, but not in Calgary. We know what is best in Calgary. You should trust us."

Samaranch was overcome with anger. He stood up, walked glacially around his chair and raged at Bill: "Listen to me. If you aren't going to keep your promises then I will not use your transport and neither will anyone else in the IOC. We will rent our own cars and drivers and you will pay the bills."

I decided to call time out. We left Samaranch with assurances that our word was our bond. The IOC system was in. There were several other issues on my mind, both major and minor, that I wanted to discuss with him, but there was no point in trying to get him to focus on anything else for the moment. We left for the opening of the athletes' village with all the other issues unresolved.

IOC member Kevin Gosper, who sat in on our meeting, told me later he had never known Samaranch to be so angry. Samaranch told me he did not want to deal directly with Bill Pratt again.

Although our VIP transportation system involving a radio-equipped pool of cars had been criticized and rejected by the IOC, it has now been accepted as "the best possible system" for 1992 in Albertville, France. In Calgary, many IOC members learned to take advantage of the "taxi service" we offered, even though dedicated cars and drivers were also available. It's a much more efficient system once the participants appreciate how to use it.

The Countdown

My wife Jeanette and I moved into the Palliser Hotel the next day, February 4th, to facilitate our hectic schedule and frequent daily changes of clothing over the next month. Our suite was small, and crowded with special OCO'88 communication and computer gear and several television sets, directly linked to host-broadcaster signals from all venues.

Like most senior members of the OCO'88 team, I wore a pager on my belt so our headquarters could reach me instantly if needed. The system was a lifesaver.

We established a daily schedule of meetings starting at 7 a.m. to deal with last-day ticket distribution and last-minute accreditation approval, followed by meetings with our management team, then the IOC Executive Committee and finally with the OCO'88 board of directors. By 10:30 every morning we had dealt with the problems of the previous day and were ready to see what a new day would bring.

The IOC members and administration staff had descended on Calgary early in February 1988. Val Wheeler had prepared well for their arrival and for the 93rd session of the IOC in Calgary, which preceded the opening of the Games by three days.

During the final year leading up to the Games, Val Wheeler had graduated from being my executive secretary to taking over the important role of IOC liaison. Her job included organizing the IOC session and arranging for IOC rooms and administrative offices in the Palliser Hotel. She arranged for all the needs of the IOC members.

The IOC session is an important part of Olympic tradition. It is roughly equivalent to the annual general meeting of shareholders in business. It opens with what is called the Solemn Ceremony. The Solemn Ceremony consists of the playing of the Olympic Hymn, some cultural performances, and brief speeches from the president of the National Olympic Committee, the head of state, and the president of the IOC. Any new IOC members who have been elected are also invited to pledge their allegiance to Olympic ideals during a short induction ceremony. The symbol of our session was the head of a horse integrated with the Olympic rings in teal green.

The Solemn Ceremony held in Calgary's new Performing Arts Centre was superb. Entertainment featured the toe-tapping Calgary Fiddlers, a young violin virtuoso, Corey Cerovsek (who played on in spite of a broken violin string) the Toronto Children's Choir singing the Olympic Hymn, the Foothills Brass, and the Calgary Youth Orchestra. It was a program dedicated to youth. Roger Jackson, president of the Canadian Olympic Association, spoke about the importance of the Games in the development of Canadian sport, and Don Mazankowski, deputy prime minister of Canada, welcomed the IOC members.

At the IOC Sessions over the seven years since we had been awarded the Games in Baden-Baden, our team had reported on the progress of our Olympic plans. From a humble beginning with no facilities in place, we were now able to report, in Calgary, that we were ready.

The IOC members responded warmly to our welcome, but a deep freeze had a grip on Calgary as the temperatures fell through the bottom of the thermometer at −28°C. The air was very dry. For many of our visitors from warmer places the weather provided new meaning to the term freeze-dried. We placed our hopes on the weather forecast, which predicted the arrival of warm westerly winds in the next few days. But by the evening of February 12th, Olympic Eve, the warming trend had not yet arrived.

Our Olympic Eve Gala was set for the Jubilee Auditorium. The program was to feature country-and-western music and an appearance by the Right Honorable Brian Mulroney. Michael Tabbitt and his clever gang of cultural event organizers had planned a sensational entry for the prime minister. They would have him enter from the rear of the auditorium and go right down the aisle through the audience to the front stage—riding

CHADDERTON · TRACY WEICKER · MABEL CHILLACK · GRANT SAWCHUK · DOUG WARD · WOODY FREAKE · GIL CARLSON · TRICIA IRVINE · MARY-JO WOOLGAR · BRUCE MACDONALD · LYLE SPEERS · MICHAEL JOHNSTON · CHARLES SMART-ABBEY · JUDITH HOOD · MARY CRAIG · MARY ELLEN WYSS · DEBI WHITE · GARY VANDERGRIFT · DOROTHY MUIRHEAD · JINNY WARNER · SURINDER KHANNA · RAY ZELL · GARTH LYNCH · ROBERT STOWELL · KELLY LEECH · JEAN MACGREGOR · WILF HELMS · PEGGY WILSON · DAVID RENCZ · GERALD FORSETH · HIESEM AMERY · LIONEL SINGLETON · DONNA FOURNIER · JUNE PEARSON · ELAINE GOLD · CHERYL BOURASSA · TROY STOOKE · MICHAEL

a horse. I would ride a second horse down the other aisle and we would greet each other in a typical western way in front of the audience and on national TV.

When I heard the idea I loved it. I recalled I had promised Dick Pound years earlier that someday we would find a perfect Olympic setting to ride our Calgary horse. This was our last chance. But just a few days before the gala, Tabbitt called to tell me the prime minister's office had nixed the plan. The P.M., it appeared, was not happy riding horses.

I said, "Call the PMO and assure them we will have a very tame horse and a good handler at his side. Tell them it will be a great public-relations move and will be something everyone will remember." Unfortunately, the PM could not be convinced. Eventually the reason came out: Mulroney suffers from a fear of heights, and even being up on a horse would be enough to bother him. We were forced to abandon our plan. Instead we entered in an old-fashioned stagecoach (alas horseless) on a rotating platform, the prime minister and myself up front and Mila and Jeanette as our passengers.

I made some brief remarks about Olympic Eve being as exciting as New Year's Eve with all the expectations of Christmas Eve, and then I introduced our special guest as "The Downright Honorable Brian Mulroney."

After visiting the Olympic Volunteer Centre to hear that Brian Orser would be the flag bearer for the Canadian team, we ended our Olympic activities at a CTV host-broadcaster shindig. CTV had rented the large dining hall at the nearby SAIT campus for a celebration with 800 of their closest friends.

To provide a climax for an evening of excitement the Coca-Cola chorus sang David Foster's Olympic themesong "Can't You Feel It" for the CTV guests. Coke had selected two of the best young singers from each of about 15 different Olympic countries and brought them together in Calgary. It was an exciting preview that created a real buzz among the crowd.

Jeanette and I drove home to the Palliser Hotel at 1 a.m. tired but happy, and hopeful that these would be the wonderful Games so many had worked for since November 1978.

CHAPTER TWENTY-ONE

Three to Get Ready and Four to Go

To strive, to seek, to find and not to yield.
ALFRED LORD TENNYSON

ON THE MORNING OF FEBRUARY 13TH, 1988, I rose a few minutes before the alarm sounded and peered out into a grey morning sky over downtown Calgary.

"How are you this morning, dear?" asked Jeanette.

"I'm ready!" I replied, thinking I should be feeling nervous or worried. I felt calm and confident. The years of effort and planning, of checking and double-checking, provided a psychological soother. We were ready to go for it—and I knew it.

A Family Support System

Two nights earlier, I had received a special note from our daughter Linda.

Dear Dad,

I wanted to let you know just how proud I am to be your daughter. Of all the lessons you could have given me on how to make a dream come true, none could be so meaningful as seeing it happen.

And this time your dream has become the dream of thousands of others who will never forget the next three weeks.

"Mr. Sunshine," "Captain Calgary," "the smooth-talking visionary". . . that's my Dad. Through all the controversy and pressures, you've kept your eyes straight ahead on reaching the ultimate goal. I think about what you taught me about running—visualizing reaching out for a pole, then another, pulling myself forward, pole after pole, faster and stronger with every step. Being the best ever! It is happening just as you said it would.

The next three weeks will be the toughest, funnest time of your life. Thank you for sharing your dream come true. Have fun—and give 'em snoose!

All my love,
LINDA

The letter had reminded me of the extraordinary support and love I had received from Jeanette and all our family. It had been difficult for our family to endure all of the public criticism and controversy from the sidelines. I felt like the luckiest person alive to have survived 10 years with only good feelings. Everyone who has ever served in public life understands the importance of a strong family.

Even before the Games were over our oldest daughter, Diane, who is married and lives in Ottawa, had encouraged me to record my recollections of the Olympic story. We sat for hours, at her insistence, on the deck at our cottage in the mountains talking together while the tape recorder kept track of the Olympic tales. Diane, a graduate in journalism from Carleton University, not only pushed me into action but produced the first organization of my thoughts for this book. I needed her support, but more importantly, I enjoyed the common bond of working together to reach a goal. And Linda, even though she lived in Toronto, had become an active Olympic volunteer as part of the Olympic Speakers' Bureau.

The First Day

Jeanette and I arrived 10 minutes late for the 10 a.m. mayor's brunch because I was held up at our morning meetings attending to the issues of opening day. Our seats beside the Governor-General were still vacant but brunch was already under way. City protocol chief Sheila-Marie Cook admonished us for being late, obviously feeling that her party at city hall had priority over the opening-day preparations for the Games themselves. I ignored her comments with a smile. Nothing was going to faze me.

We left on buses direct for McMahon Stadium. The weather was blustery and –9°C as we entered the VIP lounge at the north end of the stadium. Our sons David and Stephen had managed to talk their way into the lounge. They appeared suddenly in front of me with Mary Hart, host of the television show *Entertainment Tonight*, and with devilish grins on their faces. Mary had become our friend through Marjoe Gortner, TV personality and organizer of deluxe charity celebrity events throughout North America. Marjoe and OCO'88 had collaborated with the Province of Alberta on two great celebrity events.

I did a quick TV interview with Mary Hart and then the call came from OCO'88 protocol chief Art Smith and his deputy Bill Warden that it was time to assemble for the opening ceremonies. Unfortunately, many IOC members had been transported directly to the stadium and were left shivering in the cold for almost an hour before the ceremony started. Ten minutes before the hour, the 1,100-person Olympic choir assembled at the north-end seating area. Dressed in robes in the five Olympic colors, they formed the Olympic rings and sang "Come Together." It helped to warm up the chilled crowd.

As we emerged from the concourse into the stadium I was overwhelmed by the sight of 60,000 people, all wearing colored plastic ponchos. It was Calgary's largest sit-down audience ever, and it looked superb. On the west side of the stadium the ponchos made a giant red maple leaf on a white background. On other sides of the stadium they made the CODA snowflake logo and the five Olympic rings. People loved the idea of being included in the picture during one of Calgary's finest hours. Our concern that some spoilsports might not put their ponchos on proved unfounded. Given the temperature of –9°C and the brisk wind, the chance to put on an added windbreaker was welcomed by everyone.

As we reached our seats the stadium seemed sparkling clean and new. My thoughts went back over the years, when I had visited other stadiums used for opening ceremonies. In 1964 and 1976 Innsbruck had used its ski jumping bowl for about 50,000 people who stood during traditional ceremonies lasting about 45 minutes. In 1972 Sapporo had used a stadium built from earth with timber supports, creating stepped seating areas for 50,000 spectators in the outdoor speed skating oval. I had sat on those same earth seats in 1979. In 1980 Lake Placid organizers erected a 25,000-seat temporary stadium in a farmer's field about five miles out of the village. The temporary seats we had placed at the north and south ends of McMahon Stadium reminded me of the seats at Lake Placid. I recalled being bitterly cold as we huddled in the Lake Placid Stadium in temperatures of about –20°C. At Sarajevo in 1984 the main stadium held about 50,000 people but only the VIP section had bench seats—all other people stood throughout the 75-minute spectacular.

How fortunate we were in Calgary to be able to accommodate a record number of spectators for our opening ceremonies. Over the next 16 days our Games would have as many spectators as the previous three Winter Olympics combined! Nearly two billion people would watch our citizens at work and play on television.

Jeanette and I took our seats beside the Olympic dignitaries gathered in McMahon Stadium for the opening ceremonies. I noticed that something was missing. I had expected to see a large lump in the middle of the field but it was nowhere in sight. The lump was a large plastic inflatable set of Rocky Mountains which were to rise from the field during the opening number. At the end of the 11-minute segment the mountains would split open at the top and thousands of helium balloons would emerge. During a dry run half an hour before the opening ceremonies, the wind, which was gusting up to 50 kilometres an hour, played havoc with the inflatable mountains. Paddy Sampson decided not to take a chance, so the Rocky Mountains were "gone with the wind."

The announcer counted down each of the last five minutes before the opening ceremonies were to begin. Then, at exactly 1 p.m., a trumpet fanfare sounded, and the announcer said,

"Welcome to Alberta's Rocky Mountain salute to the XVth Olympic Winter Games." The moment had come.

The opening number included Indian chiefs, the RCMP musical ride, and an array of western trick riders, barrel racers, and chuckwagon racers. Two giant green-and-yellow dinosaurs came onto the field and were held down in the bold winds by extra-beefy players from the University of Calgary Dinosaurs football team. The colored balloons were released by hand to a roar of approval from the fans, who did not know they had missed the mountain scene.

Hundreds of Canadians dressed in ethnic costumes ringed the floor of the stadium. Governor-General Jeanne Sauvé arrived in a horse-drawn landau to a musical vice-regal salute. Samaranch and I greeted her on the field and escorted her to the Royal Box, located 25 rows above the field.

One of the highlights of every opening ceremonies is the entrance and parade of the athletes. At Calgary, though, they would not just parade in and parade out, but get a chance to enjoy the event themselves. When the Australian team entered and the music changed from a lively march into an even livelier rendition of "Happy Birthday," the fans erupted with appreciation. In 1988 Australia was celebrating 200 years as a country. We received dozens of letters of thanks for that birthday greeting from Australians who were watching the Games on television in the middle of their summer.

The teams received a warm welcome as they travelled around the stadium walking on a pure white, packed-sand base covering the green Astroturf. Few people realized the centre field area used by the dancers was actually plywood and carpet laid over a giant artificial ice rink already frozen in place for the closing ceremonies 15 days away.

Attractive young ladies, bearing the name-boards of each participating nation, were dressed in pale green, fur-trimmed outfits. They were happy and elegant as they led athletes from 57 nations around the stadium floor and to the seats provided at the north end of the stadium.

The Canadian team, led by figure skater Brian Orser and *Chef de Mission* Jean Grenier, entered last, to a standing ovation from

GARRETT · RON MILLER · TIM LYNCH · SHAWNA MACDONALD · DAVID FLEMING · PAT MCLELLAN · DEBRA MORGAN · LINDA HUNTER · LOUISE VIEN · ED DUKE · SYLVIANE GREENE · LOIS WEERSTRA · KEVIN KERR · JANICE EVANS · EVA DUNCAN · WILLI MULLER · FOREST WOOD · RICHARD KENT · RALPH SIMONE · RON MOYNIHAN · JAMES CHASE · RONALD GOODISON · MANFRED LUKAS · RICHARD BREAKENRIDGE · JULIA BURNS-SENIOR · LAWRENCE LEMIEUX · PAM MULHALL · KIM ATKINS · ROBBERT HOFFMANN · SANDRA KAUTZMAN · BRUCE AITKEN · CARMEN CARRON · ALLAN FEIR · ALEX WILKINSON · DJUMA DUMISIC · DEE READ · MARION WOLFF · TERESA VANDERWEIDE · MARGARET

the international audience. They were dressed in colorful red and white long coats with western-style leather fringe and white Stetsons. They had managed to trade ceremonies parade passes with other teams to ensure the whole 165-member team was present. Canada's famous red maple leaf flags sprouted throughout the audience, which formed a spectacle of pride and color for the athletes while they did the same for a world audience.

The giant Olympic flag that would fly over the host city was marched into the stadium by 10 of Canada's past winter Olympic heroes: Frank Sullivan (hockey), Nancy Greene-Raine (skiing), Anne Heggtveit (skiing), Lisa Savijarvi (skiing), Steve Podborski (skiing), George Mara (hockey), Lucile Wheeler (skiing), Gaetan Boucher (speed skating), Kathy Kreiner (skiing), and Vic Emery (bobsleigh).

The Olympic choir then sang the Olympic anthem in Greek. Many IOC members remarked that it was the best presentation of the anthem they could recall. The colors were brilliant in the winter sunshine, which had broken through the patches of cloud.

During the kaleidoscopic dance of the Caloco Dancers, Unni Claridge, chief of our outstanding group of hostesses, escorted Samaranch and me to the stage in front of the athletes, who were now seated beneath a giant blue steel teepee structure that crossed in an arch above them. Hidden behind them was a bronze cauldron patiently waiting to rise into the view of more than a billion people watching on television. As we walked to the stage I remembered how I had spent one Sunday morning with this great group of dancers offering a few encouraging words about the importance of doing something great rather than doing nothing. This was their chance, and they did themselves proud.

Gary Arthur and I had written my welcoming speech the day before. We tried to mention as many participants in the Games as possible. I had only two minutes to make it happen, and as I approached the microphone the famous "wave" had already begun in the crowded stands. It was an incredible sight to see, but my mind raced between thoughts of similar dangerous loads on the temporary seating structure that had collapsed at the Los Angeles Olympics, and the tight two-hour television schedule.

I decided to proceed with my speech, making my protocol acknowledgements right in the middle of the raucous third round of the wave rippling around me. By the time I began my remarks the wave had gone calm.

> On behalf of the Calgary Olympic Organizing Committee, I am pleased and honored to welcome our neighbors of the world who have come together in Calgary.
>
> These Games will have different meaning to many different people. Across Canada, Canadians have already been deeply touched by the sharing of the Olympic flame.
>
> For the people of Alberta, today marks the beginning of a lasting legacy of sports facilities. For the people of Calgary—what the world's athletes are going to do over the next 15 days is real. The dream has become a reality.
>
> And to all the people who have done so much to help: Look now at what you have created—and be proud. To the outstanding athletes of snow and ice assembled here today—your dedication to the pursuit of excellence brings honor to yourself, to your family and to the Olympic movement.
>
> To all of you—remember the Calgary Winter Games with the knowledge that you have inspired the youth of the world and the leaders of tomorrow. For all members of the Olympic Family working tirelessly for youth and sport, we are sure these Games will make your efforts worthwhile. We want the XVth Olympic Winter Games to encourage even more people to join in your powerful push toward a more peaceful world.
>
> And finally, for one man—I know these Games are very special. Earlier this week he described them as a miracle of shared friendship.
>
> It is my great honor to introduce the leader of the Olympic movement—the president of the International Olympic Committee, Juan Antonio Samaranch.

Samaranch spoke briefly and then invited Governor-General Jeanne Sauvé to declare the Games open. As we returned to our seats 1,100 exuberant children ran onto the field to create a dynamic display of each of the sports of ice and snow. The audience loved them. Samaranch remarked to me what an excellent idea it was to include so many children in such a creative way. The children ended up forming a giant image of a dove, the symbol of peace. They pulled giant white feathers from beneath their shimmering blue uniforms and the huge Olympic dove fluttered its silent message from the children of Calgary to the people of the world.

ALPHONSE VAILLANT · ROB MACKENZIE · KENT EDINGA · ANNE PEARCE · DIANNE WILLOTT · DARLENE DODDS · AUDREY BAKEWELL · STEPHEN KENNEDY · STEPHEN LESLIE · STAN PARKER · ROSEMARY WINKLER · PERSIS CLARKSON · ALEX STIEDA · CLAYTON SLACK · EARL HANES · DOUG OHRN · SID TUCKEY · CARL BOND · COLIN DICK · GORDON PAYNTER · JOHN M ARMITAGE · HEATHER WILLOUGHBY · SANDRA COOPER · PETER RUSSON · MARISE KELLY · PENNY OLAUSON · FLORA BESSELL · MICHAEL TERPSTRA · JACK DAVIS · DARYL PHILLIPS · ELFIE ELIAS · DENNIS KING · JOHN HONG · MORLEY MCDOUGALL · JERRY JOSEPH · GRANT BINDER · JUDY HORNE · JACQUELYN STONE ·

Gordon Lightfoot and Ian Tyson teamed up to sing two western songs of Alberta: "Four Strong Winds" and "Alberta Bound." The athletes in their seats clapped their hands in unison. I recalled how years earlier we had sung ourselves hoarse singing "Alberta Bound" as we winged our way home from Baden-Baden with our Olympic hopes realized.

Then the Olympic flame arrived. Eighty-eight torch bearers, one for each day of the cross-Canada torch relay, ringed the centre of the field to the beat of Native drums. Twelve-year-old Robyn Perry, representing the youth of the future, lit the huge Olympic cauldron.

Underneath the concrete stadium Hugh Dunne had arranged sonic cannons—giant loudspeakers—to add to the roar as the flame in the cauldron sprang to life. The roar of the crowd and the sonic cannons literally shook the stadium. I found out later that more than 20 other stadium loudspeakers had been revved up so high they blew out during that moment.

The lit cauldron continued to rise toward its full height. Behind the cauldron was a great steel A-frame from which guy wires ran. Giant banners were winched aloft on the guy wires to make a tribute to Canada's first people in the form of a giant teepee with stripes in the five Olympic colors: blue, yellow, black, green, and red. This was not our first effort to combine elements from the Olympic heritage with elements from the Canadian one. The design of the Calgary Olympic medals included the profile of an ancient Greek athlete with a laurel wreath beside that of an Indian chief, whose headdress contained the design of all the winter sports equipment.

The Canadian Armed Forces Snowbird precision flying team came screaming across the sky over McMahon Stadium trailing the five Olympic colors in their jetwash. The jets circled the stadium twice before disappearing.

Then a man named David Tlen appeared on the giant stage located at the north end of the stadium, below the assembled athletes. Without accompaniment, he sang *O Canada* in his native tongue, Cree. The Olympic choir joined in and delivered our national anthem again, this time in English and French.

As the ceremonies proceeded, the wind seemed to pick up. I noticed some of the giant seven-metre-wide teepee banners were beginning to ripple in response. Suddenly one of the banners seemed to lose its tension. It began to vibrate violently in increasing waves. The whole 15-storey teepee superstructure, poised above the cauldron with 2,300 athletes and officials in seats below, started to oscillate. The collapse of the structure seemed imminent!

My mind raced to Gordon Coates, who was in charge at our EMT Centre and watching on TV monitors. I muttered to myself, "Gordie—for God's sake give the orders to get those banners down!" The next 10 seconds seemed to hold the Games in their grasp. Finally the banners were winched back down, to my everlasting relief. Quick action by our site engineers had been taken to avoid a spectacular disaster at the opening ceremonies.

I found out later the clamp on one of the banner cables had come loose under the tremendous stress from the wind, causing one banner to sag and putting extra vibration loads on all the others. One of the huge concrete blocks anchoring the cables in place had been yanked right out of the ground by the enormous forces of the wind.

The athletes and officials took their oaths, and the Olympic flag, which had been brought from Oslo, was formally received. In between these ceremonial elements Paddy presented a variety of Canadian performances that reflected the strength of our national fabric. Included were modern ballet, folk dancing from French-speaking parts of the country, and square dancing from English-speaking parts. The square dancers, many of whom were senior citizens, beamed happiness out to the world. At the end of their dance they formed a huge Alberta Rose on the floor of the stadium. This was one picture that the people watching on TV got a better view of than anyone in the stands.

The ceremonies concluded with the whole cast of 8,000 ceremonies volunteers streaming onto the field to the sound of the David Foster theme, "Can't You Feel It," sung by the Coke World Chorus. The whole group clapped its hands to the beat as the song repeated itself for at least 10 minutes.

MARJORIE WALTON • TIMOTHY JAMES • DAVID HALL • SANDEE PARKIN • KATHLEEN HEWITT • REBECCA MULCAIR • PAT DE WITT • MARY GOODWIN • SIMON PARBOOSINGH • LARRY ASHDOWN • HEATH FLETCHER • LEN HUCKABAY • CAMERON DRUERY • KENNETH DAVIDSON • NORMA PRESTEGARD • STEVE NEWTON • WYNNE CHISHOLM • KENNETH LIKINS • WILLIAM BOYAR • MICHAEL REID • CHRIS SCHULTHESS • ALLYSON WANNER • MYRNIE BOYD • DANIEL GRETENER • HARRY ROMAN • JANET WEIR • CHARLIE FLYNN • TONY TAYLOR • LISA STEWART • JACQUES LAPOINTE • DON BLACK • SHIRLEY TAYLOR • SAL LOVECCHIO • SHELLEY SHEA • KATE HUNTER • CLAUDIA EMES • GENE MORES •

As I sat and soaked up the result of three years of re-hearsals, I was silently thankful for the work of Paddy Sampson. Our music director, Tommy Banks, had also de-livered a terrific show, featuring just about every sort of music you could imagine. The children had danced delightfully, the square dancers were brilliant and colorful, the ballet was ele-gant, the choir of 1,100 voices magnificent, and they all combined to win the hearts of people everywhere. It was a stunning performance that created a feeling of warmth and western naturalness. The Olympic spirit had been kindled.

There are some things about the Calgary Games that I would do differently if a second chance came—the opening ceremonies are not among them. Paddy had delivered a 10,000-goosebump version. The miracle of shared friendship had begun.

CHAPTER TWENTY-TWO

Behind the Scenes

> If a man is called to be a streetsweeper, he should sweep the
> streets even as Michelangelo painted, or Beethoven composed
> music, or Shakespeare wrote poetry. He should sweep streets
> so well that all the hosts of heaven and earth will pause to say,
> "Here lived a great streetsweeper who did his job well."
>
> MARTIN LUTHER KING

ON THE SURFACE, the Olympic story sometimes appears to
be about power, conflict, and money. There were many
games within the Games. These stories are often interesting, but they are not important. The story that matters is that
of the thousands of ordinary citizens who gave their time to
help make the Games a success.

When our organization was winding down after the
Games I took the time to talk to most of our volunteer chairmen and staff members. I asked them to share their favorite
anecdotes from behind the scenes. Some of the following
stories are theirs and some are my own.

Bringing Out the Best

Samaranch described the sporting events with insight when
he said, "The facilities and the conditions in Calgary were very
good because the best athletes won the medals." One exception

KAY MCKAY • TED SHELDON • KEITH HARE • MAUREEN NISHIDA • PAMELA FRANCIS • GORD KENT • JOHN VAN STADEN • MARK BRAY • PEGGY
MUSSON • BOB HYLAND • CHARMIAN TRAVERSO • BILL WEARMOUTH • ELIZABETH HIGGINS • THERESA STAUCH • MARIE CHIN • THOMAS
MALCOLM • PAUL BENOVSKY • DAVID SPENCER • JACKIE MAYS • BRUCE MCMANN • DON HARRISON • CECIL ANDERSON • ANNE HEWITT •
LOUIE CORRADO • JANET CROSSEN • MARK PETRIE • DARLENE WAHL • RONALD AMBROSE • GRAHAM SMITH • SHIRLEY MCKENZIE • DARYL
BAILEY • SHAWNA HICKS • CRAIG GATTINGER • MARK TOMLIN • MYRON JOST • LINDA THOM • ARCHIE SCOTT • JAMES BOYDE • PAT ALLIN •

to that might be the story of U.S. speed skater Dan Jansen, the reigning world sprint champion, who fell in both the 500-metre and 1,000-metre events to wipe out any chance for medals in events he was favored to win. His sister had passed away from leukemia only hours before his first race. Dan Jansen had the courage to compete where the world's peak level of performance is required to win. The world's thoughts went out to him.

Crown Evidence

When the King and Queen of Sweden arrived at the Olympic Village in Calgary unexpectedly, the volunteer in charge of access control at the front-desk quickly radioed to the village mayor's office requesting a hostess to greet them at once. The frantic hostess on the other end of the radio said, "I'm on my way, but how will I recognize them?" With the King and Queen standing there, the front desk volunteer replied, "They're the ones wearing crowns."

Appendix Eh

The Calgary Games included people like lawyer Francis Saville who, as a venue chairman, had worked tirelessly to prepare his venue—Canada Olympic Park—for the Games. But just as the Games began he was rushed to hospital for an emergency appendectomy. Bruce Cleveley, vice-president of operations (an appropriate designation under the circumstances), visited Francis and jokingly said he was concerned that permission had not been granted for a leave of absence. Three days later, Francis was back at his volunteer job working up to 16 hours a day.

Touchy Subjects

Paula Andrews was already the mayor of Canmore and a member of the OCO'88 board of directors when she agreed to take on the added role of mayor of the Canmore Olympic Village. We called her the mayor squared. Taking her responsibilities seriously, Paula had taken a course in protocol. She had learned that when VIPs visit, you don't ask questions about money, politics, or religion. When Governor-General Jeanne Sauvé arrived, she asked Paula about all three in the first five minutes. Apparently the Governor-General had not taken the same course! As always, Paula smiled and handled it.

A Friend Indeed

Turkish IOC member Turget Atakol was already seriously ill when he arrived in Calgary, but he wanted to spend his time, if possible, attending one more set of Olympic Games. After only a few days his condition deteriorated and our doctors decided that he must be flown back to Istanbul. We tried everywhere to find a private plane to take Atakol home for his final days, but none was available. During an official dinner, I was seated next to Prime Minister Brian Mulroney when Art Smith arrived at my shoulder to tell me about the lack of progress in finding emergency transport. The prime minister, hearing of this humanitarian need, immediately relinquished his own Government of Canada Challenger jet to take our Turkish friend home. Atakol died two weeks later, but his family will never forget their friend in Canada who cared enough.

Code Six Alert

The CTV host broadcast personnel all had mobile radios that operated on the same frequency as Team'88 workers. At Canada Olympic Park, every time there was an emergency or a problem at the bobsleigh track, CTV crews therefore had first access to the details. Doug Hansen, sports chairman for luge, decided to have some fun with his CTV buddies. Just prior to a luge final Doug activated his mobile radio, excitedly screaming, "Attention all course workers—we have a Code Six alert up here at the Omega turn!" The response expressed equal concern. "OK, hang in there, we'll get right on it." CTV spent the next three days discreetly asking around, trying to find out what a Code Six was. The Code Six alert was never used again. It was the prank invention of the luge track supervisors to help keep life interesting for eavesdroppers on the mobile radios.

Excuse Me Ma'am

The Olympic Saddledome has four box suites at the concourse level, which provide excellent views of the ice surface. We had decided to allocate one box to the International Ice Hockey

STERGIDOU • DARREL JONES • STEPHEN GOLDBERG • MIJI CAMPBELL • PAT DOYLE • SANDY NEMETH • HEATH HUTCHINGS • MARK RAYBURN • SUSAN BRODIE • WENDY BOONE • JOHN MCGRUTHER • TARA PHILP • TONY SCHNEIDER • GLEN KUHNLEIN • DONNA BROWN • MILAN CUC • BILL CORCORAN • LORI HURST • ROBB ANDERSEN • RIET WYNKER • NEL SERAFINI • ROBERT GOUDY • THOMAS MARSHALL • PERRY ROMBOUGH • JEANNE SCHNELL • DONNA LEBOUEF • BRUNO PAULETTO • PATSY CROSS • MARY RABEN • LINDA CUNDY • PETER KASIAN • DOUG MCPHERSON • JOAN PIKE • PAMELA JONES • KEN DOYLE • DAVID CUTHBERT • LES WHITE • NANCY MARSHALL • RONALD BAY

Federation (IIHF) and the International Skating Union (ISU) and their VIP guests during the Games. We placed a sign on the door of the suite that read IIHF, ISU, AND INVITED GUESTS. Some joker removed the sign and placed it on a door down the concourse a short distance. When our distinguished IIHF visitors from Germany arrived for their first visit to the Saddledome, they marched right into the special room marked for their use. The welcome sign had been placed on the door to the women's washroom.

Snow Job

The snow at the Canmore Nordic Centre had not been adequate to ensure the quality of the events, even though some snowmaking was available on site. There was a large stockpile of snow at Nakiska which, in spite of record-high temperatures, was not needed for the Alpine venues. A decision was made to truck snow from Nakiska to Canmore when the warm Chinook persisted. Getting the snow to Canmore was no problem. Spreading the snow over 50 kilometres of remote trails was a challenge.

John Rule, venue chairman, solved the problem. He hired some Alberta ranchers with manure spreaders to distribute the precious snow. This was probably another Olympic first.

Near the end of the Games John Rule, in a show of confidence, shipped one truckload of snow back to Nakiska because he didn't need it. Nakiska didn't need the snow either, but it provided the chance for some banter between venues.

After wind had caused postponement of several events, the Canmore team sent a small tree in a pot over to Francis Saville, venue chairman at Canada Olympic Park, as a practical joke to provide symbolic protection from the unrelenting wind and dust. Canmore had been free of wind problems throughout the Games. The tree never left Francis Saville's office—and the office experienced no problems with either wind or dust.

Oh No!

When Bill Pratt marched proudly into McMahon Stadium behind Mayor Ralph Klein for the closing ceremonies, the place was filled with cheers and excitement. Bill heard his pager beeping as he walked onto the stage in front of the huge world television audience. For the moment he resisted the urge to read

• ANNIE BARNES • DENIS FLEMING • ELIZABETH NAGY • DANIEL OSUCH • MIKE PANNETT • KEMO SCHEDLOSKY • DAVID KADEY • TAMMY ROTH • ELINOR SINCLAIR • DAN ADAMS • DAVID SHEREMETA • DIXIE ROBBINS • ALICE MASSINE • LEO PETERS • MICHEL CHAMPAGNE • GORDON GUNNING • INGA MOROZOFF • TOM HORVATH • CAM TIPPING • CON SARNECKI • DON SUTHERLAND • TERRY SMITH • LORNA READ • MARGARET HUBER • PAULINE MCGREGOR • LAURA WRIGHT • DALE HADDEN • TERRY CAVANAUGH • RANDY GOSSELIN • BRITT SIMMONS • EVELYN COX • DAVID WORTHEN • STEVEN FLANDERS • EARL GLIDDEN • BOB FERGUSON • JIM PANAGABKO • JACK TAUNTON • PAUL

out the message on his pager, but as soon as he got back to his seat, he checked it. It said, "Bill, your fly is open on stage in front of the whole world." It was a message from Gord Coates watching on TV from Olympic headquarters downtown.

Forget-Me-Not

Almost everyone I know, including most IOC members, has trouble remembering the proper color sequence for the Olympic rings. The rings, from left to right and top to bottom, are blue, yellow, black, green, and red. As the IOC became more familiar with the colorful management style of OCO'88's president, we collaborated in the creation of our own mnemonic device: BILL YELLS BUT GETS RESULTS. I think Pratt liked the phrase; it was consistent with how he sees himself.

Nobody's Perfect

The perilous job of preparing the slopes of the 70-metre and 90-metre ski jumps requires special equipment. Mountain climbers use spiked boot attachments called crampons. So do workers on ski jump courses, and the team at Canada Olympic Park filled in a purchase requisition for four dozen sets of crampons. The OCO'88 purchasing department sent them four dozen cartons of tampons.

Unselfish Joy

The Olympic story is one of unselfish participation by people like Joy Kosten, who worked as a volunteer for eight years doing jobs ranging from filing and typing to arranging most of the important meetings, receptions and dinners at the time of the Games. To avoid nepotism OCO'88 only hired one person from any family. Joy turned down a full-time salaried position with OCO'88 so her son Steve could work as a mail boy for the organizing committee.

Once Is Not Enough

The VIP lounge at the Olympic Oval was a great place to receive visitors, but several complaints were received about the scarcity of green plants in the area. After several days of adverse comments, action was taken. Independently of each other, two people in authority ordered a plentiful selection of tropical plants for the Oval VIP room to quell the complaints. The two shipments arrived at the same time, turning the barren room into a veritable jungle of exotic greenery. We received no further complaints—except from Bill Nield in the accounts payable department.

The Danger of Drinking on the Job

The course workers at the Canmore Nordic Centre often worked through the dark hours to keep the venue in perfect shape for competitions. Box lunches were provided, but many workers brought their own thermos bottles with coffee or hot chocolate. A common problem was that these personal thermos bottles were sometimes accidentally left on site. Security officers, when checking the course before the athletes arrived, were trained to blow up all unidentified objects as a safety precaution. Course workers lost quite a few thermos bottles before they realized what was happening.

Hair: Brown; Eyes: Brown

Security dogs were also used regularly at all outdoor venues to check any suspicious packages or objects. When the dogs came through access control, there was always plenty of joking about the fact that they had no accreditation and therefore could not enter secure areas. Word soon got out that police dog handlers were planning to show up at the accreditation office to get full official "dog tags" for the dogs. To their surprise, when they showed up the accreditation office had been tipped off and was ready with pictures, vital statistics, and paw prints so that official dog-umentation could be issued.

The Arch *Faux*

On several mornings President Samaranch and I flew out to Nakiska or Canmore by helicopter to attend events there. After the first few days, when Chinook winds had forced postponement of several events at Canada Olympic Park and Nakiska, Samaranch had gained some first-hand knowledge of what a Chinook looked like. During one of our flights toward the mountains I had pointed out to him the characteristic "Chinook arch." A Chinook arch is a band of blue sky that appears to the

• ROBERT EKLUND • BRIAN DICKSON • FRANCE PLAMONDON • DALE CHORNEY • STEPHEN RENSINK • ROBERT MCKELLAR • PATRICK GUAY • KAI HANSEN • DAVE KRALL • DONNA SIM • CLIVE JOLLY • VAL HENNIG • CHRISTOPHER BIRCHALL • VALERIE THOMAS • AL HAYKO • BARBARA GEE • PHIL GREENAWAY • BARBARA SAUNDERS • JONATHON LILAND • ANN SUTHERLAND • BERNHARD TABERT • KEITH BURGESS • BILL HAYDEN • JOHN HALUN • SYLVIA MOIR • ROBERT HOLDBROOK • HEATHER JEARY • GLORIA DAVIDSON • SUKI DAVIS • OWEN QUIGLEY • CAM WARRENDER • BILL CAMPBELL • RHONDA HUNTER • WILLIAM THORNE • DAVE SCAMMELL • NICK TOULMIN • STAN HORBACHEWSKI • DALE

west on an overcast day, heralding the approach of the warm dry Chinook wind. Stretching from horizon to horizon, the band of blue looks like a huge flattened arch.

Our helicopter took off on a perfectly clear morning with no Chinook wind blowing. But as the chopper headed west over Canada Olympic Park a ribbon of black smoke was visible, probably the result of a farmer burning something in his field.

Samaranch stiffened as he saw the arch of black smoke. He put his hand on my arm and said, "Frank, is that another Chinook on the way?" I assured him it was only black smoke but he seemed unconvinced, having been bitten by the Chinook already on several occasions. As we passed over a pile of burning brush, he relaxed again and enjoyed a perfect sunny day.

The Speed King

When King Carl Gustaf of Sweden requested permission to ski on Olympic courses at the Canmore Nordic Centre, arrangements were made for his comfort and safety. Since royal guests are always provided an official RCMP escort, a candidate with excellent cross-country skiing experience was chosen to accompany King Carl Gustaf. The only problem was that after only 10 minutes of skiing on the tough Olympic course, the police escort had fallen 200 metres behind the king and complained that he was exhausted and could no longer keep up to provide protection.

Ready, Fire, Aim

The CTV host broadcaster crews had the tough job of being everywhere competitions were held to record events in their entirety. Overall, more than 500 hours of active broadcasting were made available to TV rights holders. It took a major effort to manage the logistics of TV cameras and technical personnel.

Two cameras and crews trekked out to set up on a remote section of the Canmore Nordic Centre to catch the cross-country leg of the Nordic Combined team race. Unfortunately, the racers that day all competed on the official course, while these two lonely crews had located themselves somewhere else in the confusing maze of trails. They didn't see a soul all day.

SIVUMAKI • LARRY CHAN • LOUISE-RENEE WIEBE • REBECA VERMETTE • STEVE WARRINGTON • FERNANDE BIEN-AIME • MIKE LAZORKO • LORI FLEMONS • CALVIN HUMMEL • MONIQUE BOUCHET-BERT • LORNE HAGGARTY • SUSAN MACMILLAN • BURKE KUPKEE • TERRY DARRAGH • RUSS BAKER • STORM PURDY • JOY MCNEIL • BENT HOUGESEN • RICK SMITH • CHERYL MCNEIL • JACKIE RAFTER • JOANNE PRATT • GARRY KALLOS • JOHN DAUNHAUER • EVA NEWMAN • LINDA VAN SPRANG • RAE ROBERTSON • HUSSEINALI WALJI • CAROLINE DEMERS • ED SMALL • ELIZABETH GRIFFIN • BEV ROBINSON • JAY JOFFE • JOYCE ULINDER • NINA LOVEGROVE • SYLVIE MORIN • DARRELL

COP

Canada Olympic Park is often called COP. During the Games, the venue management at COP met often to discuss another delay in events due to weather problems. Francis Saville and Dennis Flanagan told everyone that COP now stood for "Cancelled or Postponed." But by the end of the Games, Russ Tynan, who was by then the general manager of venue operations, had more appropriately observed that COP stood for "Completed on Plan." Every event was carried out before the Games were over.

Club Fed

The Government of Canada wanted to play a special role in hosting visitors from around the world, so they set up a permanent reception area in the penthouse on the top floor of the Palliser Hotel. It was equipped with television sets, a bar with full-time bartender, nuts and nibblies and plenty of friendly conversation any time of the day or night. We dubbed it "Club Fed."

The Name Game

Throughout our Olympic period I appeared on hundreds of TV and radio shows and numerous public platforms. Dave and Steve asked me one day if I would say hi to them on a radio show I had agreed to do. The request quickly escalated into a game to see if I could work into my interview the name of an object requested by them.

The first challenge I agreed to accept was to work the word "shoe" into my radio responses at the intermission of a hockey game. I had no idea how I could do that. The announcer gave me my chance when he asked "Frank, how would you describe your chances of winning the Olympic bid?"

"Well," I responded, "I wouldn't say we're a *shoo-in*, but we probably have a good chance of winning."

The name game carried on until it became the ultimate test of nerves and wit. At the opening of Calgary's Olympic Plaza I walked with Ralph Klein behind a bagpiper as we crossed the street from City Hall to make our speeches to the crowd assembled in the plaza. As I was passing through the crowd on my way to the platform I spotted Dave and Steve grinning broadly. Dave yelled, "Hey Pop, the word today is 'potato!'"

I was hard-pressed to find a way of making a short speech to 2,000 people including the word "potato." The name game had escalated to an impossible level.

My remarks at the Olympic Plaza that day made little or no sense. I commented how pleased people would be to see the many uses for the new public square. "I can visualize skating here all winter long, band concerts and picnics in the summer, people everywhere enjoying a Coke and *potato* chips." Having completed my ridiculous assignment, I was able to return to a proper perspective of the future Olympic athletes who would be acclaimed in this permanent tribute to Olympic excellence.

The final chapter in the name game came as a request from Linda to work the word "fun" into my closing speech. That was a little easier—I managed to refer to the *fun* everyone had had at the Olympic Plaza.

Exploding Cauldron

The spectacular copper-clad Olympic cauldron was built so it could rise from beneath the elevated stage at McMahon Stadium to its full height of 15 metres after it had been lit. The giant five-metre-diameter cauldron bowl had been manufactured with an internal cover designed to distribute the natural gas that fueled the traditional flame. The inside of the cauldron bowl looked like a giant apple pie sliced into wedge-shaped pieces. The metal pie-shaped wedges had been flanged and bolted together to form a cover for the inside of the bowl. The flanged joints were designed to leak the natural gas to give a wild and random flame pattern. The flame worked well in every test but one.

A week before the Games, our workers were testing the operation of the Olympic cauldron at McMahon Stadium. Apparently, during a previous test, someone had forgotten to purge all the natural gas from underneath the internal cauldron cover. When the workers lit the cauldron, instead of receiving a rich, quiet-burning mixture, they ignited an explosive mixture of gas and air which blew the top of the cauldron to smithereens.

LARRY WOLFE • PETER TERRILL • BRUCE WATSON • KELLY PENN • RALPH LOMBARDO • DAWN PETERSON • FRANK ANDREE • DAREN TREMAINE • MAUREEN ACRES • PETER BERTHELET • GORDON TIMM • JIM BARNEY • JAN BEAVERS • MARY SNETHUN • HILDA RHODES • ROBERTA JOHNSON • SHEILA DENNIS • MELITA TSOUTRELIS • DEAN MEDWID • IAN BURGESS • JANICE MASON • KEVIN CORNFORTH • HELEN WINTHROP • DANA RICE • DON MAY • ROBERT ANDERSON • MICHELLE STAPLES • THOMAS AMUNDSEN • BILL MILNE • DELLA LUND • EVA FLADVAD • JOHN BULMER • BRUCE THORPE • LARRY MCCLENNON • JANET BOYDOL • MICHAEL MARCK • VICKI KELLER • JOHN GUY • REED

Fortunately, nobody was hurt because the explosion released its force skyward, but the internal cover was obliterated. The beautiful copper bowl that formed the visible part of the structure was unharmed, and repairs were made within 48 hours, returning the cauldron to its original condition. There were a few people holding their breath, however, when little Robyn Perry ignited the cauldron for its world debut just four days later. I admit that I was watching carefully. There was no problem; it worked perfectly.

Even Her Mother Didn't Know

Robyn Perry's mother said to me a month after the Games, "Our family has discovered so many new qualities in Robyn we didn't know existed before she was chosen to light the Olympic cauldron." That is precisely what the Olympic experience is all about. Until we are asked to do something special we are held back by natural self-doubt. Finally, often by chance, we are pushed into going for it. Then, like Robyn Perry, we find to our surprise that we have capabilities we never knew we had. We all have Olympic qualities in us. Some people find them and use them, others never do.

Home on the Range

The ceremonies stand out as the place where emotions are visible, but evidence of humanity was everywhere during the Games. Perhaps the Olympic Village demonstrates best the relationships young athletes enjoy the most. There is a natural curiosity among athletes. By their nature, they seek comparison among their peers. It starts with athletic comparisons, but it naturally shifts to social, economic and political discussions. The teams naturally tend to stick together at meals, and prior to competitions the residential area is serene and serious. But the recreation areas, snack bars, and discos have a different ambience. Athletes gather in small groups to share ideas. They dance and laugh together as if they had always been friends.

Bob Niven and Paula Andrews, as mayors of the two Olympic Villages, created a home away from home that included every possible element of comfort and safety. We had few complaints and many compliments for our athletes' accommodation.

When Bob Niven and I had visited the Olympic Village disco in Moscow, it was common to see international pairings such as a towering basketball player dancing with a tiny gymnast. The athletes often wore their team sweatsuits so you could recognize various champions of the world enjoying times together. Every size, shape, color and creed was there with one thing in common—they were all smiling.

In Los Angeles, we visited the Olympic Village disco where we witnessed two athletes dancing together. The floor cleared as this couple whirled and wheeled through an incredibly energetic and rhythmical dance routine. They were wheelchair athletes. The others clapped and cheered them on. They were magnificent.

Silent Approval

I asked Libby Brooks to type out my final speech for the closing ceremonies so we could give it to the TV broadcasters in advance. I wanted to say this was not the end of our mission, but the beginning of a new opportunity for all of us. I asked her if she thought the words were appropriate but I got no response. Libby stood silently beside my desk with tears in her eyes. I used the remarks the next day, February 28th, 1988.

❄ ❄ ❄

Every member of Team'88 has special memories and stories to tell about his or her activities during the Games. If you meet one, ask—you'll be delighted with the response.

CHAPTER TWENTY-THREE

Sixteen Days of Glory

> In the name of all the competitors I promise that we shall take
> part in these Olympic Games, respecting and abiding by the
> rules which govern them, in the true spirit of sportsmanship,
> for the glory of sport and the honor of our teams.
>
> THE OLYMPIC OATH

THERE WAS A SAMENESS to my days during the Games. Gary Arthur and Art Smith arrived at my hotel room each morning at 6:30 a.m. We checked out the remaining tickets held in an emergency pool for the events. We authorized the release of tickets based on requests from various sports federations, foreign governments, sponsors, and the media. We always tried to allocate some available tickets to the athletes, who in previous Games had had a difficult time getting into events other than the ones in which they were competing.

At 7:30 each morning the OCO'88 management team would meet to review problems of the previous day, check the latest weather forecast, and make decisions on any operational changes needed. There were few if any problems on most days. With the exception of windy weather, the advance planning was paying off perfectly.

CHONG · GERALD HUPP · TONY CLARK · GEORGE CHOPEY · RAMON GALLANT · TROY KERKHOFF · ALEX PRIMAK · MORAINE MOUAT · JOYCE MORIN · FRANK LUDTKE · CINDY VON HAGEN · DOT PADGET · ROBERT SHAW · DONNA QUON · EJ SCHIILER · BRUCE SIMPSON · MARGARET COX · TODD HANDCOCK · JANICE MALAINEY · BARBARA BRANDER · FREIDA HAMM · SUSAN NEUFELD · KAREN VITEYCHUK · MARIA WONG · PEGGY PLATHAN · ROBERT IMBROGNO · KARIN SIMPSON · PAUL KANE · PATSY HOPPS · ANN HRYNYK · MICHELE MEYER · BRENT MCKERCHER · BILL TODD · DALE DEXTER · DARREN BAYDA · DONALD WILLIAMS · NICOLE WYNKER · GEORGE HOGG · DOT WATHEN ·

The windy warm weather started on the first day of the events and never went away. The weather created a series of delays in a few key events, and the white postcard appearance of the Calgary countryside soon turned to brown. But there were benefits for everyone in the warmth of February 1988. The temperatures varied from a low of –28°C to a high of 22°C—surely an Olympic record. The wind was the strongest seen in 25 years in Calgary during February.

At 8:30 a.m. each day Bill Pratt, some of our management team, and I would meet with Samaranch and the IOC Executive Board. The IOC, based on reports from IOC members assigned to various sports venues, would raise questions or concerns. Once again there were few serious complaints from the IOC. Most of our attention was focused on the weather and the regular postponements of events.

The morning after our first night at the Olympic Plaza, however, brought a complaint from Lord Killanin. As Honorary President of the IOC, he had been asked by Samaranch to present the first set of medals. Killanin, the athletes, and I waited in a heated tent behind the stage while lively entertainment kept the huge crowd out front happy. Killanin became restless as the time for the medal presentation passed and the (South) Korean dance team seemed unwilling to surrender the stage. The dancers' music, which consisted of an incessant percussion of discordant cymbals, was earsplitting. Killanin began to grumble, mildly at first, and then when 15 minutes had elapsed his patience ran out. I ran out too, to see if I could get the stage director to give the dancers the hook. Thankfully the act ended and Killanin was able to perform the medal presentation.

To my surprise at our morning meeting the next day, Samaranch asked me to cancel the medal award ceremonies at the plaza. I resisted, and we briefly debated the issue. I found a short-term solution by getting Samaranch to agree to accompany me to that evening's ceremony, so that he could see for himself what sort of show we were putting on for the athletes and the people.

That night Samaranch stood with me in the crowd of Calgarians and visitors and watched the perfectly timed (whew!) medal presentation ceremony. The atmosphere in the plaza was charged with excitement. At the end, Samaranch, usually completely impassive, stood with a small smile on his face. He said one word: "Fantastic!" We left the plaza.

We did not discuss the medal ceremonies in the Olympic Plaza again, and they continued as before.

Typically, at 9:30 each morning during the Games, I met with members of our board of directors. They were valuable eyes and ears for us during the Games, picking up on problems as they toured the venues. Each day I used the opportunity of our meeting to brief them on the major issues so they could pass the word along to the troops in the field, the media, or others.

By 10 a.m. or later each morning, Samaranch, Marc Hodler, and I would be on our way to one of the venues. Often a helicopter or two was waiting for us at the downtown heliport to whisk us away to Canmore or Nakiska for a quick peek at something special. I was lucky enough to catch Zurbriggen winning the gold and the Soviets breaking records at the Canmore Nordic Centre.

In all, 33 events had to be rescheduled due to the warm winds. We called them Chinooks, but in fact they were part of the rare El Niño weather pattern, which occurs in North America once in a while. Almost every day before noon, my pager would sound the call for a telephone conference to arrange yet another rescheduled event. The conference calls necessarily included the representative of the international sports federation involved (for example skiing), the venue chairman and the sports chairman, the host broadcaster (CTV), several major TV rights holders (ABC, EBU), the OCO'88 managers for ticketing, security, transportation, and volunteers, and often Bill Pratt or myself.

It was always complicated to reschedule an Olympic event. Most venues were used for multiple events; many athletes compete in more than one event; and many coaches, officials, and venue workers are also committed to more than one event. Camera crews, bus transportation, food services, and ticket redistribution all had to be rescheduled. It often took several hours to reach an agreement on the best answer. Compromise was common. Co-operation was excellent.

I recall the frequent rescheduling of the ski jumping events as one of the most difficult. The events were all set for the afternoon, when the wind always seemed to be strongest. The jumpers said they would be happy to compete in the morning, when the winds were generally quite calm. But ABC said the jumping couldn't go in the morning because all the TV cameras faced east and the sun (which was shining most days) would be right into the cameras. The cameras were on fixed mounts and could not be easily moved. We had already draped a huge black screen over the top of the silver-clad ski-jump tower to keep the reflection of the sun from the west from ruining the TV pictures. The jumping stayed in the afternoon, and we did the best we could.

On a good day I would already have been to three or four venues. My visits were brief and intended to show support for the Team'88 workers. In 16 days not more than one or two of our people complained to me concerning their jobs. Our people were busy and happy.

By early evening I would usually return to our hotel room to prepare with Jeanette for an evening of obligatory social rounds. The rounds were hectic. We were often invited to attend half a dozen or more dinners and receptions, and we tried to visit a few more venues during evening competition as well. Our eating habits were modified to suit the schedule. We would have appetizers at one spot, soup or salad at another, and if we'd missed the entrée we'd settle for dessert at the last place, before heading off to the Olympic Saddledome for an hour of greeting people in the VIP lounge overlooking the ice.

More than anything else, I recall the cheery countenances of our hosting volunteers. They were often on duty 12 to 15 hours a day, working at the Palliser Hotel or the various venues, but they all seemed to be miraculously refreshed. The same was true of the drivers in our transportation fleet.

Other than the wind, we had only minor problems to deal with. The Soviets made a big fuss over the possible appearance of the Protopopovs (former Olympic pairs figure skaters who had defected a few years earlier to turn professional) in the closing ceremonies. We dropped them from the program to avoid a hassle. Gunther Sabetski, president of the International Ice Hockey Federation, tried to extract payments from us to compensate teams for scheduling changes. We had no trouble rejecting the request, because our existing agreement with the IOC and the International Ice Hockey Federation clearly gave us the mandate to adjust the schedule so the best hockey games would be in the evening at the 20,000-seat Olympic Saddledome, rather than the one-third-scale Corral.

At the only press conference I attended during the Games, the only significant questions addressed to me regarded the wind and warm weather and the fact that media people living at our Lincoln Park media village had been losing their underwear in the complimentary laundry service.

When Jeanette and I finally made it back to our bunks at the Palliser each night we would be tired and hungry. A typical day would end with a tuna sandwich and a glass of milk.

The Eagle Soars

The unbelievable beatification of Eddie "the Eagle" Edwards by the people of Calgary helped make the agony of defeat bearable for himself and others. Eddie, a ski jumper from Britain, stole the hearts of Calgarians when he arrived and gave a series of engaging interviews to the international media.

Eddie had been training for the 70-metre and 90-metre jumps for only two years. He was the champion of Britain, a country not well-known for its international ski jumping. When the media asked Eddie how he thought he would do at the Calgary Games he replied, "Optimistically a gold medal; realistically last place; but it could be worse—I could be dead!"

Eddie had trained in Scandinavia and had worked in a mental hospital there to keep his meagre fortune intact. He used old borrowed skis, and once, during a training competition before the Games, his ancient oversize hockey helmet came off and tumbled into the bowl behind him as he jumped. People on hand were shocked, thinking Eddie's head had popped off. His thick glasses added to his underdog image. He captured the popular imagination because he made it clear that the important thing in life is not to win, but to struggle and to participate.

The Calgary Games did little for Eddie the Eagle's modesty, but they improved his fortune. He returned home as a TV star to a local hero's welcome. Even now, years after the Games, Canada Olympic Park advertising urges visitors to come fly with the eagles. Calgary will not soon forget Eddie.

An Olympic Diary

During the Games I was only able to catch a few minutes of events here and there. For the record, though, I include the following account, which is taken from OCO'88's official report to the IOC. The original text, which has been adapted somewhat, was written by Rod Chapman.

February 13th

Immediately following the dramatic opening ceremony the world's attention turned to Stampede Park, site of the first official Olympic sporting events—three preliminary-round ice hockey games.

In fact, the first contest between Czechoslovakia and the Federal Republic of Germany was already well under way before the end of opening festivities at McMahon Stadium. The game, played before a small crowd of about 5,000 in the Olympic Saddledome, was won 2–1 by the underdog Czechoslovakian team with about seven minutes to play in the third period.

Later that afternoon at the neighboring Stampede Corral, the powerful Soviet Union team served notice of their intent to win Olympic gold with an easy 5–0 win over an outmatched squad from Norway.

Opening day of the XVth Olympic Winter Games wrapped up at the Olympic Saddledome before a crowd of about 16,000, who witnessed a high-scoring 10–6 win by the United States over an inexperienced but determined Austrian team.

February 14th

Gale-force 160-kilometre-an-hour winds buffeted the top of the men's downhill course at Nakiska on this, the first day of the outdoor competition, forcing postponement of the Games' first alpine-skiing event.

OCO'88's ticketing department acted quickly in announcing spectators' tickets would be refunded or honored at the following day's rescheduled event. This in turn affected the scheduling of the men's combined downhill event, which was moved to day four of the Games.

At Canada Olympic Park—which like Nakiska would soon fall victim to high winds—the Flying Finn, Matti Nykanen, captured the 70-metre ski-jumping gold medal after completing impressive 89.5-metre jumps in both the first and second rounds of competition.

At the opposite end of the ski-jumping spectrum, Eddie "the Eagle" Edwards stepped boldly onto the world stage. This two-year veteran of ski jumping captured the imagination of millions, including the international media, with his cheerful embrace of a last-place finish in the 70-metre event. For Edwards, a 24-year-old plasterer from Great Britain, simply competing in the Games was thrill enough.

At the Olympic Oval and Canada Olympic Park's luge track, new world records were set in the men's 500-metre speed skating event and in the first two runs of the men's singles luge event.

Across town at the Stampede Corral, a packed house was treated to an outstanding figure-skating performance by the captivating couple, Sergei Grinkov and Ekaterina Gordeeva. The two-time defending world pairs champions from the Soviet Union thrilled the crowd with their routine, which easily captured first place in the short program.

At the sparkling new Olympic Oval, Jens-Uwe Mey of the German Democratic Republic was the first of several people to set a new world record with a performance that shaved one-tenth of a second off the existing world mark of 36.55 seconds. This was the day the American sprint champion, Dan Jansen, fell heading into the first corner of the 500-metre speed skating race.

February 15th

This day was dominated by Switzerland.

Fast on the heels of the country's 2–1 upset ice-hockey win over a superior Finnish squad the previous evening, Swiss flags were proudly flying again on the slopes of Nakiska for the morning's rescheduled men's downhill event. Even the winds were co-operative with race organizers.

The race was a classic confrontation between two Swiss superstars—Pirmin Zurbriggen and Peter Mueller.

The first skier out of the gate was Mueller. He skied a nearly perfect run. But on this day his teammate Zurbriggen would ski better. Blazing down the course to the cheers of the crowd and the clang of cowbells, Zurbriggen shot across the finish line in one minute, 59.63 seconds—a half-second faster than Mueller. For Switzerland, the celebration began before the remaining competitors had even left the gate.

Throughout the Games the Canmore Nordic Centre, lying below the massive southeast face of Mount Rundle, was unaffected by high winds. On day three the scene was set for the men's gruelling 30-kilometre cross-country ski race. Conditions were nearly perfect. So were the Soviet competitors.

Three of the top four places in the men's classic competition were taken by Soviet racers, repeating the Soviet domination of the previous day's women's 10-kilometre event, in which four of the top five spots went to skiers from the U.S.S.R.

In their second contest of the preliminary round of ice hockey, the Soviet team continued to show it would be a strong contender for the gold medal. During a game they eventually won 8–1 over Austria, the Soviet team scored three goals in a scant 61 seconds.

At Canada Olympic Park, a 22-year-old physical education student from the German Democratic Republic carried on where he had left off on day two of the Games, when he had set a new world record on the state-of-the-art refrigerated luge course. In his first Olympic Winter Games performance, Jens Mueller captured the gold medal.

February 16th

Together, the sensational Soviet figure-skating couple, Ekaterina Gordeeva and Sergei Grinkov, brought the sold-out Olympic Saddledome crowd to its feet.

Wearing matching powder-blue outfits, they astonished the crowd and impressed the judges during a flawless long program of nearly impossible jumps and spectacular lifts.

For the Soviet Union, their skaters' performance marked the seventh consecutive time the country has won Olympic Winter Games gold in pairs competition.

At Nakiska, Canada's hopes of winning its first medal at the Games were buoyed by the third-place finish of Felix Belczyk in the downhill component of the men's combined event. Switzerland's Pirmin Zurbriggen took first place and moved one step closer to his stated objective of achieving a clean gold-medal sweep in all five alpine skiing events.

Earlier that afternoon the Olympic Saddledome was the scene of the Canadian ice hockey team's second consecutive victory. This time the opponent was Switzerland, who fell to the Canadian squad in a sluggish 4–2 contest. For Canadian fans the result held promise for their team's advancement to the medal round later in the Games.

Day four was also the first competition for the women's luge competitors at Canada Olympic Park.

ARTHUR HUBMAN • MIKE AGG • LORNE BIGGS • BRUCE HAGEN • KEN ROSS • JOSEF SPIELER • DIANE FARMER • JACK FORSTER • JOHN BURROWS • GORD ROBERTSON • TIM KEMP • BRIAN ANDERSON • DAWN CURRIE • JOSEPH FITZGERALD • FRED BELL • TIMOTHY LAMOUREUX • RANDOLPH BILLINGHURST • BRENDA BRUNSKILL • GLORIA MARCH • ANNAR JACOBSEN • WALLY HANISHEWSKI • JANE PERRY • JERRY SHEARS • JUDY BROOKER • KATHRYN GREGORY • AURORA HAMILTON • SUSAN CURRIE • CLARENCE FISHER • PATRICIA EDGAR • NICK BAUER • DEBORAH WELDER • DAWN RUPERT • WAYNE GORDON • KEITH MATHESON • JAMES DYCK • PAT MCCLELLAND • VICKI SMART •

During the first two runs, athletes from the German Democratic Republic dominated the field, posting the three fastest times of the day.

February 17th

Gusting Chinook winds took their toll at Canada Olympic Park. Despite attempts by competition officials to wait out the 40-kilometre-an-hour winds, they eventually decided to postpone both the 90-metre team ski-jumping event and the third and fourth runs of the women's luge competition until the following day.

While the morning events at Canada Olympic Park were brought to a standstill, the same could not be said for the action inside the Olympic Oval.

In a tremendous display of determination, Swedish speed-skating phenomenon Tomas Gustafson came from behind in the last lap of the men's 5000-metre race to edge two competitors from Holland in an Olympic record-breaking time of six minutes, 44.63 seconds.

Gustafson—and an amazing 28 other athletes—easily shattered American Eric Heiden's 1980 Olympic record time set at Lake Placid's outdoor track.

At Nakiska, amid lightly falling snow, the men's combined slalom event got under way, with high expectations for two competitors—Switzerland's Pirmin Zurbriggen and Canada's Felix Belczyk. Zurbriggen intended to capture his second Olympic gold medal. After the previous day's top-place finish in the downhill component of the combined event, things looked promising for the Swiss skiing ace.

To the astonishment of millions around the world, however, Zurbriggen's gold medal dreams vanished in one momentary lapse. With just 100 metres to go and with a full two-second lead over the nearest competitor, he hooked a ski tip on a gate and tumbled to the snow. For Zurbriggen the race was over.

Meanwhile, for Belczyk—sitting in third spot after the combined downhill—the possibility of securing Canada's first medal of the Games appeared within reach. But a missed gate brought him a disqualification instead and dashed the hopes of an expectant nation that today a Canadian would step onto the medal podium at the Olympic Plaza.

Later that evening, at the Olympic Saddledome, an emotional ice hockey showdown between the United States and the Soviet Union took place before a sold-out crowd. Despite outshooting their opponents 31–28, the U.S. succumbed to the superior Soviet squad by a 7–5 margin.

Day five was also the first of two days of disabled skiing exhibitions. A field of 15 blind cross-country skiers set off on the five-kilometre course at the Canmore Nordic Centre with their sighted guides. The competition captured the essence of the Olympic ideals. The three winners were from Sweden and Norway.

February 18th

The day dawned bright and sunny atop the women's downhill at Nakiska. Winds were brisk but seemed manageable. Canada was still without an Olympic medal, but this morning looked like it would provide an opportunity to rectify that situation, thanks to the strong performance expected from the Canadian women's alpine ski team.

But just as the first skier left the gate, blue skies gave way to dark clouds, and winds grew more intense. Before long, 117-kilometre-an-hour winds and blowing snow forced postponement of the event. Everyone would have to wait until tomorrow.

At Canada Olympic Park, the scene was similar. For the second straight day, the 90-metre team event was cancelled due to dangerous winds. Still, the winds were not strong enough to extinguish the German Democratic

Republic's medal sweep in the women's luge singles final—the first time one country had swept the top three places in a luge event in two successive Olympic Games.

Following the evening's men's short program at the Stampede Corral, the stage was set for yet another classic showdown, the free-skate component of the men's individual event. The combatants were American Brian Boitano and Canadian Brian Orser—two superb and evenly matched figure skaters. After day five's compulsory figures and the short program on day six, positions one through three were held by Boitano, Orser, and Soviet skater Alexandre Fadeev.

Inside Calgary's new speed-skating oval, yet another Olympic record fell on day six—this time to Soviet skater Nikolai Gouliaev in the men's thousand metres. With the addition of a bronze medal in the event, the Soviet Union had captured 11 Olympic medals before the halfway point of the Games.

February 19th

It was a warm winter's evening as an estimated 50,000 flag-waving people gathered at the Olympic Plaza to salute the day's medal winners—including bronze-medallist Karen Percy, the first Canadian athlete to win a medal at the Games. The atmosphere was electric. Flags waved, people cheered, and then suddenly the crowd erupted. Karen had stepped into view.

For Percy, who held the lead in the women's downhill event after starting from the sixth position, waiting for the remainder of the field to complete the course had seemed as difficult as the competition itself. During the slightly more than 10 minutes it took for the last skiers to negotiate the course, Percy saw her gold medal turn to silver and then to bronze.

On this day Marina Kiehl of the Federal Republic of Germany and Switzerland's Brigitte Oertli would ski just a little faster. But for Percy—and an Olympic host nation anxiously awaiting its first medal—it was clear that bronze would do just fine.

At Canada Olympic Park the powerful luge team from the German Democratic Republic continued to dominate the world's best lugers in posting gold- and silver-medal performances in the men's doubles event.

And the story from the cross-country ski trails at the Canmore Nordic Centre on day seven continued to be the Soviet Union. On a warm morning in Canmore, Soviet skiers captured the gold and bronze medals in the men's 15-kilometre event.

In the demonstration sport of curling, the Canadian women's team advanced to final round play at the Max Bell Arena while their male counterparts were ousted by a Norwegian team during semi-final competition.

February 20th

This was a story of two artists pitted against one another in what constituted one of the single greatest athletic battles of the XVth Olympic Winter Games.

The scene was a packed Olympic Saddledome. The competition—the men's free skate program. The two competitors—the United States' Brian Boitano and Canada's Brian Orser.

The event was a spectacular display of figure-skating artistry. Boitano skated first, in what may have been the performance of his life. Technically perfect, Boitano exuded the confidence of a gold medal winner. Clearly, Orser's task would be a difficult one. As Orser skated onto the ice he and 27 million other Canadians knew that he represented the country's best chance at winning Olympic gold at the Games.

Orser's performance was magnificent, but he stumbled on a triple flip jump and on a triple axel, and those mistakes cost him the gold. A surprise come-from-behind bronze-medal win by Soviet skater Victor Petrenko over countryman Alexandre Fadeev rounded out the evening's competition.

On day eight, Canadian teams won gold and bronze in the finals of the demonstration sport of curling. The women's team finished first in a close-fought contest with Sweden, while the men's team captured the bronze.

At the outdoor venues things were beginning to heat up. Record-breaking temperatures of 17°C swept through Calgary and troublesome chinook winds continued to make their presence felt.

In the first day of biathlon competition not one athlete in the men's 20-kilometre individual event would hit all 20 targets. But despite wet snow, Frank-Peter Roetsch of the German Democratic Republic skied a powerful race, overcoming the burden of skiing the required penalty laps to finish a full 21 seconds ahead of the nearest competitor.

February 21st

The first Olympian to win double gold at the XVth Olympic Winter Games was Sweden's speed-skating star Tomas Gustafson. Maintaining a steady pace throughout the gruelling 10,000-metre race, Gustafson simply overpowered the competition in the 25-lap event. In the process, the 28-year-old athlete posted new world and Olympic records, with a time of 13 minutes, 48.20 seconds. Gustafson's performance—hot on the heels of his gold-medal-winning 5,000-metre effort on day five—clearly established him as the world's best distance skater.

High on the slopes of Nakiska, France's Franck Piccard ran away with the gold in the first-ever Olympic Super G race. A native of Savoy, France (location of the XVIth Olympic Winter Games), Piccard sliced his way down the icy course a full 1.3 seconds ahead of second-place finisher Helmut Mayer of Austria. Piccard's win was his second in three outings at wind-blown Nakiska. Earlier he had captured the bronze medal in the men's downhill.

Although strong winds forced cancellation of the men's demonstration event of freestyle aerials skiing, the women managed to complete their event before conditions grew unsafe at Canada Olympic Park. The spectacular event, in which skiers perform a series of gravity-defying twists and rolls high in the air, was a crowd favorite.

On this day the powerhouse Soviet Union team earned their sixth gold, winning in the women's four-by-four-kilometre cross-country relay event and adding to its already impressive overall medal count.

On the ice hockey rink the Soviets romped to an easy 6–1 victory over arch-rival Czechoslovakia, clinching first place overall in preliminary-round play. Meanwhile the American team, a determined but inexperienced group of college players, fell at the hands of the Federal Republic of Germany by a 4–1 score. With the defeat, any dreams were over of repeating in Calgary their astounding gold-medal performance at Lake Placid.

February 22nd

To the relief of everyone but the spectators, who by now were growing accustomed to Calgary's balmy weather, cooler temperatures finally returned to the city on day 10 of the Games.

And for Canadians everywhere it was also time once again to salute the talents of their alpine-skiing heroine Karen Percy. Competing in the women's Super G event, Percy edged Regine Moesenlechner of the Federal Republic of Germany by a mere three one-hundredths of a second to capture her second bronze medal of the Games. In doing so, Percy became the first Canadian alpine-skiing double medal winner since Nancy Greene won gold and silver at the 1968 Olympic Winter Games. The event was won by Sigrid Wolf of Austria.

In the women's 500-metre speed-skating race at the Olympic Oval, a strong showing by the powerhouse German Democratic Republic was eclipsed by an even stronger showing by American Bonnie Blair. Speeding to a world- and Olympic-record time of 39.10 seconds, Blair left the competition behind from the start and never looked back. For the German Democratic Republic, second-through fourth-place finishes would have to suffice.

Short-track speed skating also began its four-day appearance as a demonstration event on day 10 of the Games. Protected with helmets, gloves and pads, tightly grouped packs of short-track speed skaters blazed around a 111-metre oval laid out on the surface of an ice hockey rink at the Max Bell Arena. The sport, which made its Olympic debut in Calgary, attracted large crowds of spectators, most of whom had never seen short-track speed skating before. On day one, Ki Hoon from Seoul, [South] Korea, took the gold medal in the men's 1,500-metre race.

At Canada Olympic Park the wind-postponed conclusion of the two-man bobsleigh event was finally completed, but not without some controversy. Cancelled the day before when blowing dirt found its way onto the track, the event began on day 10 under similarly windy conditions. After several runs the event was delayed yet again because of strong winds. Then, following the restart, the ice was noticeably faster than earlier in the day. The result was an unexpected come-from-behind win by the Soviet Union over a top-ranked team from the German Democratic Republic. Despite protests, the U.S.S.R. two-man team of Ianis Kipours and Vladimir Kozlov were awarded the gold medal.

Later that evening a capacity Olympic Saddledome crowd was treated to an impressive figure-skating display during the original set pattern dance. Performing to variations of the tango, the skaters impressed the audience but not always the judges. Crowd favorites Isabelle and Paul Duchesnay—Quebec natives but representing France at the Games—stole the show in a wonderfully choreographed performance. Upon completion of the competition, the Soviet Union held first and second place, while a young innovative Canadian duo placed third. The medal winners would be decided at the next day's free-skate event.

February 23rd

By far the largest crowd of any XVth Olympic Winter Games event gathered in the massive 90-metre ski-jumping bowl to watch an event originally scheduled to be held three days earlier. The huge turnout of more than 80,000 spectators was due in large part to an OCO'88 three-for-one ticket deal. This entitled Olympic spectators holding tickets to the 90-metre ski-jumping event, the 70-metre team nordic combined ski-jumping event, or the men's aerials freestyle skiing event admittance to all three competitions.

The decision to allow spectators access to three events with a single ticket was a reward to the thousands of enthusiastic spectators who earlier in the week travelled to Canada Olympic Park only to be sent home after winds forced postponement of the 90-metre and aerials events. Despite the large crowds, the venue operated smoothly. Spectators were also treated to a gold-medal 90-metre jump by Finland's Matti Nykanen, which vaulted the Flying Finn into Olympic record books as the first person ever to win both the 70- and 90-metre events in the same Olympic Winter Games.

Topping off a near-perfect day was the evening's long-awaited free-skate program at the Olympic Saddledome.

In this, their last public performance, a sterling athletic display by Soviet ice dancers Natalia Bestemianova and Andrei Boukine earned them a clean sweep of all three ice dance events and the coveted gold medal. The silver went to their countrymen Marina Klimova and Sergei Ponomarenko, while the bronze was captured by crowd favorites Tracy Wilson and Rob McCall of Canada.

ROSEMARY MALAHER • GERRY CASSAN • HALEY CATTERALL • LARRY NICOLAY • GLENN KRUYSSEN • AMY OKAZAKI • SANDY O'CONNOR • ANNE-MARIE PILKINGTON • PAULA RAFTREE • MARGARET MATTHEWS • LORRAINE HAMEL • PETER BRUSH • BRIAN SPENCE • TERRY BULLICK • PAUL BZETA • RENATE WICHMANN • MONIQUE GAMES • ROSS BAXTER • BERNICE B MATTSON • WAYNE SMITH • CHERYL BARON • CHRISTINE KOVAC • ANNE PETERSON • BURKE TAYLOR • OLIVER HANNULA • MARILYN WEBSTER • ROSEMARY HOWATT • RAY THOURET • CAROLYN JACKSON • GLENN LARSEN • KELLY KAYELICH • CATHERINE ORBAN • EILEEN BEDDOES • CAM WILLIAMS • PAUL JOHNSTON •

February 24th

In the first-ever Olympic Winter Games 90-metre team ski-jumping event, the Finnish four-man team easily won the gold in a performance led by the world's best in the sport, Matti Nykanen. For Nykanen it was a day to jump into the record books yet again. Never before had a ski jumper won three gold medals at one Olympic Winter Games. Nykanen made the task look easy.

Millions of ice hockey fans across Canada were silenced by the Soviet Union's easy 5–0 win over the Canadian team. With the defeat, Canada's hopes of winning a medal in ice-hockey competition were virtually eliminated. It was clear that the Soviet Union would now be the team to beat for the gold.

On the sunny slopes of Nakiska, the stage was set for the women's giant slalom. Switzerland's Vreni Schneider and Maria Walliser captured the gold and bronze medals respectively, while Christa Kinshofer-Guethlein of the Federal Republic of Germany came from behind to win the silver.

The first stage of the final battle between two of the Games' highest-profile competitors got under way early in the morning at Father David Bauer Olympic Arena. Debi Thomas of the U.S.A. and Katarina Witt of the German Democratic Republic—two of the world's premier figure skaters—would finally get their chance to settle the issue of who was the better. Following the day's compulsory figures, Soviet skater Kira Ivanova led the way, with Thomas and Witt in hot pursuit.

February 25th

For Olympic athletes and spectators the day's events were overshadowed by a tragic accident on the slopes of Nakiska.

Shortly after noon, a physician with the Austrian Olympic team, Dr. Joerg Oberhammer, fell into the path of a snow-grooming machine following a collision with another skier. He was killed instantly.

Shaken by the accident, which he had witnessed from a nearby chairlift, Switzerland's Pirmin Zurbriggen carried on to win the bronze medal in the men's giant slalom event. Italy's Alberto Tomba earned the gold, and Austria's Hubert Strolz won the silver. A total of 14 competitors, including the entire Canadian team, were disqualified from the event after it was discovered their ski suits had not previously been approved by the International Ski Federation.

Despite warm temperatures at the Canmore Nordic Centre, the Soviet Union made easy work of the final women's cross-country skiing event—the gruelling 20-kilometre competition. To no one's surprise, the powerful Soviet team took all three medals.

Later that evening, the close-fought women's short program at the Olympic Saddledome was held. Although at the end of the competition the two top positions were predictably occupied by Debi Thomas and Katarina Witt, it came as a pleasant surprise to the Calgary crowd when Canadian Elizabeth Manley skated a strong performance and took third spot.

February 26th

At the Olympic Saddledome the Soviet ice-hockey team proved as unbeatable as it had seemed. Powering their way to an easy 7–1 victory over Sweden, the Soviets recorded their seventh gold-medal performance in their last nine Olympic ice-hockey tournaments. For the remainder of the medal-round contenders, all that was left was to strive for Olympic silver and bronze.

Biathlon competition wound up at the Canmore Nordic Centre on day 14 with yet another Soviet victory. This time the U.S.S.R. raced to a strong gold-medal finish in the four-by-7.5-kilometre relay event. The Federal

Republic of Germany and Italy rounded out the field with second and third place finishes respectively.

In the women's alpine-skiing event, Switzerland's consistently strong Vreni Schneider raced to her second gold medal of the Games with a flawless performance in the slalom competition.

Day 14 closed on yet another record-breaking note, when Christa Rothenburger of the German Democratic Republic set a world record in the women's thousand-metre event with a time of one minute, 17.65 seconds. Ironically, the record she broke had been set only moments earlier by her silver-medal-winning teammate, Karin Kania.

February 27th

This day the question the world had been asking for 15 days would finally receive an answer. Who would win Olympic gold in the women's individual figure-skating program?

Would it be the German Democratic Republic's Katarina Witt, with her emphasis on artistry, or American Debi Thomas, who relied on her pure athletic talent? On this night the winner would be Katarina Witt. Skating an efficient but cautious program, Witt took the gold after Thomas landed unsteadily following several jumps. The much-talked-about Witt–Thomas confrontation was overshadowed, however, by an outstanding performance from Canada's Elizabeth Manley.

Skating the program of her life, Manley vaulted from the tenuous position of third place overall heading into the competition to record a solid second-place finish to win the silver medal. For Canadians everywhere, Manley's medal finish was the surprise of the Games.

In another unexpected development, Midori Ito, a figure-skating dynamo from Japan, stole the show from everyone with her awesome jumps and brilliant smiles. Although a crowd favorite, the tiny Ito would not win a medal at these Games.

Olympic competition at Nakiska came to a close on an exuberant note with the second gold medal win for Italy's Alberto Tomba. The flamboyant Italian raced to victory in the men's slalom.

At Canmore, Sweden's cross-country skiing phenomenon Gunde Svan sailed to victory in the demanding 50-kilometre men's competition.

Day 15 of the Games was also the first day of competition in the four-man bobsleigh event at Canada Olympic Park. After the first round, a team from the German Democratic Republic led the pack.

February 28th

All too soon it was here. The final day of the XVth Olympic Winter Games.

Switzerland's continued strong showing throughout the Games was capped off with two last-minute gold medal performances—one in four-man bobsleigh and the other in nordic combined.

At the Olympic Oval—the scene of so many exciting record-breaking performances—Yvonne van Gennip of the Netherlands propelled herself to a third gold-medal finish, winning in the women's 5,000-metre event. The win made her only the second athlete at the Games to win three golds. Her other winning efforts came in the women's 3,000-metre and 1,500-metre events.

And for the ice-hockey teams from Finland and Sweden, who already knew gold was out of reach, today meant playing one final game to determine who would take home silver and who would take home bronze. Both Finland and Sweden won in close-fought games. Finland edged out the U.S.S.R. 2–1, giving the U.S.S.R. its only defeat of the tournament. The win for Finland, that country's first-ever against the Soviet Union in either Olympic or world-championship play, came as a surprise to Finland's arch rivals, Sweden, who were forced to settle for bronze. It was also Finland's first Olympic ice-hockey medal ever.

Throughout the day, however, there seemed to be an underlying current of expectation in the city. Tonight the Olympic flame would be extinguished and the Games would officially draw to a close. For many people it was difficult to believe the time to bid the world goodbye had come so quickly.

But in true western tradition, the closing ceremonies presented a golden opportunity to do what Calgarians do best—celebrate.

And so people returned to McMahon Stadium much the same way they had arrived 16 days earlier. Bundled up against the crisp winter evening, they streamed into the stadium, looking forward to a show to end all shows.

CHAPTER TWENTY-FOUR

A Midwinter Night's Dream

The true legacy of the Games comes from the seeds
we sow in the hearts of our children.
1981 CALGARY BID FILM

O N FEBRUARY 28TH, 1988, Olympic Winter Games history
was recorded as 60,000 spectators and more than 2,000
athletes and officials gathered for the closing ceremonies
at McMahon Stadium. It was the first time the ceremonies had
been held outdoors for the Winter Games. It was by far the
largest audience to witness the dramatic farewell.

Included in the enthusiastic crowd were nearly 10,000 members of Team'88 who were given complimentary tickets as
recognition for having been the heart and soul of Calgary's
Olympic effort.

Members of the Olympic family and its partners in the
Calgary project gathered in the Olympic Volunteer Centre an
hour before the closing ceremonies. The sky was clear but
growing dark as the sun's memory dropped behind the saw-
tooth Rocky Mountains to the west.

LAZZAROTTO • FRANCES PRESTON • DIANE MCANDREWS • LENORA PIKE • KEITH FREEMAN • TERRANCE HAMEL • NOELLE PHAN-
BRODERICK • JIM POMEROY • GUY BERNDTSSON • STELLA VAN BEUSEKOM • ROSS MCLEOD • MARG MCMULLEN • GERRY POOLE • GARY
MACRAE • RICHARD LUCKASAVITCH • PAUL O'NEILL • PEGGY WILLEMS • MARJORIE BRIDGE • BILL RICE • HEATHER SINCLAIR • PAULINA
VELDMAN • GISELLE LECLAIR • LINDA SALMON • JAN WINKLER • BILL NOELCK • LEAH PELTON • BRENDA LOMORE • GWEN WINTER • DON
ROBART • GAIL LIKINS • MALCOLM TETLEY • VIC KROEGER • GARY BROWN • KENDRICK CHARLES • GREG CHALMERS • ROBERTA RONAYNE •

Even before the emotional climax, a round of warm embraces and congratulations was quietly taking place among old and trusted friends. The years of preparation were over. The fears and concerns were behind us. The freak weather had helped, not hurt us—Calgarians had turned from underdogs to overachievers.

Jeanette and I walked with Juan Antonio Samaranch and his wife Maria Theresa under the west seats at McMahon Stadium and toward our place in the royal box with the other members of the official party. People on their way to their seats for the Olympic finale waved and yelled positive comments to the Olympic boss, confirming my feeling that few leaders can claim the universal admiration and respect accorded this man. We took our seats next to Margaret and Don Getty, the premier of Alberta, and our old Olympic friend, Marc Hodler.

To the beat of stirring march music, the athletes of the world entered the Olympic stadium. Each of them carried an Olympic candle with a red plastic wind guard. The members of the audience held candles too. Hugh Dunne had always wanted to provide the candles to the audience, but had feared the fire marshall would nix the idea because of the fire hazard. Hugh had come to me with an apprehensive look when he learned that his idea might be doused. We had first tried the idea of lighted candles for the audience at the closing night of the Calgary Stampede in July 1987. I stood on the stage as part of the platform party, spellbound, as 15,000 Stampede patrons lit their candles in salute to the coming Olympics. I urged Hugh to go ahead because the idea was too good to suffer a premature bureaucratic death. I was relieved that no hazard had been created and gratified by the spectacular effect of 60,000 lighted Olympic torches at the closing ceremony.

Paddy Sampson had planned to light the candles later in the ceremony when the cauldron was extinguished—a symbol that the spirit of the flame lived on. But the athletes had their own idea of sharing the flame and it was a better one because it came from the heart. The athletes lit up the lights and the lives of the audience by passing on the Olympic flame. The lights spread up the elevated audience like a prairie fire as the athletes marched in.

Athletes from every country intermingled, marching together now as champions of the world. Two crazy Canucks
from the Canadian bobsleigh team performed exuberant back-
flips, to the delight of the crowd. We recognized one of them to
be Calgarian John Graham, a world-class 400-metre hurdler
and member of the bobsleigh team. He is the son of good
friends of ours and has competed in two Olympic Games in
one year.

When the athletes were seated, the announcer's voice
boomed out: "Athletes of the XVth Olympic Winter Games—
Calgary thanks you!" The bright stadium lights were turned
down, revealing a brilliant black starlit sky with an almost-full
moon and 60,000 candlelit stars circled around a large blue ice
surface with Olympic rings at the centre.

A single skater with a huge plumed headdress skated onto
the ice—the largest outdoor refrigerated rink ever built. Now
that the Chinook had arrived we were glad we had not relied
on natural ice for this important show.

The familiar melody of "Come Together in Calgary" was
discernable as the opening number developed with beautifully costumed skaters carrying flags circling the huge ice
surface. Skaters dressed in brilliant red and carrying banners
shaped like the flame of the Olympic torch wove their way
around the ice surface. I recalled seeing them practise on the
frozen pond at Bowness Park and then again at the Olympic
Oval. They were members of figure-skating clubs from several
cities across Canada.

While the skaters performed an exciting opening number,
the giant teepee sat in quiet repose at the north end of the stadium, sheltering the Olympic cauldron, which had burned for
16 days. The great Olympic flag draped limply beside the tall
silver pole that had supported it there since the opening day.
The warm Chinook wind was bidding farewell to Calgary too.

At the end of the first act, Samaranch and I proceeded to
the stage. The audience chanted, "Frank, Frank, Frank," as we
approached the podium. There was so much I wanted to say
to the people, to the athletes and to my teammates seated opposite me in this Olympic stadium they had built. No matter

how carefully I chose my words, they would always seem inadequate.

My remarks at the closing ceremonies were brief:

> These have been wonderful Games. Sport has focused the world on friendship and the future.
>
> As Canadians, we brought the Olympic flame from ancient Greece. It left millions of smiles. Those who touched it were touched by it.
>
> As Calgarians, in the beginning we offered "only who we are." We said, "Come together—share our warm western way of life." (It turned out to be warmer than we expected.) People came from everywhere—they had so much fun that we expect to see them back soon in the Olympic Plaza.
>
> To all the athletes—you have captured our hearts and filled us with memories. You have broken world records, established many personal bests, and some of you even have soared like an eagle. Thank you for the unbelievable feeling of pride we all shared in your accomplishments.
>
> Yes, these have been wonderful Games. Most of all, it's because they have been volunteer Games.
>
> To all of you who worked so hard, you have done enormously well. You chose to believe in a dream and to expect the best—people everywhere will long remember how well you did your job.
>
> Remember today, not as the end of our Olympic experience, but as a highlight in our lives as we seek ways of making our world a better place. The flame will soon be gone—but the spirit of these Games will live forever.
>
> Now we pass on the bright promise of the Olympic challenge to those who follow.
>
> To the youth of the world—the future depends on you.
>
> Thank you.

After I spoke, Samaranch and I turned on stage to witness the traditional flag-raising ceremony to recognize the founding nation, Greece, the host nation, Canada, and the next host nation, France. When it came time to hear *O Canada*, the Canadian flag was stuck at the bottom and could not be raised. Samaranch, standing quietly beside me, whispered, "Why is the Canadian flag not going up?" I didn't know but I said, "I don't think we're ready to say good-bye." Reluctantly, the Canadian flag did go up—five minutes after the French flag had been elevated flawlessly.

Then, to the rousing cheer of the audience and the Calgary song, "We Are the Neighbors of the World," Ralph Klein and

Bill Pratt marched into the stadium. Klein stopped to salute Team'88 at the south end while Bill Pratt threw his white hat into the crowd. In spite of many differences that had divided them over the years, it was a pleasure for me to see these two men walking together receiving the acknowledgment of a grateful crowd. Both of them would later receive an Olympic Order in Silver as recognition of their outstanding service to the Olympic movement. The audience chanted, "Ralph, Ralph, Ralph" as the mayor, carrying the original Olympic flag, which was introduced for the first time during the 1952 Oslo Olympic Winter Games, crossed the stage where Mayor Dujold of Albertville waited to receive one of the longest passes completed in McMahon Stadium in years. Bill Pratt gave me a big bearhug as he reached centre stage.

The second act of the closing ceremonies was pure Paddy Sampson at his best. A Currier-and-Ives snapshot of a perfect old-fashioned winter scene appeared on the ice as the lights came up. The snapshot came to life as the familiar music of the *Skaters' Waltz* was heard in the cool Calgary night air. The audience in Calgary and around the world saw scenes of curling, hockey, skiing and skating, along with chestnuts roasted over open fires, children flying kites, and gentlemen and ladies waltzing to the music.

In the midst of this wonderful Canadian winter scene we were delighted by individual performances from famous skating champions of past Olympic Winter Games. It began with Dorothy Hamill, sweetheart of the 1976 Innsbruck Games. She was joined by Don Jackson (1960); Toller Cranston (1976), who performed four straight split jumps; and Brian Pockar (1980), who had orchestrated this section of the show as part of Paddy's artistic team. The parade of stars continued with favorites Barbara Ann Scott King (1948), Bob Wagner and Barb Paul (1960), Frances Dafoe (1956), Petra Burka (1964), Debbi Wilkes (1964), and Karen Magnussen (1972). There were others too, but a favorite for me was the return of Otto and Maria Jelinek (1960)—they were a great Canadian athletic pair and former world figure-skating champions. I also recalled with a smile the positive influence of Otto Jelinek as a sports minister who had supported Calgary throughout his term.

Then, careening onto the ice, a solo figure dressed in plus-four trousers and sweater appeared. After teasing the girls and stealing a fur muff, he thrilled the crowd with two perfect back flips in a row—stopping to a roar of approval as his name, Robin Cousins, the champion of Lake Placid (1980), was announced.

As the skaters left the ice, a little girl was seen to fall at centre ice. Her four-year-old boyfriend was trying to help her up, but only when Dorothy Hamill arrived were they able to toddle off the ice together.

Then, to the march-time version of "Come Together," Samaranch and I returned to the stage at the north end of the stadium. Calgarians were in the mood and began the wave. As we walked to centre stage, I warned Samaranch that he would have to start his speech even if the wave was still rippling around the stadium. He sensed that it would not be easy to curb, but he began his final speech, which signalled the end of the official part of the Calgary Games.

When he declared that the Games were over, there was a profound sense of loss. "God keep your land glorious and free!" he said, and the stadium was quiet. The cadets dutifully lowered the Olympic flag and marched it out of the stadium.

At this point I had taken my place again back in the stadium seats with my wife. I had just received the Olympic Order in gold from President Samaranch. Only six others had received that honor. I accepted it on behalf of our whole organization. It now rests in the Olympic Hall of Fame at Canada Olympic Park.

When I returned to my seat, Jeanette's tearful embrace had set me up for the emotional finale. As the Olympic flag passed in front of us and then out of the south exit, tears streamed down our cheeks.

Then the flame went out—not only at the stadium, but simultaneously at every venue as well as the Olympic Plaza and atop the Calgary Tower. In McMahon Stadium, a pair of skaters performed at centre ice. They were Barbara Underhill and Paul

Martini, Canadian favorites and Olympic athletes in Sarajevo (1984), and later world champions. Their skating was accompanied by music from a haunting female voice and solo cello.

From this point on the pace picked up again. There was a musical introduction of athletes from Albertville, France (1992), dressed in the red, white, and blue of the French tricolor. The mascots put in an appearance, and then there was a peppy number involving a western shoot-out. We saw Robyn Perry and her brother skating in that number. The Olympic torch candles continued to burn, now the only Olympic fire remaining in the stadium.

Then k.d. lang, the country singer, came onstage to knock the audience out of any possible lingering gloom. She belted out a rockabilly song about peace and harmony called "Turn Me Round," and the stadium felt it. The place became a whoop-up, a love-in, a Calgary happening. Athletes poured onto the stage—hugging, dancing, and singing with k.d. lang. She ended: "Thank You—Peace on Earth."

Finally, the World Chorus arrived on a crowded stage to sing our song, "Can't You Feel It," written by David Foster and Tommy Banks.

> Now the trumpets have sounded, and the drums are still
> And you've vowed that you'll do your best,
> And we know you will
> We're not here just to cheer for fame
> But for honor and truth, that's why we came
> It's not whether you win that counts, but only how you play the game.

Fireworks exploded overhead signalling the end of the Games. Signs appeared in the stands—THANK YOU CALGARY and WE DID IT. The music played over and over a dozen or more times. There was a special feeling in the air as the audience cheered and swayed to and fro, waving their candles, smiling, jumping, and dancing in a collective outpouring of emotion. We were sharing a moment that will be a lifetime memory for all of us.

As the spectators left the stadium they were greeted by half a dozen huge hot air balloons tethered in the parking lot and glowing under the light of their propane-powered flames.

HANSEN • JOHN ROONEY • BRENTON SHERICK • SEATH KARDELL • MICHAEL GAU • CATHY GLOVER • HEATHER ANDERSON • GAIL MCQUEEN • BETTY PARK • EILEEN KWAN • IAN HAYHOW • ROGER MCKELLER • LINDA THOMPSON • ROSS MANNEN • DOUGLAS MOORE • MICHAEL ROACH • GWYNNETH MORICE • EDDIE TANTAY • ROBERT HERMAN • KATHRYN OSTERBERG • GREGORY SIM • PETER WILLIAMSON • LAURIE TARVES • TERESA KOLISNIK • DENISE BARRON • TIFFANY WATSON • ELLEN SIMONE • ANNE KILROY • BRUCE BONKOWSKY • OLE VALMESTAD • ROD SKOG • STEVE KRUPER • JANET POYEN • ART GLASSFORD • ZENA DRABINSKY • PENNY WORDEN • DOREEN BRISBIN •

It was a warm and friendly sight for people who had to be urged to go home.

One hour after the final sound of "Can't You Feel It," about 5,000 volunteer members of Team'88 still sat in their places in the Olympic Stadium. They had been part of the best-ever. It is seldom that anyone is asked to be that good.

CHAPTER TWENTY-FIVE

Great Perils—Wide Hopes

The gaze of those who take part . . . is directed
toward a future full of great perils and wide hopes.
Let us labor to remove one and to realize the other.

PIERRE DE COUBERTIN

W HEN CALGARY WAS AWARDED the Games in 1981, it
was assured a place in history alongside all the other
Olympic host cities. Calgary became part of the
Olympic legend. The journey from Baden-Baden to McMahon
Stadium took 2,327 days and was probably the most significant
period of growth in the city's history. That growth was not so
much measured in financial terms as in human ones.

The Right Reasons

Immediately following the Calgary 1988 Olympic Winter
Games, our offices were deluged with calls and visits from
hopeful future host cities. Our first question was always, "Why
do you want to host the Games?" The answers never extended
beyond the usual reasons: a boost for local facilities, funding,
tourism, economics, and sports.

The next question for bid organizers is more difficult: "What
feature of your bid distinguishes you from others?" The answer

GODDARD · DONNA MATHISON · LINDA HOLLINGSHEAD · PAT MCCAULEY · DEBORAH MILLS · JAMES NEGREY · LYNNE WORTHINGTON ·
WAYNE TRUMBLE · SUSAN GLENN · BERNARD SKINNER · JON ED · LINDA PENLINGTON · ALEX CUMMINGS · VIT JANKOVIC · KAJ JACOBSEN ·
BENO HUBER · SHANNON BRUCE · JOHN CASSELS · FLO SMITH · ARTHUR VARNES · MORAG LOGAN · KATHY MATTERN · ALLEN CLOW ·
DOROTHY DE ST JORRE · BENTE PEDERSEN · NANCY MCGILLIGAN · SHERRY DELANTY · SYD GRIMSLEY · CHRIS SPENCE · JOCELYN
RUNQUIST · MARIO STAMILE · LISA HUNT · JOAN LAST · JOHN CYBULSKY · BETTY BOON · KEN REYKJALIN · MARIANNE SAIK · RICK BATYCKY

usually centres around bricks-and-mortar items—"All our venues are within 13 minutes of the IOC hotel and the press centre," or "We have a superb four-lane highway to the ski hill." These sales pitches are reminiscent of the early position taken by members of CODA, whose speeches and presentations usually focused on major community benefits. But the difficulty with bid cities emphasizing local benefits when presenting their bids to the IOC is that almost every bid city can claim similar potential benefits.

No matter what city wins an Olympic bid, the city will benefit from the influx of tourists, the construction of new facilities, the promotion of sport, and the enhancement of civic pride. From the IOC's standpoint, that's not an argument for holding the Olympics in one city versus another. Assuming local benefits will accrue to any region awarded the Games, a much larger consideration faces IOC members.

How will the selection of a host city contribute to the Olympic aims? Baron Pierre de Coubertin created an Olympic plan to promote physical and moral development, educate young people through sport, and thus develop in them a spirit of understanding and friendship that would foster international goodwill. The Olympic aims have little to do with local benefits in one region of the world; they are universal.

One of the best selling points a bid city can present to the IOC is that the city's games will be well-organized. This is because the Olympic Games are to the Olympic movement what the Olympic finals are to an athlete—the acid test, a showdown, and a showcase. Although the Olympic movement works continually in support of its mandate, the IOC has to wait four years for feedback on its progress. The feedback comes from around the globe, and if the Games are poorly organized, it reflects very badly on the IOC. If the Games are well-organized, it makes the IOC look great. The most successful bidders and organizers figure this out before long; the unsuccessful ones never do.

Oil and Water

Over the years I often found myself trying to sort out in my mind the relationship between sports and politics. Some people say sports and politics are like oil and water: they don't mix. But as any oilman will tell you, oil and water are usually found together. The Games should be free from political meddling, but to date it has never rested in anyone's power to make them so.

As we began to forge a strong management and volunteer team known as Team'88 during 1987, I often thought about the far worse political problems faced by other organizers. The Olympic Winter Games have never experienced a boycott. "Snow falls on cool heads," I had once joked at a news conference when asked why the Winter Games had eluded serious political gamesmanship.

Boycotts are not successful. The Games go on regardless of absent friends. The cohesive and co-operative spirit of the Games always overcomes those who try to use factionalism and dissension to accomplish political goals. Samaranch hit the nail on the head when he addressed the IOC session in Los Angeles during the Soviet-led boycott:

> If I have learned one thing in my life, it is that only through human contact can our differences be overcome and dialogue opened. Perhaps that is what our world today lacks the most.
>
> It is our responsibility therefore, to struggle firmly to convince world leaders that to hold sport hostage for political purposes only serves to create new sources of conflict, for thus we lose irrevocably one of the greatest opportunities open to us to meet as friends and to seek mutual understanding.
>
> The International Olympic Committee does not have at its disposal any measurable or conventional powers, as do the governments of the world. However, if it were suddenly necessary for governments to repay all those people who have freely and generously given their time to sport, very few states would be in a position to do so. That is why it is so important, as I have stressed many times already, that the Olympic movement be recognized for what it is—a nonpolitical voluntary body—and that our rules be respected and honored by all. This is what I continually stress during my numerous contacts with those in positions of responsibility throughout the world. The National Olympic Committees and the national sports organizations must work in close collaboration with their governments and must maintain good relations with them. At the same time, governments must accept our approach to life, our rules, and our traditions, and respect our independence and autonomy.
>
> This is all the more essential when one considers the current international situation. Today's world consists of many radically different political systems, each one having developed its own

definition of the role of sports. It is totally unrealistic for one to try to impose its ideals upon the other. The Olympic movement, and more particularly the International Olympic Committee, has accepted the heavy responsibility of forming a bridge between these ideals and countries by offering athletes equal opportunities to train and compete under the Olympic flag.

One of the aims of the Olympic movement is in fact to educate young people through sport in a spirit of better understanding and friendship, therefore helping to build a better and more peaceful world.

Current events are a clear indication of to what extent this ideal is necessary, not only in the domain of sport, but in all walks of life. I can assure you that the Olympic movement will do everything in its power in order to preserve this ideal.

A Sacred Cow

There are several major aspects of organizing the Games that can make a real difference to the world. One of them concerns money. For some reason, the question of funding sport is a sacred cow. It is time for open, honest discussion of how sport will be financed. The Calgary Winter Games provided some important feedback concerning financing Olympic sports.

I have travelled to nearly one-third of the Olympic countries in the world. With few exceptions, they all have the same problem in sport—not enough funding. Yet when appropriate steps are taken to reduce or eliminate this universal constraint, strange cries of commercialism arise. It's time we defined commercialism. If selling sponsorships and television rights to the world's most inspiring athletic event benefiting sport in 167 countries is commercialism, then I'm in favor of it. If commercialism means turning our athletes into walking billboards or our sports venues into Times Square advertising opportunities, then I'm against it. The focus at Olympic competitions should be on the athletes. The focus on the marketing side of the Olympic Games should be on maximizing private revenues and minimizing public (tax) contributions.

Taxpayers have one thing in common: they resent increasing taxation. If the Olympic movement had chosen to rely mainly on funding from tax sources, it would have invited certain resentment. Instead, Olympic leaders decided to raise money privately to expand sport. By doing so they invited support from grassroots people in countries everywhere. The main weakness in the funding formula that we saw in Calgary is that a disproportionate amount of revenue came from the United States. The IOC is working on achieving a better balance in the future.

If the Olympic Games are run efficiently, sponsors and television networks will want to be associated with this world-class event. The IOC and organizers share the revenues received in a fair way that leaves incentives in place for everyone involved to contribute to the success of the Games. It's an effective arrangement where everyone who participates wins.

One of the great potentialities of the Olympic Games is to provide benefits to all regions of the world similar to those enjoyed by the host region. There are several ways this can be achieved, but the simplest is through financial aid. The IOC recognizes its chance to help sport by providing funds to the National Olympic Committees in 167 countries through its Solidarity Program. Similarly, the International Sports Federations receive direct payments from the IOC for their operations. The money is used for sport programs in every corner of the world—children on the Ivory Coast playing football; children in Chile attending a ski school; children in China receiving better coaching in diving; children in Bulgaria attending the Olympic Academy. The money for these programs comes from one major source—the Olympic Games.

The Olympic movement today is completely self-financing, so, theoretically, it could be independent of political meddling. The Olympic movement is expanding its role and increasing its membership and, as a result, it is achieving its aims. Few movements exist that can make the same claims. The Olympic movement can be justifiably proud of the unique formula for success it has achieved. Juan Antonio Samaranch has done much, as IOC president, to combat the "great perils" and realize the "wide hopes" for the future that Pierre de Coubertin once spoke of.

Samaranch has said, "The Olympic movement will be one of the leading social forces in the world at the end of this century." I think it may be already.

BIENVENUE • JEFFREY HOLDEN • CARMA FLORENCE • DIANE RATNIK • JANET HILDEBANDT • SHIRLEY KELLY • MAC LINDSAY • LARRY TURNER • SIDNEY GAUDRY • ELLIE TIMS • SANDRA FOLLETT • EMMA PATEL • AGNES LEBLANC • DOUG SHERRIS • BIRTHE PERRY • CORRY DEYDEY • WAYNE ODEGARD • GERTRUDE THIRNBECK • KARI-LOU ANTOLIC • JOEL TOBMAN • DIANA BION • BETTY ELKINS • MARLENE SUMMERS • ANNE MARIE PLESA • KEN LUNN • LINDA TAYLOR • LORI MENZIES • HARRY BULLEN • JACK FOURNIER • RICK CROSSEN • GEORGE SHORT • JOHN RUTTAN • GRACE SARDO • ELENORA WILSON • RICK SHAUGHNESSY • GARY HAZEN • VONNIE MCLEAN • AUDREY DONNELLY •

A New Feeling

Organizing the Games can make a difference to the world in a second way—a way that is much more difficult to describe but which is perhaps contained in the main question asked by our Olympic song, "Can't you feel it?"

The people who come into close contact with the Olympic Games feel something special. When the Olympic flag was being lowered and marched out of the stadium and then the melancholy music of the harp proclaimed without words that the Games were finished, I had a different point of view than I'd ever had before. During the previous 10 years I had seen a different world, but I was able to place the importance of Olympic Games into proper context only at the end. If you were a member of Team'88 or a visiting team, or a spectator or TV viewer, you will always remember the tingles the Games produced. There was a smile on every face.

It goes without saying that world leaders face a troubled agenda of social and economic issues. The biggest challenges are man-made, so they must be solved by men and women with courageous vision or things will not get better.

We raise our children in a global climate of conflict and gloom. The list of world problems is long and bleak: environmental damage, nuclear threats, famine, disease, illiteracy, crime, hatred, intolerance, drugs, and so on. Every media outlet in every part of the world is dominated every day by stories about these issues. Each passing day bombards young people with so much bad news that it is easy for them to fall into despair.

It is against this background that the Olympic Games arrive every four years. Suddenly during the Games things are not as they were for those lucky enough to become involved. All the things that trouble and divide us are pushed aside, and ordinary people everywhere come together in friendship. This one story is so powerful in its effect on people that it blows the negative stories off the front pages for 16 straight days.

Admittedly those who have the opportunity to participate directly in the Olympics are a privileged few out of the five billion or so people on this planet, but our Olympic Games reached an estimated two billion of them through television. No other celebration of human achievement or international brotherhood reaches anything like that number of people.

The Olympic movement still has enormous room for improvement, but if the Olympic Games continue to promote Olympic ideals, then the whole idea works.

CHAPTER TWENTY-SIX

The Flame Burns On

Life is either a daring adventure or nothing.
HELEN KELLER

DURING THE 16 DAYS between February 13th and February 28th, 1988, Canadians found their worthy cause—the XVth Olympic Winter Games. Brand-new facilities greeted winter sports champions from a record 57 countries. Nearly two million tickets were used at Olympic events and almost two billion people watched the Games on television. But even more remarkable was the nearly perfect effort of more than 20,000 volunteer workers and performers, and the people of Calgary, who made the Games a special experience for visitors and viewers alike. The Games brought people everywhere together through sport.

With memories of the Calgary Winter Games still fresh in their minds, people who had been touched by the experience sent letters to OCO'88 and Calgary City Hall. Thousands of letters from viewers around the world poured in, each expressing the feelings of a grateful public in a different way. Each had been witness to the Olympic ideals in action at a new and friendly location.

HUTTENBRINK • NORMA SIEPPERT • BARRY PARDELL • ROLAND MANSELL • RICK SCHLEYER • ROBERT WATT • JOYCE TORJAN • JOAN SUMNER • LYLE ROBINSON • ROD GORDON • SUSANA MARTINS • KIM DOBSON • JUDY CHRISTOU • SUSANNE WIENS • WILLIAM HARRIS • DAYLENE SLIZ • GLORIA MORSE • DWAINE ELDER • DAVID JOHNSON • ALEX JARVIE • BRIAN WALSH • LAURIE WHITE • SANDY DEERE • MARK KIBZEY • ALISON LAURESHEN • PURVIS MCDOUGALL • JULIE MARLATT • BLAIR COOK • HEATHER HATTIN • LILO DEIMEL • JOHN COX • JANET DAVIES • MARILYN RIEGEL • MIKE MCELROY • SID RUDMAN • RANDY SADNICKI • GRAHAME BLUNDELL • BRIAN GASTALDI • COLLEEN CROWE •

Here are only two of the more than 5,000 letters received after the Calgary Games.

Dear OCO'88,

The best athletes won gold; the Russians had 11 and the East Germans garnered nine. Very impressive.

But the Calgarians won the hearts and minds of all those who had visited the XVth Winter Olympics, including myself who had covered three Olympics as a foreign correspondent.

No one can ever forget the smiles of the "Cowtown" citizens, smiles warmer than the ice-melting Chinook. They are the best hosts in the world. Everyone agrees with Juan Antonio Samaranch, president of the International Olympic Committee, who described the Games as the "best ever."

As years go by, few would remember who won how many golds in Calgary, but many will vividly and fondly remember their golden time in that friendly city. Who says the Canadians did not win a gold medal? Their prize is better than gold.

I, for one, was deeply touched by the spirit of Calgary—the western hospitality, volunteerism, and the way they welcomed the world. The pictures of ubiquitous volunteers, the cheers at the Saddledome and the enthusiastic crowds at Olympic Plaza which was like Times Square on New Year's Eve, form a kaleidoscope that revolves before me. I, like the gregarious Calgarians, hated to see the party end.

Thank you, Calgary, it was a lifetime experience.

DAVID TING
OTTAWA

Dear Mr. King:

For so long now, I've wanted to write you a letter, but I've never been able to find the words to explain what I feel. Even now, everything feels so inadequate, but I've got to give it a shot. First of all, I need to say thank-you to you and the group of men and women who made the XVth Olympic Winter Games possible. The work and time you have put in are unimaginable and you all deserve all the credit in the world.

I was a ceremonies host during the Olympics and I led in the athletes for the opening and closing ceremonies. Never in my life have I felt so proud and never in my life will I again feel that ecstatic high of thousands of people yelling for my country as I brought them in.

I could go on forever with my praises but basically what I want to thank you for is hope. I am only 20 years old and sometimes I would wonder if I was going to make it to 21. All the crazy stuff going on in the world is making our youth awfully short. We feel like we have to grow up now, so maybe we can stop all the craziness. Our childhood was grabbed away. But for those few weeks in February 1988, everything was given back to us. Our hopes and dreams were restored. There was a chance for peace in our lifetime and for a short time, the rest of the world was forgotten. All of those athletes and young people, we were friends. And even though I'll never see them again, I'll never forget the friendships made in a few seconds of eye contact and a smile. Nor will I forget when an American took a Russian's picture and then they shook hands and hugged. It was a wonderful sight and it made me believe if they can do it, and all the other athletes, why not everybody? So now I feel I can hope again and believe. And that is what I and the rest of my generation want to thank you for. Thank you for giving us back the ability to dream and to make our dreams possible.

Yours sincerely,
PATRICIA

The Living Legacy

After the Games were over, we produced a short film in collaboration with the Alberta government to be shown at our final Team'88 Recognition Night at the Olympic Saddledome. The film was entitled "The Dream Came True." For those who ask why did so many people volunteer to give so much, the answer is found in the final words of this great film: "For those who have had the experience, no explanation is necessary. For those who have not, none is possible."

The people of Calgary, Alberta, and Canada felt excited, proud, and grateful for the opportunity they received to host the "best-ever" Olympic Winter Games. The spirit of Calgary will become part of the new Olympic spirit and the next Games will benefit from that.

The living legacy of the Calgary Winter Games will grow from the feeling of true friendship that thousands of workers and Olympic athletes contributed to a world that hungers for harmony. At the end of the day they knew that their dream had come true.

This book is about them all.

HEATHER SAGAN • DARRIN WHITNEY • DAVID LAWSON • GASTON GRENIER • GRANT FAGERHEIM • LISBET VAILE • VIVIAN ZANDER • PAM BARRETT • ROB MONK • CAROLYN DOZEMAN • VERNE WETTSTEIN • DEDRHA RIPLEY • MEL LA POINTE • GRAHAM MCFARLANE • COLIN CRANDON • BEVERLEY KLIPPERT • DELL SUDNIK • JIM MULDREW • DIANNE VAN DYL • HALEY EGAN • TOM ATKINSON • KAREN EDWARDS • BEV JULIEN • PATTY BECKSTEAD • DUNCAN MCNAUGHTON • KELLEY WORMAN • FRANCINE BELAND • CHERYL CARR • ALLISTER KEENE • STACY KIRK • MICHAEL CARR • SUSAN HOLLOWAY • BETTY LOU COURAGE • BRUCE GALE • ROXANNE MCKENDRY • EILEEN DEFREITAS

Index

PHOTO CREDITS ▶ PLATE 1 courtesy OCO'88 • PLATE 2 courtesy OCO'88 • PLATE 3 from the author's personal collection • PLATE 4 courtesy OCO'88 • PLATE 5 from the author's personal collection • PLATE 6 by Peter Brosseau, courtesy OCO'88 • PLATE 7 courtesy the International Olympic Committee • PLATE 8 from the author's personal collection • PLATE 9 from the author's personal collection • PLATE 10 from the author's personal collection • PLATE 11 from the author's personal collection • PLATE 12 by Rolf Gottwald, courtesy OCO'88 • PLATE 13 by Rolf Gottwald, courtesy OCO'88 • PLATE 14 courtesy OCO'88 • PLATE 15 from the author's personal collection • PLATE 16 courtesy OCO'88 • PLATE 17 from the author's personal collection • PLATE 18 courtesy OCO'88 • PLATE 19 courtesy OCO'88 • PLATE 20 from the author's personal collection • PLATE 21 by the *Calgary Herald,* courtesy OCO'88 • PLATE 22 courtesy Bob Niven • PLATE 23 from the author's personal collection • PLATE 24 courtesy OCO'88 • PLATE 25 courtesy OCO'88 • PLATE 26 courtesy OCO'88 • PLATE 27 from the author's personal collection • PLATE 28 courtesy OCO'88 • PLATE 29 from the author's personal collection • PLATE 30 from the author's personal collection • PLATE 31 courtesy the City of Calgary Archives • PLATE 32 from the author's personal collection • PLATE 33 from the author's personal collection • PLATE 34 courtesy the City of Calgary Archives • PLATE 35 courtesy the City of Calgary Archives • PLATE 36 by Larry Fisher, courtesy OCO'88 • PLATE 37 by Patrick Price, courtesy OCO'88 • PLATE 38 by Patrick Price, courtesy OCO'88 • PLATE 39 by Patrick Price, courtesy OCO'88 • PLATE 40 by Patrick Price, courtesy OCO'88 • PLATE 41 from the author's personal collection • PLATE 42 by Patrick Price, courtesy OCO'88 • PLATE 43 by Larry Fisher, courtesy OCO'88 • PLATE 44 by Mike Ridewood, courtesy OCO'88 • PLATE 45 by Larry Fisher, courtesy OCO'88 • PLATE 46 from the author's personal collection • PLATE 47 from the author's personal collection • PLATE 48 by Larry Fisher, courtesy OCO'88 • PLATE 49 by Mike Ridewood, courtesy OCO'88 • PLATE 50 by Mike Ridewood, courtesy OCO'88 • PLATE 51 courtesy the City of Calgary Archives • PLATE 52 by Larry Fisher, courtesy OCO'88 • PLATE 53 photo courtesy the City of Calgary Archives • PLATE 54 by Larry Fisher, courtesy OCO'88 • PLATE 55 from the author's personal collection • PLATE 56 from the author's personal collection • PLATE 57 courtesy the City of Calgary Archives ■

Additional copies of *It's How You Play the Game* are available from the publisher. To order yours now, complete the order form below (or a photocopy) and mail it along with a cheque or money order for $35.00 for each book ordered.

Please print clearly; this will be your mailing label.

I would like to order _____ copy (copies) of *It's How You Play the Game: The Inside Story of the Calgary Olympics* (ISBN 0–9694287–5–8) at $35^{00} for each copy of the book ordered (includes handling, postage, and GST).

I have enclosed a cheque or money order for _____ copy (copies) for a total of $ _____.

Name: _____

Address: _____

City, Province: _____

Postal Code: _____

Clip this form and mail it to:

Script: the writers' group inc.
Suite 200, 839 - 5 Avenue S.W.
Calgary, Alberta T2P 3C8

Please allow two to three weeks for delivery.

GST Registration # 124167594